North Dakota
The Heritage of a People

North Dakota
The Heritage of a People

by D. Jerome Tweton and
Theodore B. Jelliff

North Dakota Institute for Regional Studies • Fargo

Second Printing, 1983

Copyright ©1976 North Dakota Institute for Regional Studies
All Rights Reserved

Library of Congress Catalog Card Number: 76-27123

ISBN: 0-911042-19-9

Printed in the United States of America
by Knight Printing Company, Fargo, North Dakota

Cover photograph: Haying time on the Hultstrand Farm, Fairdale, ND., 1911. From the Fred Hultstrand History of Pictures Collection at North Dakota State University, Fargo.

To the young people of
North Dakota who like
Karin, Karla, Eric, and David
will write the next
chapter of North Dakota's
history.

North Dakota American Revolution Bicentennial Commission

John Conrad, Chairman, Bismarck
Ron Abrahamson, Fargo
Earl Azure, Bismarck
Christine Barks, Devils Lake
Anna Bridston, Grand Forks
Wallace Dockter, Bismarck
Sophie Hansen, Denhoff
Brynhild Haugland, Minot
Lorne Hillier, Hensel
Dr. John Hove, Fargo
Janice Johnson, Fargo
Stanley Moore, Jamestown
Corliss Mushik, Mandan
Dr. Frank Pearson, Dickinson
Sheila Robinson, Coleharbor
Dan Rylance, Grand Forks
Q. R. Schulte, Stanley
Del Shipman, Watford City
Dennis Smith, Jamestown
Oscar Solberg, Rolla
Rod Tjaden, Medora
Dr. Merton Utgaard, Bottineau
Jeanne Wagner, Richardton
Eleanor Wilcox, Devils Lake

PREFACE

This is a book about people — the people who came to a place called North Dakota. It is a story about many kinds of people — Sioux, Chippewa, Metis, Mandan, Hidatsa, Arikara, Norwegians, Poles, Germans, Irishmen, Frenchmen, Hungarians, Swedes, Danes, Austrians, Canadians, Icelanders, and those who came from other regions of the United States. They spoke different languages, worshiped in different ways, wore a variety of dress, and came to the prairies and plains for various reasons. Yet, they had something in common: they had to adjust to a new land. This history tells that story. It emphasizes the people and the institutions that touched their lives — the school, the political party, the farm organization, the labor union, the church, *the tiospaye*, the clan.

Many people have helped in the preparation of this book. Several have read all or part of the manuscript and made many helpful suggestions: Robert P. Wilkins, Glenn Smith, and Thomas Howard, Department of History, University of North Dakota; Arthur Raymond, Director of Indian Studies, University of North Dakota; Vera Facey, Robert Seabloom, and William Wrenn, Department of Biology, University of North Dakota; John Bluemle, North Dakota Geological Survey; Lynn Davidson, Lowell Jensen, and Ronald Stastney, the Department of Public Instruction; Bill Reid, North Dakota Institute for Regional Studies, North Dakota State University. Many secretaries typed the several drafts of the manuscript: Kathy Peterson, Kelly Ames, Cindy Nichols, Dorothy Steiner, Debbie Ray, Betsie Deitz, and Suzanne DeLaPointe. Frank Vyzralek of the State Historical Society of North Dakota courteously helped with photograph selections. Elwyn B. Robinson and Weisert Graphics did excellent photographic reproduction work for the book. The State Historical Society of North Dakota, the *Grand Forks Herald*, the University of North Dakota (University Relations, Archives, and Orin G. Libby Manuscript Collection) graciously provided most of the photographs. Daniel Rylance, John Davenport, and Audrey Kazmierczak of the North Dakota Room of Chester Fritz Library at the University of North Dakota gave the authors exceptional reference service. Phyllis Tweton and Jan Jelliff proofread the manuscript. The authors are deeply indebted to all these people.

Our gratitude also goes to the North Dakota American Revolution Bicentennial Commission, which had enough confidence in the project to help fund the preparation of the manuscript. Finally, we are indebted to the people of North Dakota for giving us such an exciting story about which to write.

D. Jerome Tweton
University of North Dakota
Theodore B. Jelliff
Red River High School

PHOTOGRAPH CREDIT ABBREVIATIONS

GFH — *Grand Forks Herald*
SHSND — State Historical Society of North Dakota
UND-LC — University of North Dakota, Orin G. Libby Manuscript Collection
UND-A — University of North Dakota, Archives
UND-UR — University of North Dakota, University Relations
ND-DPI — North Dakota Department of Public Instruction
FSA/UND-LC — Farm Security Administration Photographs in the Orin G. Libby Manuscript Collection, University of North Dakota

CONTENTS

1. The Heritage of the Land — 1
2. Nature's World — 7
3. Seven Council Fires: The Sioux — 16
4. From the Woods to the Plains: The Chippewa — 29
5. Other Campfires — 40
6. Four Flags Over the Land: The Fur Trade — 47
7. Conflict on the Plains — 56
8. Carts, Stages, and Steamers — 66
9. The Iron Horse — 75
10. Day of the Bonanza — 82
11. Dakotaland, Sweet Dakotaland — 91
12. Now It's North Dakota — 103
13. The People at the Turn of the Century — 114
14. The Golden Age — 125
15. Political Prairie Fire: The NPL — 135
16. Road to Depression: The 1920s — 147
17. Years of Despair: The 1930s and the War — 155
18. The Boom Years: Since 1945 — 167
19. Political Change: Since 1945 — 185
20. Progress of a People — 200

Epilog — 217
North Dakota Atlas — 219
Picture Album of North Dakotans — 226
Index — 235

THE ROYALTIES FROM THE SALE OF THIS BOOK ARE EARMARKED FOR NORTH DAKOTA'S HERITAGE CENTER.

1 The Heritage of the Land

North Dakota is at the very center of the North American continent. The geographical center of North America is located near Rugby in Pierce County. With a total land area of 70,665 square miles, North Dakota is a rectangle of 336 miles from east to west and 210 miles from north to south. The state is bordered by the Canadian provinces of Manitoba and Saskatchewan on the north, and the states of Minnesota to the east, South Dakota to the south, and Montana to the west. North Dakota is smaller in land area than any of its neighbors but ranks 17th in size among the 50 states.

I. The Geological Past

The earth is about 5,000,000,000 years old. Over those billions of years North Dakota was formed and shaped. Human history is a very small fraction of those years. If one could compress those 5,000,000,000 years into one make-believe calendar year, primitive man would appear at about 10:20 p.m. on the evening of the very last day of the year. The American Revolution would have been fought with only two seconds remaining, and North Dakota would have become a state during the last second of the year.

Geologists are the scientists who study the solid earth. Their studies explain the formation of rocks and soils and the changes that have taken place in and on the earth. Geologists have developed a time scale, a calendar of prehistoric events, which charts the progress of early life and the changes in the earth. The geological time calendar has four main divisions called eras. Eras are divided into periods, and periods into epochs.

The Cryptozoic Era covers that time from the beginning of the earth to about 620,000,000 years ago. Few traces of life have been found from this era. Many of the earth's rich metal deposits, such as the iron around Lake Superior, were formed during this era. North Dakota's oldest known rock formations, called Precambrian, come from this time. The Precambrian formations have many, many layers above them and are 16,000 feet below the surface throughout much of the state.

The Paleozoic Era extends from 620,000,000 to 225,000,000 years ago. During these millions of years, land-animal life, fish (including sharks), and amphibians appeared; primitive plants flourished. Near the end of the Paleozoic Era, insects and reptiles appeared. Over North Dakota the seas invaded and receded, leaving sediments which became limestone, sandstone, and shale deposits. Containing much marine life, these deposits would provide North Dakota with some of its oil reserves.

The Mezozoic Era, from 225,000,000 to 70,000,000 years ago, saw the appearance of dinosaurs and flying reptiles. Dinosaurs roamed North Dakota. The brontosaurus with a long neck, small face, and huge body shared the North Dakota landscape with the armored stegosaurus, which had a row of vertical plates along its backbone. Geologists have uncovered Mezozoic dinosaur bones and skeletons in southwestern North Dakota. Most of North Dakota's oil deposits and clay that is used for brickmaking date back to the Mezozoic Era.

The Cenozoic Era, the most recent geological era, began 70,000,000 years ago. The Cenozoic Era is divided into two periods: The Tertiary (70,000,000 to 1,000,000 years ago) and the Quaternary (1,000,000 years ago to recent times). The Tertiary Period of the Cenozoic Era was a time of mammals. Some of them reached gigantic proportions, exceeding elephants in size. Crocodiles, monkeys, mastodons, four-toed horses, and others lived on the land. Whales appeared in the seas. Modern plants were developing. Volcanic activity was changing the face of the western United States. The climate was becoming cooler. Many Tertiary Period fossils (traces of prehistoric life) have been uncovered in North Dakota. In Billings County, geologists unearthed the skeleton of a 16-foot-long crocodile. The remains of a rhinoceros and a titanathere were found in the White River formation of this geologic period. The official state fossil, "teredo wood," dates back to the early Tertiary Period — about 65,000,000 years ago. Teredo wood is a fossil wood which has been riddled with the borings of worm-like clams. During the early years of the Tertiary Period of the Cenozoic Era, North Dakota's uranium and much of its lignite deposits were formed.

The Quaternary Period of the Cenozoic Era began about a million years ago. North Dakota's landscape changed dramatically. Glaciers invaded the region. As climate in the north grew colder, snow began to build up, forming large masses of ice sometimes thousands of feet thick. As the glaciers moved southward inch by inch, they altered the shape of the land, picking up earth and all sizes of rocks. Warming of the climate made the glaciers melt, and the last one, the Wisconsian, left the state about 13,000 years ago. Because the glaciers covered all of the state

A geologist examines a North Dakota dinosaur skull. (UND-A)

except the southwest corner, most of North Dakota was affected by the huge sheets of ice. The glaciers left large deposits of drift. The state gets its sand and gravel from these deposits. The glaciers created many potholes, sloughs, and lakes. The glaciers also altered the state's drainage pattern. Before the coming of the glaciers, all of North Dakota's rivers flowed northward toward Hudson Bay. The ice masses and their huge deposits of drift blocked the ancient Missouri and its tributaries and forced them to flow southward. When the ice melted, it formed a large glacial lake, Lake Agassiz. The lake was 300 feet deep, 700 miles long, 200 miles wide, and covered the Red River Valley. The Red River drains the old lake bed, and lakes such as Winnipeg and the Lake of the Woods are remnants of the glacial lake. Although North Dakota had other glacial lakes in areas now drained by the James and Souris rivers, Lake Agassiz was the largest.

The advance of ice over North Dakota and the shift to a cold climate drove out the animal life. With the retreat of the ice and the return of a warmer climate, animal life began to return to the North Dakota area. The most important biological event of the period was the arrival of humans. Scholars do not know exactly when man first came to North America. Estimates range from 12,000 to 60,000 years ago. Man might have been in North Dakota as early as 10,000 to 13,000 years ago. Along the Missouri, archaeologists (those who study the remains of ancient people and places) have discovered villages that may be 1,300 years old. Very little, however, is known about the thousands of years before the Mandan made their way up the Missouri to become North Dakota's first permanent inhabitants.

II. The Shape of the Land

North Dakota lies within two large land regions. The northeastern half of the state is part of the Central Lowlands, which stretch east to the Appalachian Mountains and south to the Coastal Plain on the Gulf of Mexico. The southwestern half of the state marks the beginning of the Great Plains, which rise westward to the Rocky Mountains. As one travels west across the state, the land rises from 750 feet above sea level at Pembina to 3,000 feet on the plains.

The Central Lowlands part of North Dakota has two main topographical regions: the Red River Valley and the Drift Prairie. The Red River Valley is a flat strip of land which is 30 to 40 miles wide. The Valley is the lake bottom of glacial Lake Agassiz and is North Dakota's most fertile land. The Pembina Escarpment (also called the Manitoba Escarpment) separates the Valley from the Drift Prairie with a sharp rise in elevation. The rise is most noticeable at the northern end where the Pembina Hills rise from 300 to 500 feet. West of the Pembina Escarpment lies the Drift Prairie, a region of gently rolling prairie and thousands of potholes, lakes, and sloughs. Glacial deposits are evident everywhere. The Drift Prairie is about 200 miles wide at the Canadian border and 70 miles wide at the South Dakota border. Two hilly regions, the Turtle Mountains on the Canadian border and the Prairie Coteau on the South Dakota border near the Valley, rise to elevations of 700 feet above the Drift Prairie. Elevations on the Drift Prairie range from 1,400 to 1,700 feet above sea level.

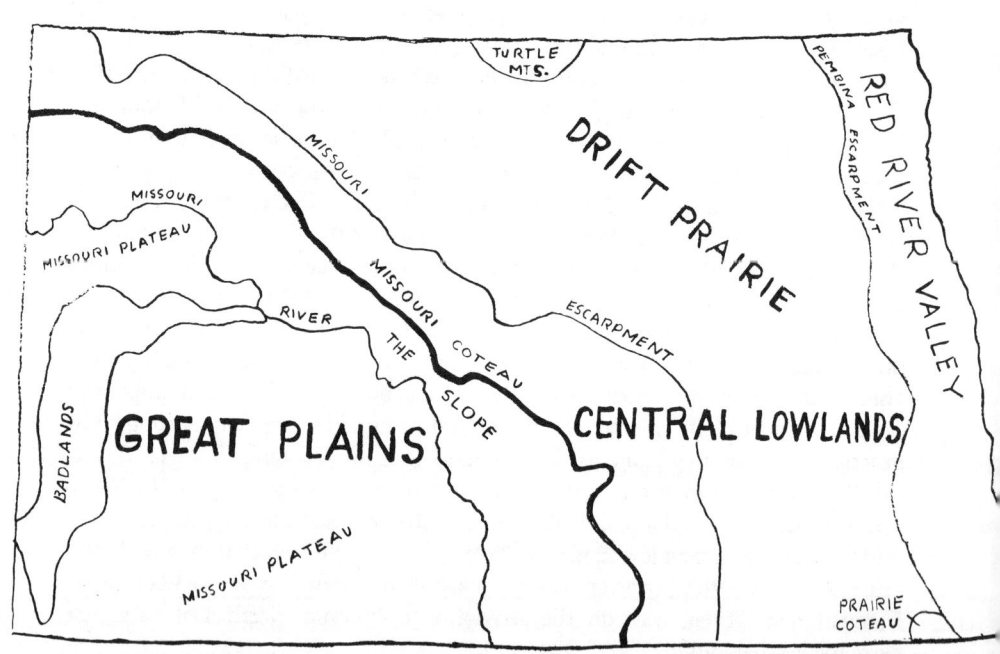

In North Dakota, the Missouri Escarpment divides the Central Lowlands from the Great Plains. The steep rise in elevation of up to 700 feet marks the western boundary of the Drift Prairie. The Great Plains area is about 200 miles wide at the South Dakota border and 20 miles wide at the Canadian border north of Williston. The Great Plains region of the state has three main topographical regions: the Missouri Coteau, the Missouri Plateau, and the Badlands.

West of the Missouri Escarpment lies the Missouri Coteau, also called the "Hills of the Missouri." The Missouri Coteau is a 30- to 50-mile wide strip of hilly country. Because glaciers left thick deposits of sediment in this region, many lakes and sloughs developed. The Missouri Coteau slopes into the Missouri Plateau, through which the Missouri River flows. The Missouri Plateau covers almost the southwestern half of the state. All but the southwestern third of the Plateau is covered with a thin cover of glacial deposits. The Plateau country is rolling and hilly with frequent buttes. The elevation of the Plateau generally runs between 2,000 and 3,000 feet above sea level. Near Bowman, White Butte rises to 3,506 feet above sea level — the highest point in North Dakota.

The Badlands, which run along the Little Missouri River, is one of the most striking regions of North Dakota's Great Plains. The glaciers did not cover the Badlands, and erosion has carved a land of ravines and broken bottomlands. Running water and the winds have exposed colorful rock strata. The Badlands, rich in geologic and historic color, offers the traveler a western-movie type landscape.

Drift Prairie landscape. (UND-A)

THE HERITAGE OF THE LAND

Badlands landscape. (UND-LC)

Most of North Dakota is covered with soil which is capable of supporting extensive farming. Soils are classified according to their qualities into the Great Soil Groups. Soils are further divided into series which describe more specific qualities of soils found in specific places. The soil of the state's Central Lowlands (the Red River Valley and the Drift Prairie) belongs to the Great Soil Group, Chernozem, a Russian word meaning "black earth." This soil is rich in organic material and is among the most productive soils in the world. In the Red River Valley the principal series is the Fargo, a heavy clay and clay loam. On the Drift Prairie, the most common series is the Barnes, a loamy soil which reflects the glacial deposits which characterize the Drift Prairie.

The soil of the state's Great Plains belongs to the Great Soil Group, Chestnut, called that because of its brownish color. Over 20 soil series, such as the Williams series in the northeastern counties and the Morton series in the southwest, exist on the Missouri Plateau. Although not as rich as the soils of the Valley or Prairie, the soils of the Plains are productive when they receive enough moisture.

*   *   *   *   *   *

The land — its shape and makeup — plays an important role in determining the activity of the people on that land. The economy of a region is based on such factors as the fertility of the soil and the mineral resources deposited in the land. Northern Minnesota prospered because of its iron ore; Kansas and Oklahoma boomed because of oil discoveries; coal and oil helped diversify the North Dakota economy and are essential resources in an energy-conscious world. More important, however, were the soils. The richness of the land determined that North Dakota would be an agricultural region — a world leader in the production of grain. Throughout its history, North Dakota has been tied to a one-crop wheat economy. Wheat has been king because of the land.

2 Nature's World

Many humorous stories are told about North Dakota's climate. An often-heard wisecrack is that the climate in North Dakota is six months of good sleighing and six months of bad sleighing. A standard joke tells about the person who left the state for two days in July and missed the summer season. Knowledge of the state's climate and plant and animal life is important for understanding its history. The nature of a region's climate and land determines the kinds of activities in which its inhabitants can engage.

I. The Climate

Because North Dakota is located at the center of the continent, it has what is called a continental climate. A continental climate is characterized by light to moderate precipitation, low relative humidity, great changes in seasonal and daily temperatures, many sunny days, almost constant wind, and four distinct seasons. North Dakota's distance from mountains and its relative flatness allow weather systems to move quickly across the state.

Precipitation does not fall evenly throughout the state. Annual precipitation ranges from 13 inches in the northwest to over 19 inches in the Red River Valley. North Dakota receives most of its moisture during the spring and summer months. Winter precipitation is light, compared to the other states which border Canada. By the time the winter weather systems have moved into North Dakota, they have lost much of their moisture.

The continental-type climate is reflected in the great annual temperature variations. For example, in 1936 both the hottest and coldest records were set: 60

degrees below zero at Parshall in January, and 121 degrees above zero at Steele in July. Although temperature varies greatly from season to season, the state's yearly average is about 40 degrees. North Dakota receives more sunshine than any of the other states which border Canada — 2,600 to 2,800 hours per year. Wind seems to be ever present. The average surface wind speed is 12 miles per hour. The Red River Valley is generally windier than the rest of the state.

North Dakota's seasons vary in length and are distinct. Summer is a pleasant time of the year. The days are long and warm; the nights are cool. Summer is North Dakota's frost-free season, stretching from mid-May to early September. Summer weather can be very hot, but usually just for brief spells. July temperatures average between 67 degrees in the northeast to 73 degrees in the southwest. North Dakota receives most of its precipitation during the summer. When and where it falls makes a vital difference to the farmers. Thunderstorms are frequent. Occasionally, the dreaded tornado strikes. On the evening of June 30, 1957, one of the worst tornadoes in North Dakota history descended on Fargo. The tornado ripped a path three blocks wide, running from the western edge to the northern part of the city. It killed 10 people and injured over 60. The violent winds uprooted trees and smashed buildings. The damage from the storm reached $10,000,000.

In 1896 a tornado smashed the Great Northern's Gassman Coulee trestle near Minot. For a picture of the trestle before the storm, see page 80. (SHSND)

Fall is harvest time. Farmers work feverishly to harvest the crops before the coming of cold and snow. Hunters stalk the fields for pheasants or watch the sky for ducks. This season runs from September into November. By November, the average temperatures are below freezing. Rainfall is usually light, and temperatures range from the 60s during the day to the 30s at night. Usually, each fall North Dakota experiences "Indian summer," short periods of summer-like weather.

The first snows come in November, marking the beginning of the winter season. Winter is the longest season; it extends from November into March and sometimes April. Although sub-zero temperatures are common from December through February, the average January temperature ranges from two degrees above zero in the northern Red River Valley to 17 degrees above zero in the southwest around Dickinson. Winter precipitation is light. Snow depths vary from nine inches in the southwest to 15 inches in the northeast. The blizzard is the most extreme example of winter weather. Winds that sometimes reach 70 miles per hour drive the falling snow into whirling walls of white. The state has experienced many ferocious storms. In January 1888, a blizzard brought death to over a hundred people and covered houses and barns with mounds of snow. Again, in March 1941, a blizzard swept into the state, leaving in its wake a death toll of 39 people. Many of those who perished in the storm might have saved themselves if they had heeded the warnings that were broadcast over the radio. Today, with modern communications, storm warnings are instantly broadcast on radio and television. Few people are foolhardy enough to travel when a warning of a blizzard is heard. In March 1966 a severe blizzard roared through the state, but adequate radio and television warnings prevented any loss of life. In 1975, however, several people perished in a blizzard which hit suddenly.

Above, Senator Quentin Burdick inspects Red River flooding. (GFH)

Below, banks of snow on the main street of Hague after the 1966 blizzard. (SHSND)

Although cold at times, most winter days are filled with sunshine and little wind. With the advent of the snowmobile and the increased interest in winter sports, such as hockey and cross-country skiing, the winter season is a great recreational time for those who love the outdoors. Improved winter clothing, rapid snow removal, and a widespread communications network have taken much of the worry out of the winter season.

Although North Dakota spring is short, it is a most welcome season. After a long winter season, the people are eager for the snow to melt. Farmers await planting time; students anticipate the end of the school year; summer sportsmen begin to limber up for competition. In some years, spring lasts from early April into June; in other years, spring is only a brief interlude between winter and summer. Sometimes, spring is a wet season; sometimes, it is warm and sunny with light rains.

Springtime is flood time. The melting of snow brings problems to people who live along the rivers. Grand Forks' worst flood occurred in the spring of 1979, when the water reached a level of 49.9 feet. Flood stage at Grand Forks is 28 feet. In 1970, Fargo and Minot experienced flooding which caused hardship and property damage.

Although most flooding occurs during the spring, in the summer of 1975 a most unusual flood occurred along the Red River. On June 28, a violent rain storm dropped a deluge of water on the drainage area, resulting in the first summertime flood that anyone could remember. Permanent and hastily built dikes protected most of the homes in the cities, but many parks and golf courses were left damaged and unusable. Thousands of acres of crops were lost. Federal, state, and local flood-control programs, however, have helped to control the dangers of flooding.

II. Plant Life

North Dakota is part of a vast grassland which extends from Mexico into Canada. When white settlers came to the prairies, North Dakota was 98 percent grassland and two percent woodland. Although much of the state's grassland has fallen victim to the plow, grass is one of the state's important natural resources. Grass provides a natural feed for cattle and sheep. It can also be cured for hay or used as silage or feed during the winter months.

Many varieties of grasses grew in North Dakota. In the Red River Valley, the original native grasses were of the tall kind, reaching six feet or more. Many varieties appeared in the Valley: bluestem, Indian grass, porcupine grass, cordgrass, green needlegrass, prairie dropseed, switchgrass, and bearded wheatgrass. Because most of the Valley has been cultivated, very little native grass has survived. On the Drift Prairie, which receives less precipitation than the Valley, medium-height grasses developed: needle-and-thread, blue gramma, junegrass, green needlegrass, western wheatgrass, and bluestem. The Drift Prairie is a transitional grass zone which has some of the grasses of the Valley and some of the Missouri Plateau. Short to medium-tall grasses dominate the

Missouri Plateau. Wheatgrass and needle-and-thread are medium-height grasses; threadleaf sedge and blue gramma are short varieties. Blue gramma is considered to be the best grass for grazing.

The hunger for land and the need for lumber have reduced North Dakota's original woodlands by half. About 30 percent of the state's woodlands are in the Turtle Mountains. Aspen dominates the landscape, but the American elm, poplar, cottonwood, boxelder, green ash, bur oak, and birch are common. The area around Devils Lake is the second largest wooded region. There, one can find bur oak, green ash, American elm, aspen, boxelder, and basswood. The only evergreen woodlands are located in the southwest. The ponderosa pine grows in dense clusters and as scattered trees. Timbered belts along rivers such as the Red, James, and Sheyenne contain most of the trees common to the Devils Lake region. The majority of the clusters and rows of trees that dot the landscape today are not native. Settlers planted most of these as shelter belts for farmsteads. Those who gained land under the Timber Culture Act had to plant trees. During the drought years of the 1930s, many farmers began extensive tree planting to fight soil erosion.

Several native types of shrubs still exist in North Dakota. In the drier western areas, sagebrush and bullberry grow extensively. Buckbrush and the wild rose, the state flower, thrive east of the Missouri River. Juneberry, chokecherry, wild plum, and raspberry appear in areas of sufficient moisture.

III. Wild Life

The wide, open prairie of North Dakota was a suitable habitat for those animals that ran in herds, roamed large areas in search of food, and flocked together for long migratory journeys. Before the settlers turned the prairie sod, the area was a great refuge for the animals of the prairie. Alexander Henry, who operated a trading post at Pembina in the early 1800s, described buffalo herds that covered the land as far as the eye could see. Other early explorers told of seeing great herds of elk, antelope, and deer.

Fur-bearing animals — mink, otter, and beaver — lured the early trappers into the area. The black beaver had the most valuable pelt. Although not as numerous as in other states, the black bear and moose lived along the river banks and forested area of the Turtle Mountains. Along the Missouri, Lewis and Clark saw many grizzly bears. Wolves and coyotes roamed the plains. The large buffalo wolf ran in packs and attacked the old and sick buffalo as they fell behind the herd. On the open prairie, the long-legged, whitetailed jack rabbits, gophers, ground squirrels (also called flickertails), and prairie dogs made their homes. North Dakota is named the flickertail state because of the numerous ground squirrels.

With the coming of settlement, many of the once-numerous animals disappeared or were driven from the land. The buffalo was the first to go; by 1873, commercial hunters and Indians had killed off most of the herds. Because their pelts were in great demand, the beaver were trapped almost to the point of extinction.

In 1843 Maxmillian, Prince of Weid, published his *Travels to the Interior of North America in The Years of 1832 to 1834.* His journey took him through North Dakota. Carl Bodmer, a Swiss painter, went with him to capture the people and landscape on canvas. He painted the above scene of buffalo. The originals are in the Joslyn Art Museum at Omaha, Nebraska. (SHSND)

As the land fell under the plow, much of the wilderness habitat of the wildlife disappeared. Since those days of reckless destruction of wildlife, things have changed. Today, one may find white tail and mule deer, as well as pronghorn antelope, in many parts of North Dakota. The number of white tail deer has increased because of the planting of shelter belts and the increased availability of food, due to agricultural activity. Audubon sheep, once numerous in the western part of the state, were hunted to extinction. In 1956, the state placed some bighorn sheep in Theodore Roosevelt Park. By the mid-1970s, because the herd had increased so greatly, limited hunting was permitted.

Many predatory animals still roam the prairie. Coyotes are found in the Badlands and in other parts of the state, though not in great numbers. The red fox has largely replaced the coyote as the most numerous predator. The bobcat makes its home in wooded areas. The beaver, mink, muskrat, and weasel still live in wooded lands along streams and numerous prairie marshes. The skunk and raccoon can be found throughout the state.

Flickertails and gophers still inhabit the state's pasturelands. Prairie dogs, which have been largely destroyed by poison, are now found mostly in the Badlands. North Dakota has six types of rabbits. Three species of cottontails make their home in areas where there is brush cover, around farmsteads, and on the outskirts of the cities and towns. The jack rabbit, actually a true hare, is a prairie-roving animal. In the more forested areas, such as the Turtle Mountains, the snowshoe hare is prevalent.

Almost a hundred kinds of fish inhabit North Dakota's waters. With the creation of reservoirs, fishing has greatly improved and has provided many hours

The Richardson Ground Squirrel (at the right) is referred to as the flickertail from which North Dakota gets its nickname, "The Flickertail State." The Western Meadowlark (below) is the state bird. (ND-DPI)

of recreation for those who love the sport. The Game and Fish Department has stocked these waters with fish such as walleye, northern and sand pike, and trout. Smaller school-fish (crappie, sunfish, bluegill) are common.

Of the almost 2,000 kinds of birds that breed in the United States, 180 breed in North Dakota. Over 200 other kinds migrate through the state or visit it now and then. North Dakota's bird population numbers about 53,000,000. About a third of the bird population is made up of the horned lark, the chestnut-collared longspur, the red-winged blackbird, and the western meadowlark, the state bird. The other most numerous birds are the bobolink, mourning dove, brown-headed cowbird, American coot, blue-winged teal, and several kinds of sparrow. Most of the state's birds are those typical of a grasslands region.

Since North Dakota is a part of the central flyway for ducks and geese, these birds stop off here for food and rest. The Drift Prairie with its many potholes and sloughs provides the ducks and geese with wetlands. Upland game birds inhabit most of the state. The ruffled grouse, sage grouse, sharptail grouse, and the prairie chicken are found in most wooded areas. Three game birds have been introduced into the state: the ringneck pheasant, the wild turkey, and the Hungarian partridge.

Because of its climate, North Dakota has fewer amphibians (frogs, toads, salamanders) and reptiles (turtles, lizards, snakes) than other states. More amphibians inhabit eastern than western North Dakota. The reptile population is equally distributed around the state. The garter and bull snakes are most common. The only poisonous snake is the prairie rattlesnake, which lives mostly on the Missouri Plateau.

*　　*　　*　　*　　*　　*

The activities of North Dakotans are influenced by the state's continental climate and the plant and animal life that can adapt to it. The land and the climate dictate how North Dakotans make their livings. The Indian survived because of the animal life which the prairie could support. Spring wheat has become the main support of the state's economy because of the soil and climate. The abundance of certain kinds of grasses has made cattle ranching possible. The history of North Dakota is the story of adjustment to the land and the climate.

3 Seven Council Fires: The Sioux

Of the Indians who claimed North Dakota — or part of it — as their land, the Teton Sioux were the strongest and the most aggressive and were the last to yield to the government of the United States. The Santee Sioux remained in southern Minnesota. The Yankton Sioux stayed for the most part in South Dakota. Both, however, had tribes who hunted in what is today North Dakota. The Teton had three tribes which lived in southwestern North Dakota and claimed the western part of the state as their hunting ground. The story of the Sioux in North Dakota in the period before the coming of the white man is essentially the story of the Teton.

I. The Westward Journey

During the 15th century the Siouan people who were living between the Appalachian Mountains and the Atlantic Ocean began a slow migration toward the west through the Ohio Valley. During the long and hazardous journey, some groups split off and went south. The largest group, however, continued northwest. Most of them settled by the 1600s in the forest and lake country west of Lake Superior.

By this time, these Siouan people were divided into three groups. They had developed different language patterns or dialects: Dakota, Nakota, and Lakota. For example, the term "thank you" in Dakota is *pidomiye*; in Nakota it is *pinomiye*; in Lakota it is *pilomiye*. Sometimes these three groups are named for the dialect each spoke. Besides language, the three groups had differences of physical characteristics, dress, and living style.

The "Eastern Sioux" — called the Santee — spoke the Dakota dialect. They consisted of four tribes: the Mdwakantowan, the Wahpekute, the Sisseton, and the Wahpeton. They were the smallest physically and wore their hair in four braids. All the Siouan people originally had been woodlands Indians, and the Santee remained a people of the woods. They built permanent homes and depended on the forest and lakes for their food. They farmed and remained in Minnesota. The Wahpekute lived in the region of the Blue Earth and Cannon rivers, while the Mdwakantowan made their home along the Mississippi between the St. Croix and the Upper Iowa rivers. The Sisseton and Wahpeton centered in the Big Stone Lake and Lake Traverse region on the border between Minnesota and South Dakota. Close to the plains, the Sisseton and Wahpeton hunted on the plains of Dakota.

The "Middle Sioux" — called the Yankton — had two tribes, the Yankton and the Yanktonnai, and spoke the Nakota dialect. They were middle-sized in stature and wore three braids. About 2,500 Yankton moved into the region of the lower James and Big Sioux valleys in South Dakota. The Yanktonnai, about 5,000 to 6,000 in number, lived in the territory of the headwaters of the James, Sioux, and Red rivers. The "Middle Sioux" practiced a mixed way of living; some built permanent homes, some did not. Many farmed, but they also held semiannual buffalo hunts.

The "Western Sioux" — the Teton — spoke the Lakota dialect. Numbering about 12,000 they were the largest and strongest of the groups. Stretching from western Nebraska to western North Dakota and from the Missouri River into Wyoming, the Teton became the masters of the plains, claiming hunting grounds from Oklahoma into Canada. The Teton group was made up of seven major tribes. The largest was the Oglala, who mainly lived in Wyoming, northwest Nebraska, and westernmost South Dakota. The Sicangu, also known as the Brulés, lived in northwestern Nebraska and southwestern South Dakota. The Miniconjou and the Oohenonpas (the Two Kettle) resided north of the Brulés in South Dakota. The Hunkpapa, the Sihasppa (Blackfeet), and the Itazipchos (Sans Arc) were smaller groups which occupied the northern part of Teton territory in southwestern North Dakota.

Physically, the Teton were taller than the Yankton and Santee; many Teton warriors were over six feet. They wore only two braids. The Teton were the most nomadic of the three groups; they gathered and hunted food, but never farmed.

The Sioux began leaving the forests of Minnesota during the mid-1600s to continue their westward migration for two main reasons. First, the Chippewa, allied with the French, were beginning to pressure the Sioux from the east. Second, buffalo were plentiful on the plains and offered a bountiful food supply.

The Teton were the first to leave. As they migrated out of Minnesota and across the plains of Dakota, they had to force other tribes out of their way. War was the only answer if the Teton were to continue their westward movement. The Cheyenne, the Iowa, the Otoe, the Omaha, and others yielded to the Teton. By the 1750s the Teton had reached the Missouri. Now the Arikara — 20,000

```
        ASSINIBOIN            PLAINS CHIPPEWA

                        MANDAN         YANKTONNAI
                        HIDATSA
                        ARIKARA
    TETON
    HUNKPAPA
    SIHASPPA                              SISSETON
    ITAZIPCHOS                            WAHPETON
```

Locations of Indian groups and their hunting grounds — early 1800s.

people with fortified villages in northern South Dakota — stood in the way of Teton control of the Missouri. For 20 years the Teton and the Arikara carried on a bloody struggle. In 1792 the Arikara gave up their land and moved up river into North Dakota.

The Yankton followed the Teton out of Minnesota, pushing the Omaha out of southwestern Minnesota and eventually claiming eastern South Dakota. The Santee remained in Minnesota and until 1736 lived at peace with the advancing Chippewa. For 44 years the Chippewa, allied with the French, the Cree, and the Assiniboin, fought with the remaining Sioux. In 1780 the Santee lost their last battle to the Chippewa. In 1825 the United States government restricted the Santee to southern Minnesota.

II. Government and Society

Sioux life was structured; the Sioux were master organizers and they were democratic. The Seven Council Fires (the seven tribes) met each summer. Multitudes gathered together to decide matters of common importance and to perform the Sun Dance. This annual meeting symbolized the unity of the great Sioux Nation.

At this meeting the *Wicasa Yatapickas*, the four great leaders of the nation, met to discuss Sioux problems. Elected from the outstanding chiefs of the tribes by a national council, they were the most honored men in the Sioux Nation. They formed policy and approved or disapproved of actions taken by the individual chiefs.

A Teton Sioux horse race painted by Carl Bodmer. (SHSND)

Since the *Wicasa Yatapickas* met only yearly, each tribe within the Sioux Nation had great independence and had as many chiefs or Shirt Wearers as the tribe needed. The Shirt Wearers decided matters of tribal concern and looked after the welfare of the people. The *Wakincuzas* or Pipe Owners served under the Shirt Wearers and were elected by the *Naca Ominicia*, the tribal council. Their tasks were to organize camp moves and to appoint the *Akicitas*, the tribal police. The *Akicitas* was open to all able young men and was responsible for maintaining order in camp and on buffalo hunts.

The *tiospaye*, a group of individuals banded together under a common leader and often related through marriage to the same father, was the heart of the Sioux society. Its members cooperated in hunting, homemaking, rearing children, caring for the aged, burying the dead, and worshipping. The *tiospaye* was composed of one or more families and was a very tightly-knit organization. No man would marry a girl with whom he shared a common grandparent, and ideally the man should choose his wife from outside the *tiospaye*. The family of the grandfather, father, and son, together with blood brothers, was the basis of the *tiospaye*. The *tiospaye* assured the Sioux of security.

The Sioux prepared their young for marriage and family responsibility at an early age. As children reached adolescence, their parents advised them about matters of sex and marriage. Courting for young people varied from place to place. Sometimes a young man, wishing to meet and talk to a young woman, would meet her in front of the tepee. He might cover their heads with his robe and talk in private. The girl had the choice, and if she did not wish to marry a certain man, she could refuse the embrace. Sioux marriages were, however, generally planned by the parents. A Sioux man could take up to six wives, but more than two was rare for both economic and peace-keeping reasons. Divorce was simple. All a man needed to do was beat the drum publicly and announce that he had parted with his wife. Women, too, could divorce men.

III. Religious Beliefs

The Sioux believed in one God — the Great Spirit — called by some the Great Mystery. The Great Spirit's name was *Wakan Tanka.* The Great Spirit or *Wakan Tanka* was in all things and all people. The great Spirit was the Earth, *Maka*; the Sky, *Skan*; the Sun, *Wi*; the Rock, *Inyan*; the Moon, *Hanwi*; the Wind, *Tate*; and the Buffalo and the Bear — in all things. Man was but a very small part of the mysterious universe.

The Sioux believed that good and evil powers controlled the universe. They knew that the powers of good were more powerful; but they also realized that evil power, represented by *Iya*, the Cyclone, and *Itom*, the Trickster, had to be reckoned with. They called these competing good and evil spirits the Controllers.

Among the Sioux, the Holy Men interpreted and transmitted knowledge of the universe to the people. Being able to communicate with the Controllers, they could give proper advice. Inheritors of all tribal legends, the Holy Men were keepers of the vast treasuries of tribal memories and lore. Prayer and worship through ritual were the only effective ways of insuring life. Rituals were patterned to the universe, and only the Holy Men possessed the knowledge of ceremonies and rituals.

Of special importance in religious life was the visit to earth that *Whope,* the daughter of the Sun and Moon, had made. Arrayed in dazzling dress, the beautiful *Whope* had appeared to Sans Arc scouts. They were awestruck at Her beauty. "I am of the Buffalo People. I have been sent to this earth," she declared, "to talk with your people." She appeared the next day at the camp holding a pipe stem in Her right hand and a red pipe bowl in Her left. She entered the council tepee, sat in the place of honor, and told those present that *Wakan Tanka* was pleased with the Sioux and that She was proud to be their sister. Because the Sioux had preserved good against evil, harmony against discord, She would give them the pipe which She held on behalf of all mankind. Smoking the pipe would be a symbol of good faith and peace. She told the women that their role was one of faithful mother and wife. In kindness, despite their own troubles, they should comfort others. The children, She said, should respect their parents and make sacrifices for good. She informed the men that the pipe was to be used to offer sacrifices to the Great Spirit for all the blessings of life and that it be offered daily. She also told them to be kind and loving to women and children. Finally, speaking to the chief, *Whope* entrusted the pipe to his care. After four days and a final pipe-smoking ceremony, She left. As everyone watched Her disappear, She was transformed into a white buffalo calf. In this way She had come to earth to teach the Sioux.

An artist's version of the Sun Dance. (SHSND)

The Sioux had a moral system which declared that good outweighed evil. Moral codes such as that brought to them by *Whope*, the Beautiful One, directed their lives — lives which demanded self-denial and sacrifice. Four main rules were stressed: help one another; be kind to one another; pity one another; be of one people.

The Sioux believed that man could not succeed without power and that with power almost anything was possible. This power was a force coming from the Great Spirit. To a few it came easily; to some, with great difficulty; and to many it never came.

Power came to men in dreams or visions. Once obtained, it became a part of the person. Some gained power early as children as they slept. Most had to seek it, and they sought it in several ways, all of which called for self-sacrifice. They might fast on the top of a hill or drag buffalo skulls attached to the skin of their backs with pins of wood. Men who were successful became known as Dreamers and were held in high esteem.

The Sun Dance was the most important Sioux religious ceremony. It symbolized their relationship with the Great Spirit. The Dance was very complicated. Men might participate in the Sun Dance to fulfill a vow in return for a favor. Some danced to secure supernatural aid for themselves or for someone else.

The Sun Dance ceremony was held during the moon of the ripening of chokecherries and lasted 12 days. The first four days were devoted to the preparation of the campsite. The next four days were spent giving instructions to the dancers, who were isolated in a lodge with the Holy Men. The final four days were the Holy Days. On the first Holy Day the Sioux established a ceremonial camp, erected a Sacred Lodge, and held the Buffalo Dance. The second and third

Holy Days were devoted to the capture of the "enemy," represented by a cottonwood tree. Everyone sang and cheered joyfully as the tree was felled and trimmed. After the pole was placed in the lodge, the warriors danced the War Dance.

On the fourth and last day the Holy Men prepared the Sun Dancers for their part in the ceremony. The Holy Men, carrying buffalo skulls, led the dancers to the Dance Lodge. During the ceremony, each dancer took the role of a captive and danced one of the forms of the Sun Dance. Those who danced the "Gaze at the Sun Buffalo" had wooden pins placed through their back shoulders with two to four buffalo skulls attached. Those who did the "Gaze at the Sun Staked" were placed in the center of four upright poles with ropes running from each pole to the wooden pins in the dancer's chest and back. In the highest form, "Gaze at the Sun Suspended," the dancers had ropes tied from the sacred pole to pins in their breasts. Each successive dance became more frenzied, and the singing grew louder. The dancers struggled to free themselves, being careful, however, not to do so. During intermissions, friends might clean the dancers' wounds. It was often late at night before the men began to free themselves. When the captives were free, the Dance was over and the sacrifice completed.

The Sun Dance was the center of the Sioux religious experience and was characteristic of the great importance of religion in their lives. The men publicly demonstrated their selflessness by submitting to capture and unbelievable pain.

IV. Life Cycle

The birth of a child was the fulfillment of a woman's role in Sioux society. During birth a woman was usually assisted by her mother or sister. Four days after a birth, a feast for naming the baby was announced. The Sioux generally named a baby after its oldest living grandparent or in honor of a deceased and respected grandparent. If a child in the family had already been given such a name, the new child was often named for a warlike deed its father had performed. Boys received a secret name which insured long life. The father provided the boy with bow and arrow; and as soon as the boy was able to straddle a horse, his father gave him a colt and trappings. The boy's first war party marked the transition from childhood to youth. At 13 or 14 a boy hoped to join one of the police societies.

For a girl, the first ten years of life were similar to those of the boy. Instructed by her mother, she learned rules of conduct and household skills. If the girl had a younger sister or brother, much of her time would be devoted to child care.

When someone died, the family waited for a day and night in case the person revived. Then the relatives dressed the body in finest attire. The body, along with highly cherished possessions, was wrapped in a robe and in a tanned skin, forming a great bundle. For four days the family mourned and the men performed a worship ceremony. The body was then placed on a high scaffold out of reach of wild animals. The dead person's horse was killed and its tail fastened to the

Scaffold burial. Right, artist's view. (UND-LC) Below, an early photograph. (SHSND).

scaffold. At death, the Sioux believed that the spirit left the body to travel the Spirit Trail to the Land of Many Lodges. The Land of Many Lodges was a beautiful place where all the ancestors pitched their tepees amid lush prairies. This was a good land where all things which had once existed on earth lived forever.

V. Life in a Warrior Society: The Teton Sioux

The Teton Sioux became the masters of the plains. Before coming to the plains, they had been a people of the woods. Their new environment brought changes in their way of life. By the 1750s the Teton had developed into a nomadic hunting society — aggressive, independent, and economically secure in the middle of the great buffalo range. The horse gave the Teton control of the range, and the buffalo became the center of their lives. To maintain their domination, the Teton frequently had to fight other tribes. Therefore, they developed a strong warrior class.

The Teton had a nomadic way of life. They followed wandering buffalo herds, which determined the location of their camps. Their dwellings and property were very mobile, and a camp could be ready to move in fifteen minutes. An average day's march was 25 miles, but under pressure, bands could travel 50.

They made no pottery which might be broken while moving, but cooked in pouches made of buffalo skins. They stored their belongings in leather cases and carried their babies in cradles. Everything they owned was portable. They chose campsites which provided water, wood, grass, protection from the weather, and security from enemies. Winter camp was more permanent, and often, reflecting their woodlands heritage, the Teton preferred the Black Hills. During the winter and spring, many moved into wigwams which were permanent hut-like dwellings made of poles permanently fixed in the ground and covered with bark, grass mats, or hides. In the spring the Sioux repaired their tepees, began breaking horses, and hunted smaller game. During the summer, bands usually moved to camps on higher ground. Family hunting continued and raiding parties were active. Summer was also the season for ceremonial affairs. Fall was a busy time of the year. Women gathered nuts and vegetables, and men concentrated on hunting the buffalo and planning war parties. When the first heavy snow fell, the scattered groups gathered to decide upon a permanent winter camp.

The Teton lived off the land, hunting and gathering. Hunting was not a sport; it took work and meant survival. They divided hunting into two categories: the *tate*, the family hunt, and the *wani-sapa*, the communal buffalo drive. Individuals hunted daily for food or for decorations such as bird feathers. In the fall, bands dispersed as *tates* to hunt and collect winter supplies. Men usually hunted in small parties or as a family group.

The *wani-sapa* was the most efficient way of getting food. It was a tribal matter and was used solely to obtain buffalo. When a *wani-sapa* was held, everyone was expected to work hard for its success. Those who did not were whipped or had their property taken away. The Teton divided the meat equally,

A Teton Sioux warrior, a painting by Carl Bodmer. (SHSND)

but those who contributed most to the success of the hunt received the choice pieces.

The Teton also fished the many rivers which flowed through their territory. They used a bone hook, a long line of sinew, and grasshoppers for bait. Obtaining food was a task for all: the men hunted and fished; the women gathered the berries and roots of the woods. At times they obtained corn, beans, and squash in trade with the Omaha or the Arikara.

Conquest was an important aspect of Teton life. Their economy was not only based on the buffalo, but also on the capture of enemy property, especially horses. War became a way of life. Boys fought make-believe wars. Adolescents prepared themselves for war. Men engaged in actual warfare. Glory belonged to the successful warrior. They saw obvious values in waging war. The individual could gain personal wealth as well as prestige and a position of leadership. For the tribe, war meant security; enemies were forced farther away from the buffalo, and safety from attack became more certain.

Retaliation, defense, conquest, and obtaining goods were the primary reasons for war. Men became adjusted to a life of risk, violence, and self-assertion. A war honor system, called the *coup*, was very important. The first to touch an enemy was entitled to wear a golden eagle feather upright at the rear of his head. The second to touch the same enemy would wear an eagle feather tilted to the left; the third, an eagle feather horizontally; and the fourth, a buzzard feather hung vertically. Rivalry for war honors was keen, and success meant personal gain and glory.

Along with the serious business of hunting and war, the Sioux enjoyed playing a wide variety of games. In winter the children had ice-sledding contests or played the sticking-together game in which boys and girls would spin tops on the ice to see whose would spin the longest. The moccasin game was a popular winter night game and involved guessing the location of sticks.

Older boys played rough contact games. In the fire-throwing game two teams attacked each other with lighted brush. In the spring a similar game was played using mudballs, some of which held a burning coal. Knocking-the-ball was the favorite team sport. As in soccer, two teams attempted to kick or hit a ball with sticks at the opponent's goal. The swing-kicking game was the roughest. Two teams using robes as shields would attack each other, kicking their opponents, trying to knock them down. The game was over when one side gave up. These rough games were, in part, a way in which the Teton conditioned their youth for later combat.

Women found delight in shooting dice in a basket. The dice were three pairs of plum seeds. One set was painted with the images of a buffalo; one, with a swallow; while the third set was totally black. A complex scoring system made the game very exciting. The Teton, like most Sioux, loved to gamble and played most games for high stakes.

The old folks enjoyed telling tall tales and stories about pranksters and fools. Storytelling about the past was a part of any evening's entertainment. In this way

A Sioux camp, mid-1800s. (SHSND)

myths, tales, and history were passed down from generation to generation.

The main dwelling was the tepee. The construction of the tepee was the responsibility of the woman. The hunt provided the required number of buffalo hides: seven for a small tepee and 12 to 18 for a large one. The women tanned the hides — a task which might take two weeks. Cutting the hides to a tepee pattern was an exacting job and took much experience. Twenty or more 15 to 20 foot long poles provided a frame upon which the women sewed the hides. A door was cut and a smoke flap sewn. A "dew cloth" made of hides was fastened around the inside of the tepee to serve as insulation against the dew and extreme temperatures. The tepee was warm in winter and provided shade in the summer. The Teton placed beds of folded buffalo robes around the inside edge of the tepee, and leather storage bags between the beds. A water bag hung on a pole by the door. The fire pit was located directly under the smoke flap. The altar was placed behind the fire pit. The tepee belonged to the woman; it was her property and responsibility.

Throwing Stick, a Teton Sioux girl. (SHSND)

The buffalo robe was one of the most essential and decorative articles of clothing worn by the Teton, who were the flashiest dressers of the Sioux tribes. Fine robes for dress and ceremony were brightly adorned with quill work and/or paintings. Women's robes were mostly decorated with buffalo pictures, and older men's with war exploits.

The men's clothing consisted of an undecorated leather breechcloth and moccasins. Leggings, reaching from the ankle and covering the thighs, were tied with a decorated belt. Poncho-like shirts were reserved for *Akicita* and other dignitaries of the tribe. Only the *Wicasa* could wear painted shirts. The Teton — like most Sioux — also wore ornaments such as shell earrings, quilled armlets, bear claw necklaces, beaded chokers, and quilled braid wrappings. Women's attire consisted of a dress made from two elk skins, knee-length leggings, and moccasins. For everyday use the garments were rarely decorated. For ceremonial occasions, the women decorated their dresses with quill work and later with beads. Leather belts with geometric designs were worn around the waist. Leggings and moccasins were also adorned with quill work.

* * * * * *

The Sisseton and Wahpeton tribes of the Santee Sioux — the "Eastern Sioux" — remained a woodlands people, even though they hunted on the plains of Dakota. The Yankton and Yanktonnai — the "Middle Sioux" — were a mixture of woodlands and plains cultures. The Teton — the "Western Sioux" — became a people of the plains. The Teton adjusted to their new environment; they became nomadic, following the great herds of buffalo across the plains. To protect their domain and to gain what they did not have, they developed into a warrior society. The Teton became the masters of the plains.

4 From the Woods to the Plains: The Chippewa

The Chippewa were originally a people of the woods who depended on the forests and lakes to provide their livelihood. Those of them who left the woods of Minnesota for the plains of Dakota faced a new environment. The story of the Chippewa in North Dakota is the story of adjusting to a new land — a land very much different from the one they had known before.

I. The Westward Journey

The Chippewa, also known as the Ojibwa (which means "to roast until puckered up"), came from the valley of the St. Lawrence River and are members of a large language group of Indian people called Algonguian. Other Algonguian-speaking Indians are the Cheyenne, the Cree, the Arapaho, the Shawnee, the Sauk, and the Fox. During the 1600s, as European fur traders and settlers moved west, the Chippewa began their westward migration. The Chippewa actively traded with the newcomers. In exchange for furs, they received firearms, metal-made items such as axes, and other goods. Moving west with the fur-trading frontier gave them a steady supply of important European goods.

As the Chippewa moved into the region of Lake Superior, they came into contact with the "Eastern Sioux," or Santee, who controlled the lands of northern Minnesota. In 1679 the Sioux agreed to let the Chippewa hunt on the eastern fringe of their land. In exchange, the Chippewa agreed to trade French goods to the Sioux. This friendly agreement lasted for 50 years. The Chippewa were in a favorable position as go-betweens for the French traders and the western

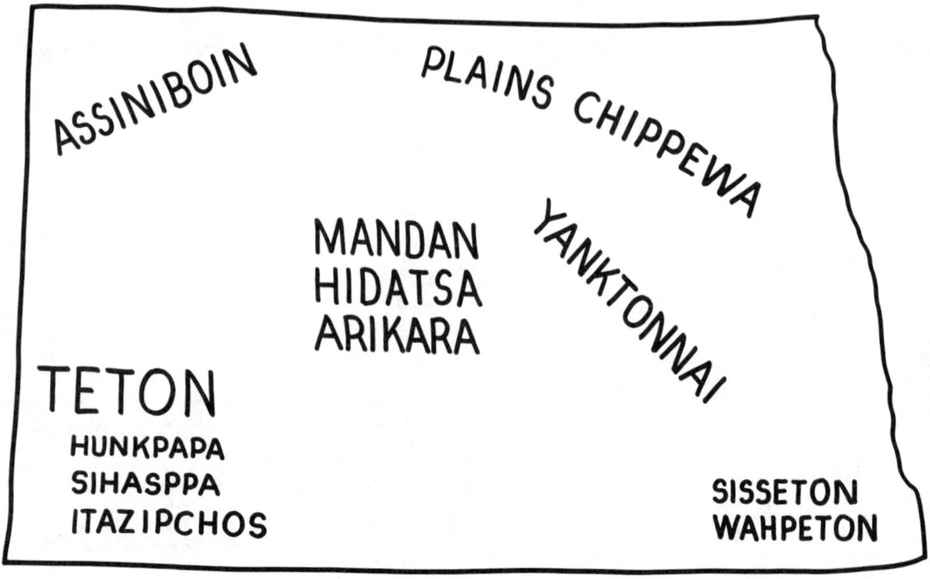

ASSINIBOIN

PLAINS CHIPPEWA

MANDAN
HIDATSA
ARIKARA

YANKTONNAI

TETON
HUNKPAPA
SIHASPPA
ITAZIPCHOS

SISSETON
WAHPETON

Locations of Indian groups and their hunting grounds — early 1800s.

Indian groups. As the Chippewa pushed westward into northern Wisconsin, conflicts with neighboring tribes developed. They joined the French in war against the Fox, who were competing with the Chippewa for hunting space. By the 1730s the Chippewa and French had defeated the Fox, and the Chippewa claimed much of Wisconsin as their hunting grounds.

In 1736 the long peace between the Chippewa and the Sioux ended when a party of Santee Sioux killed a party of Frenchmen. The Chippewa came to the aid of their allies, the French, and a war was on. The Cree and the Assiniboin, long-time enemies of the Sioux, joined the Chippewa. In a series of bloody battles over a span of 44 years, the Chippewa and their allies, who had more European guns than their enemies, gained firm control of northern Minnesota and Wisconsin. In 1780 at St. Croix Falls, the last Santee attempt to drive back the Chippewa failed. In 1825 the United States government set up a boundary line between the Santee and the Chippewa.

The Chippewa were a people of the woods. Their experiences from the St. Lawrence Valley to the lakes of northern Minnesota had made them accustomed to and dependent upon the forests. The Chippewa of the woodlands trapped for furs, fished the lakes, made sugar from the abundant maple trees, harvested wild rice, hunted deer, and picked wild berries. Since the necessities of life were always near at hand in the woods, the Chippewa built permanent dwellings. Their wigwams and lodges were constructed of poles driven into the ground and covered with birchbark or matted bullrushes.

Most Chippewa were happy with life in the forests of northern Minnesota and Wisconsin. But some, perhaps looking for better trapping or hunting grounds, began to move westward. This brought them to the Red River Valley. By the 1790s Chippewa were hunting beaver over a wide stretch of territory from the Red to the Souris River and as far north as Lake Manitoba. The first Chippewa migrants to the prairies tried to live the same way they had in the Minnesota woods — hunting, fishing, and trapping. But they soon found that they would have to adjust to their new environment. Wild rice and maple trees were scarce; fish were not as abundant; buffalo hunting was difficult without horses. This, along with Sioux war-parties, made it impossible for them to live in permanent communities. During their early years in North Dakota, the Chippewa developed a more nomadic way of life. Not until the early 1800s did they form a permanent band near Alexander Henry's Pembina trading post. This was the beginning of the Turtle Mountain Band, which was becoming a plains group.

By the 1830s the Chippewa in Dakota had adjusted to life on the plains. They acquired many horses, which made it possible for them to hunt the great buffalo herds as far west as the Yellowstone River in Montana. The Chippewa drove the Cheyenne and the Hidatsa out of eastern North Dakota, and by treaty with the Sioux in 1863 acquired a claim to the northern third of North Dakota. They maintained friendly relations with the Plains Cree and the Assiniboin, but continually skirmished with the Sioux, the Mandan, the Arikara, the Blackfoot, and the Hidatsa.

II. Government and Society

The Chippewa, unlike the Sioux, were not a single, well-organized political nation. Despite common language, beliefs, customs, and way of life, each Chippewa band was a unit which acted independently of the others. A dozen bands of Plains Chippewa resided on the northern plains, and each usually took its name from the territory where it lived, such as the Turtle Mountain Band. The Plains Chippewa were also divided into clans named after animals, birds, or fish. Clan membership was inherited and passed on through the father. Marriage between two people belonging to the same clan was prohibited, and often clans were made up of many different families. The clan was the most important group to the Chippewa. It held them together. The members of a clan looked after one another.

Each band usually had several chiefs, one of whom acted as the head chief. A head chief inherited his position and held it for life. The tribal council, made up of the adult men, could, however, remove a chief who failed to carry out his duties. The powers of the head chief were limited, and the band usually obeyed an order only when it was accepted by the majority. The head chief kept order in camp, settled serious disputes, distributed gifts at ceremonies, entertained visitors from other bands, and led the tribe in war. The chief was assisted by four (in some cases 12) counselors who were elected by the tribal council.

A group of Chippewa leaders, late 1800s. (SHSND)

The *okitsita*, the tribal police, were men who had good war records and judgment. The *okitsita* had a special tepee in the center of the camp and wore special facial paintings and bonnets. Besides keeping order, the *okitsita* settled minor disputes and punished those who broke tribal laws.

The most serious crime in Plains Chippewa society was murder. Murders were dealt with by private blood revenge. Relatives of the murdered person traditionally killed either the murderer or one of his relatives. The chiefs and *okitsita* took no part in these affairs.

Next to murder, crimes against the tribe as a whole were most serious. Going ahead of the main hunting party to fire at a buffalo was such a crime, since the whole group might suffer. The punishment for a first offense was loss of belongings and a whipping. A second offender might be thrown out of camp, and a third offense sometimes resulted in the death penalty.

III. Life on the Plains

Although the Chippewa continued to fish, harvest some wild rice, make what sugar was possible, and hunt small game, life on the plains meant that the buffalo would, as in the case of the Sioux, play the important role in their lives. The Sun Dance, unimportant to the Chippewa when they lived in Minnesota, now became very important. A buffalo skull on the altar reminded them that the buffalo was now their source of life, and they did the Sun Dance in part to bring rain, grass, and buffalo.

An annual buffalo hunt took place each summer. Directed by a hunt chief, a party would scout out suitable herds. The hunters would encircle the herd and charge, firing at the heart of the buffalo. The women, children, and older folks would follow to do the skinning and butchering. Most of the meat was cut into long strips, dried, and stored for winter use. Hides were tanned for use in building tepees.

Fishing was not so important to the Chippewa after they left Minnesota. The Plains Chippewa, however, did fish with line and hook, spear and nets. The Chippewa in the Red River Valley harvested wild rice and made maple sugar. Blueberries, plums, and chokecherries were picked in season and dried. Some Chippewa in North Dakota grew corn, but farming was no longer very important. Most food was distributed equally among all members of the group.

The horse was very important in helping the Chippewa live on the plains. Horses were essential for the buffalo hunt and for transporting belongings. Although the horse travois, a pole and leather thong device which was pulled behind a horse, was important, the Chippewa also adopted the use of the Red River cart, which had two wheels and was made of wood.

The dress of the Plains Chippewa combined the dash of the plains with the skilled craft and color of the woodland people. Men wore buckskin breechcloths as an apron in front and back. Older warriors and chiefs wore long breechcloths which touched the ground, but the usual length was "four hands." Men wore deerhide leggings, some coming up to the knee and others to the hip. In cold weather and on ceremonial occasions, men put on poncho-type shirts of leather. Shirts were brightly trimmed with bead work and other ornaments such as ermine skins. Capotes, parka-like garments made of moose or elk hide, were worn in the cold season. Both men and women wore decorated bison robes. Women's dresses were made of either hides or blankets. The dress hung from the shoulders by two beaded straps and was gathered at the waist with a wide belt. Women's leggings were usually short and were held up by a woven garter or buckskin thong.

The Plains Chippewa used several kinds of moccasins. Some retained the soft-sole type of the Minnesota woodlands. Most, however, switched to a hard-sole type used by other plains Indians. The Chippewa, unlike other plains tribes, added a floral-beaded cuff.

The Plains Chippewa were very fond of horned bonnets; any sort of headgear might have horns on it. The tribal police and distinguished warriors wore horned bonnets with a single row of feathers on a tail piece running down the wearer's back. Buffalo headdresses were worn on certain occasions. Both men and women wore earrings of shell, and later, of silver. Silver brooches often adorned entire garments. The Plains Chippewa commonly fastened a small wooden hoop with a spider-web-like filling of yarn to Sun Dance costumes.

Both men and women commonly painted their faces in a decorative way. The police painted one side of their face and upper body red and the other side yellow. In some dances, men painted their battle scars red to make it appear that the

A Chippewa family stands by its tepee. These Chippewa of the late 1800s have adopted the white man's dress. (SHSND)

wounds were fresh. Members of the Midewiwin lodge were the only persons allowed to use blue paint.

In a busy life the Plains Chippewa found time for relaxation and play. Their favorite sport was *wapaskawsn*. It was played on a field about 100 yards long with a goal at each end. Each side had eleven men, including a goal tender, and each player carried sticks with a bend at the end. The object of the game was to get a ball, deerskin stuffed with hair, through the goal. The ball could be tossed or carried by stick. The game was rough, with blocking, tripping, and even clubbing allowed. Sometimes they played the game on horseback. *Pakesank* was also popular. In this game one player attempted to throw a spear through a hoop rolled by his opponent. In the winter they played "snow snake." A smoothed stick was thrown over a snowy surface to see who could make his stick slide the farthest.

The moccasin game was the most popular indoor sport. Four pads cut to resemble moccasins were placed over four objects — one of which was different. One player tried to guess which pad concealed the different object. If he guessed correctly, he received one point; if not, his opponent gained the point. After 11 chances the game ended. At times heavy betting accompanied the moccasin game, and occasionally a bettor would lose all his possessions.

Young boys played with tops made of wood, stone, or horn, and with sling shots and pop guns made of willow shoots. Girls played with dolls, usually made of sticks and grass or stuffed buckskin.

IV. Religious Beliefs

The Chippewa believed in a single, all powerful God named *Kitse-manito,* or Great Spirit, who resided in the heavens from where He looked down upon the earth and His children. Because *Kitse-manito* was so powerful, usually He was worshipped through lesser spirits found in the forests, water, sky, and many other objects. The Chippewa also saw the Sun as a powerful force. The Earth was the mother of mankind and was often spoken to in prayers. The Stone was an important symbol of great strength. Of the animal spirits, the Bear was the most powerful; the Buffalo and the Horse were also very important. The Chippewa prayed to the Thunderbirds, giant eagle-like birds, to bring the rain. The Thunderbirds constantly fought with the Underground Panthers, enormous creatures resembling panthers with scales and with bulls' horns on their heads. The Panthers possessed great knowledge of medicine and were masters of underwater creatures. The Thunderbirds represented the sky and the upper world, light and good. The Panthers stood for the lower world, darkness and evil.

A Chippewa Sun Dance lodge. (SHSND)

Like the Sioux, the Chippewa believed that the forces of good and evil were struggling for control of the universe. Because man had both within him, they believed that both forces had to be pleased. A Chippewa would worship the Thunderbirds but also pay homage to the Panthers.

The *Wihtigohanek* or Ice Giants were a race of cannibalistic giants, made of ice, who lived in the far North. Occasionally the Ice Giants would venture into Chippewa territory. The Chippewa associated *Pagek* or Bony Spectre with the winter season. *Pagek* had once been mortal and had died while on an extended vision quest seeking knowledge. Because of His sacrifice, *Kitse-manito* made Him a spirit. He was the center of the Trade Dance and was a patron of small children.

The Chippewa could contact these spirits in a number of ways, and the most important was through dreams or visions. A child would not possess a spirit until he had a dream, which might be brought about by fasting. Children would inform their parents about their dreams, and if a pattern occurred in which birds or animals appeared, the dreamer's guardian spirit was revealing itself. When the child was sure of the spirit, he would obtain some part of the bird or animal and keep it to be used when he needed spirit power.

The Chippewa held several important ceremonies. The Trade Dance was important to the Chippewa of the woodlands and to the early Plains Chippewa who depended upon fur trading for a living. Performed in early winter, the Trade Dance helped to bring a heavy snowfall that would make it easier to track game. The ceremony was dedicated to *Pagek*, and offerings were made to Him during the dance.

As the need for the Trade Dance declined, the Sun Dance became the major annual ceremony of the Plains Chippewa. During the early 1800s the Plains Chippewa began using the Sun Dance of the plains tribes. They performed the ceremony in mid-June and used it primarily to ask for rain, good health, and good fortune. A person might vow to perform the Sun Dance for recovery from illness for either himself or a member of his family. The ceremony began with an all-night singing session at the Sun Dance camp in a tepee or wigwam prepared for the purpose. At dawn, men who were dressed as warriors went in search of the sacred tree which would form the center pole of the dance lodge. After informing the Holy Man that a tree had been found, the warriors brought the tree to camp. All but the upper branches were removed; a nest for the Thunderbirds was made at the top, and cloth offerings were tied to the base. They built a lodge around the pole and an altar on the north side of the lodge. A pipe resting on a decorated buffalo skull formed the center of the altar. Two eagle-wing fans were crossed behind it. The Dance lasted for four days and three nights, during which singing and prayers were offered to the spirits. On the fourth day those who were going to perform the dance were pierced in both shoulders with a bone knife. Thongs were placed through the slits in their shoulders and attached to heavy ropes fastened high on the center pole. The participants then danced to the accompaniment of a number of songs. A feast concluded the Sun Dance. The Chippewa version of the Sun Dance was much shorter and less painful than that of the Sioux.

THE MÉTIS

Métis (French for half-breed) culture began during the 17th century when French traders began to marry women of the Chippewa and Cree tribes. The Métis commonly refer to themselves as Mechif. In legal definition, the Métis are classified as Indians, but their culture has been greatly influenced by the French. Their language is a mixture of Chippewa, Cree, and French.

The Métis hunted and trapped in Canada and North Dakota and played a role in the Pembina trade. The traders adopted the Red River cart which the Métis had developed. In the 1880s the Métis agreed to reside on the Turtle Mountain Reservation with their brothers, the Chippewa. Because not enough land was available on the reservation, many Métis received land in Williams County. The village of Trenton in Williams County became a center for Metis activity.

In spite of many hardships, the Métis were and are a people who enjoy life. They enjoy dancing. The Red River jig is a famous Métis dance. They especially celebrate holidays. The New Year's celebration (LaShur-de-la) began the day after Christmas and continued with many festivities until the Friday after New Years. The Métis have a deep-rooted pride in their French and Indian heritage.

The picture above is an early artist's view of a Métis hunting camp. (SHSND)

The *Midewiwin* was a religious society brought to the plains by the Chippewa. It emphasized a ceremonial "death" and "rebirth" of the members, and its purpose was to secure health and long life. There were two ways of becoming a member: to be cured of an illness by a member of the society, or to have a dream in which a spirit suggested that the dreamer join the society. Members progressed through four degrees. Each degree was obtained after receiving instruction in the secrets of the order, memorizing a ritual formula, and paying initiation fees.

The meetings of the *Midewiwin* were usually held in the spring in a large lodge, and the ceremony lasted for four days. The priests of the society carried out the initiation and the healing rites. These rites brought the natural and supernatural together, since the members learned not only practical medical knowledge but also supernatural medicine which gave immortality.

V. The Cycle of Life

When a Plains Chippewa child was born, a midwife was present to assist with the delivery. The child would be named for an unusual event at the time of birth, for a war exploit of a relative, or for some personal characteristic. Later in life, men often acquired a new name in war. Usually an elder male relative, known for his supernatural power, selected the name. The entire family lavished affection on the child, and he was rarely spanked or disciplined.

At puberty a boy was sent into the woods or to a hilltop to fast for several days. He blackened his face with charcoal and prayed that some spirit would become his life-time helper. If the boy were unsuccessful, he would go on other vision quests. For some, the initial fast was the only one; some fasted at various times during their lives to gain some special goal or to acquire additional power.

At the time of their first menstruation, girls were secluded in a small hut and were given very little to eat. During this time of seclusion, spirit helpers often visited the girls and gave them curing powers. Some became powerful medicine women.

Parents usually arranged the marriages of their children. If a young man's parents noticed his fascination with a certain girl, they might negotiate a marriage. A feast and gift exchange marked the marriage. Young men married between the ages of 20 and 25, and girls between 15 and 18. Some important men had more than one wife, but rarely more than two. Divorce was an easy matter. Either person merely picked up his or her belongings and left. The wife retained the tepee and common property.

Plains Chippewa used several types of burial, depending upon the season. The most common type was the "house." A burial pit about six feet long, three feet wide, and four feet deep was dug, and the body was placed in a sitting position. A small gabled roof was built over the pit, and food and water were placed in the house for four days to sustain the dead person's spirit on its trip to the hereafter, a wonderful place where everything desirable was found. Sometimes the dead were buried in shallow graves filled with earth and covered with rocks. In

Chippewa children. Shirts, pants and cotton print dresses have replaced the native dress. The tent, not the tepee or wigwam, has become their home. (SHSND)

winter, tree burial was practiced. The body, wrapped in hide, was placed on a platform in the tree. The Plains Chippewa often thought of the dead and held feasts in their honor.

* * * * * *

When some Chippewa migrated from the woodlands of Minnesota onto the plains of North Dakota, they faced a new environment. Their earlier lives had been centered in the forest. Their religion and their economy reflected the woods. Trapping for furs and eating wild rice, fish, berries, maple sugar, and small game had been their way of life. Once on the plains, however, things had to change, and very rapidly the Chippewa developed a distinct plains way of life. The horse replaced the birchbark canoe; the movable tepee replaced the stationary wigwam; hard soles replaced soft soles on their moccasins. And the buffalo became the heart of their livelihood. With fewer fish and little wild rice or maple sugar, they became almost totally dependent upon the buffalo. Since fur trading became less and less important, the Trade Dance declined. In its place came the Sun Dance, which would bring rain, grass, and buffalo. The Buffalo became an important spirit, and its skull became a religious symbol. By the 1830s those Chippewa who had left the Minnesota woods had become the Plains Chippewa of North Dakota.

5 Other Campfires

In addition to the Sioux and the Chippewa, seven other Indian groups are a part of North Dakota history. The Cheyenne and the Crow spent a short time in the state before moving on to new grounds. The Cree and the Assiniboin lived in Canada, but they traded and hunted in North Dakota. The Three Tribes — the Mandan, the Hidatsa, and the Arikara — made the Missouri Valley their permanent homes. Like others who came to the state, their story is one of adapting to a new environment — the plains.

I. The Three Tribes: Mandan, Hidatsa, and Arikara

The Mandan was the first tribe to make its way into North Dakota. A member of the Siouan language group, the Mandan simply called themselves *Numakiki*, which means "people." The Mandan once lived in the East in the vicinity of a lake. They probably moved west from the Mississippi River Valley and followed the Missouri River toward the north. By the mid-1700s the Mandan had built nine villages at the mouth of the Heart River. Smallpox killed off several thousand Mandan. Reduced in numbers, they migrated north, building two villages near the mouth of the Knife River for their 1,300 people.

The Hidatsa (also called Gros Ventre of the Missouri) were also Siouan in language. The Hidatsa lived near a lake to the northeast of the Missouri River — probably Devils Lake. More powerful tribes, such as the Chippewa, forced them west. They located near the Mandan, with whom they became good friends. When Lewis and Clark visited the region in 1804, the Hidatsa numbered about 2,000 and were living in three villages near the mouth of the Knife River.

The Arikara came to North Dakota on the same pathway as the Mandan — the Missouri River Valley. They were unrelated to the Mandan or Hidatsa and belonged to the Caddoan language family. Originally, the Arikara were a part of the Pawnee Nation east of the Mississippi. The Pawnee and the Arikara split; the Pawnee allied themselves with the Omaha, and the Arikara began moving up the Missouri River. By the mid-1700s they were living in earth-lodge villages below the mouth of the Cheyenne River in South Dakota. During the late 1700s the Arikara became locked in a bloody struggle with the Teton Sioux; the Arikara lost and moved northward into North Dakota near the Cannonball River. Later, with only 2,800 people left, they migrated northward toward the mouth of the Knife River and settled near the Mandan and Hidatsa.

The Mandan, the Hidatsa, and the Arikara eventually became known as the Three Tribes. After the white man's smallpox had drastically reduced their numbers, they sought security in some kind of friendly cooperation. At first, however, each tribe maintained its independence. The Mandan and the Hidatsa got along very well, and both were friendly toward the United States government. Relations between the Mandan-Hidatsa and the Arikara were sometimes strained. In 1837, for example, the Mandan quarreled with the Arikara and moved across the Missouri River. The Arikara then took over the vacated lodges, sometimes stealing Mandan women. The Hidatsa did not always side with the Mandan. Fearing the Teton Sioux, the Hidatsa often looked to the stronger Arikara for protection.

In spite of the difficulties that arose among the Three Tribes, they had much in common. The Mandan and the Arikara brought a sedentary way of life to North Dakota; to say that they were a sedentary people means that they lived in permanent villages and farmed. The Hidatsa also accepted this kind of life when they migrated to the Missouri country. They were good farmers. Corn was their main crop, but they also raised pumpkins, beans, sunflowers, squash, and tobacco. Each family worked a half or full acre of land, and they got an average yield of 20 bushels of corn to the acre. The women and children did most of the farm work.

Corn was the most important crop. The Arikara held an elaborate festival to bless the corn crop. In a good year they traded hundreds of bushels of corn to the fur companies and to other Indians. They also traded tobacco, which was a high-priced item. Once the tobacco leaf was cured, they mixed it with buffalo tallow. The Three Tribes viewed tobacco as a delicacy. They depended on the buffalo for meat and hides. Often, but not always, they moved to winter camps for purposes of hunting.

The Three Tribes lived in villages of permanent, mound-type homes. The lodge, a circular building about 40 feet in diameter, was constructed by covering logs with brush, grass, and clay. Its vaulted ceiling had an opening for the fire's smoke to escape. The lodge was cool in the summer and warm during the cold winter season. At first the villages were not fortified, but as warfare with other tribes increased, ditches and palisades were built around the villages.

Left — the earth lodge. Top, ceremonial lodge. Middle, log-wall lodge. Bottom, interior painting by Carl Bodmer. Right — the Arikara section of the Three Tribes' village. (SHSND)

The making of pottery was another characteristic of their sedentary culture. The Teton Sioux, for example, made no pottery because they were often on the move and pots broke easily. The women of the Three Tribes excelled in pottery making as well as in basket weaving.

Tribal councils elected the chiefs. During their days of power, each of the Three Tribes had more than one chief. The Mandan had two: a war chief and a village chief. The war chief was responsible for military defense, and the village chief cared for the day-to-day needs of the people. By the 1830s, after so many people had been killed off by smallpox, one chief was all that each tribe needed. Each of the groups had a society called the Black Mouth, which carried out the police duties.

Among the Indians who came to North Dakota, the Mandan and Hidatsa developed a unique social structure. The Arikara, like the Sioux and the Chippewa, had clans in which membership was determined by the father. In Mandan and Hidatsa society, however, one's membership in a clan was determined by the mother. Society was divided into two groupings; the "west side" and the "east side." Children inherited the "side" to which their mother belonged. A person could not marry within his or her social "side." The groups were of equal number and represented all villages. The "sides" determined one's position at ceremonial occasions and even on which team one would play games.

The religious beliefs of the Three Tribes were much like those of the other plains Indians. The Great Spirit was in all things, and the Indian sought help from the Great Spirit during his life. The vision quest was just as much a part of Mandan life as it was for the Sioux. To the plains Indians the Sun Dance was the center of ceremonial life. The Mandan, however, celebrated the *Okipa*, a four-day dance which featured the re-creation of historical events from the tribe's past. The *Okipa* was much like the Sun Dance. Men pledged to dance a certain number of dances to secure an abundance of buffalo and prosperity for the village. As in the Sun Dance, the participants underwent very painful rites.

The Three Tribes, like the Sioux and the Chippewa, believed that life after death was very happy. The Hidatsa believed in a Spirit Village, located somewhere in the earth. Life there was a continuation of earthly life. Murderers and those who committed suicide, however, were not allowed to enter the Spirit Village. The Mandan believed that the dead went back into the past and lived in the old villages.

The Mandan, the Hidatsa, and the Arikara were people of the eastern woods who adjusted to the plains of North Dakota. Their ways of life were similar, but each group maintained its independence. Only when death from smallpox reduced the population (after 1837 only 135 Mandan survived) did the Mandan, Hidatsa, and Arikara become the Three Tribes.

An elderly Hidatsa woman, 1910. (SHSND)

Assiniboin breaking camp near Fort Union, Carl Bodmer painting. (SHSND)

II. Cheyenne, Assiniboin, Crow, and Cree

The Cheyenne (their name means "the people of alien speech") belonged to the Algonquian-language family. Before 1700 they lived in the wooded areas between the Mississippi and Red rivers in Minnesota. As the Teton Sioux moved west, they pushed the Cheyenne out of Minnesota. The Cheyenne moved to the valley of the Sheyenne River, a tributary of the Red. They lived in southeastern North Dakota for some time, but roamed as far as the Turtle River area. As the Sioux and Chippewa pushed farther west, the Cheyenne once again had to move. During the 1700s they migrated to the Missouri River Valley; they had to move again when the Mandan and Hidatsa drove them to the south. By 1800 they had found a more permanent home in the Black Hills at the headwaters of the Cheyenne River.

While in Minnesota and southeastern North Dakota, the Cheyenne relied on the woods and farming for their livelihood. By the time they established their territory in the Black Hills, they had adjusted to the new environment, and the buffalo became important to their lives.

The Assiniboin hunted the plains of Canada and the northeastern part of presentday North Dakota. They broke away from their parent group, the Yanktonnai, sometime during the early 1600s and moved into the region between Lake Superior and Hudson Bay, northwest of Lake Winnipeg. By 1775 the tribe had gone westward to the Saskatchewan and Assiniboine river valleys, where they occupied the land between the Sioux, who were to the south of them, and the Siksika, who were to the west. The Assiniboin was a large tribe numbering between 10,000 and 12,000 people. The smallpox epidemic of 1838, however, killed over 4,000 of them.

The Assiniboin, like their relatives the Sioux, had been woodlands people before they came to the plains. Although the Assiniboin adapted like the other plains tribes to the new environment, their culture was a mixture of plains and woodlands. They hunted buffalo and moved about the plains, but they continued to call the wooded river valleys their permanent home. The Assiniboin traded with the Mandan and later with the whites at Fort Union. Their close ally was the Cree, with whom they intermarried. In the early 1800s, and especially after the smallpox outbreak of the late 1830's, they joined the Cree. Because of conflict over the buffalo range, the Assiniboin and Cree were often at war with the Teton Sioux.

The Crow and the Cree played less important roles in the history of North Dakota. The Crow moved west with the Hidatsa and joined the Mandan at the mouth of the Heart River. During this period of close relationship with the Hidatsa, the Crow began to live in permanent villages. Sometime in the late 1600s, the Crow moved into the region of the Yellowstone River Valley in Montana, but they still occasionally hunted on the plains of Dakota. After leaving the Hidatsa, the Crow became more nomadic and gave up village living. The Plains Cree influence was limited to the extreme northeastern part of the state. The Cree, like the Chippewa, were part of the Algonquian family, and they often allied themselves with the Chippewa. Although most Cree lived in Canada, some hunted the territory of northeastern North Dakota, but they never permanently occupied the land.

* * * * * *

The Three Tribes suffered the most from the ravages of the diseases which the white man brought to the frontier. Weakened in numbers, they became easy prey for other Indian tribes — especially the Teton Sioux. They gradually lost their land to the United States government through a series of treaties made in the nineteenth century. Weary of trouble with the Sioux and continual poverty, many people of the Three Tribes welcomed the coming of the government reservation at Fort Berthold.

6 Four Flags Over the Land: The Fur Trade

The search for furs brought the first Europeans to North Dakota. The fur traders and trappers were not interested in becoming permanent settlers. They wanted only beaver pelts and buffalo robes. The flags of four nations — Spain, France, England, and the United States — flew over North Dakota during the age of the fur trade, which lasted from the 1730s to the 1850s. But nationality made no difference — all four countries looked at the American West as a place which would provide rich furs.

I. The Early Trade on the Missouri

To the European, the Indian was important for economic reasons. The newcomers wanted the goods — especially furs — which the Indians had; therefore, they actively traded with them. The first European to trade with the Indians of North Dakota was an adventurous Frenchman from Quebec, Pierre Gaultier de Varennes, Sieur de la Vérendrye. After fighting for France against England on the New England frontier and in Europe, he entered the fur-trade business and moved to a trading post north of Lake Superior. In 1731 he and his son began a search for new sources of furs and for a river-route to the Pacific Ocean. Near Winnipeg he traded with the Cree and Assiniboin, urging them to hunt more beaver and adopting them as children of France.

On October 18, 1738, with a party of 52, he began his journey to visit the Mandan on the Missouri. A short time later, a large band of Assiniboin, who were on their way to trade with the Mandan, joined him. After 46 days, they arrived at a Mandan village near present-day Menoken. Vérendrye received a friendly welcome, and he observed the trading between the two tribes. The Assiniboin gave the Mandan muskets, axes, powder, and tools in exchange for corn, tobacco, and deer and buffalo skins. During his ten-day visit, the Mandan told Vérendrye that the Missouri River eventually emptied into a great ocean. On December 3 the Vérendrye party decided to return home. In 1742 his sons returned to the Mandan country, but neither Vérendrye nor they found the hoped-for route to the Pacific Ocean. They did, however, find new sources for furs, and they were the first non-Indians to set foot on North Dakota soil.

The French traded with the Indians of the northern Great Plains until their defeat by the English in the French and Indian War (1754-1763). The Treaty of Paris of 1763, which ended the war, gave France's land claims in North America to England. By the 1790s the English Hudson's Bay Company and the North West Company of Montreal were trading on the Assiniboine River with the Assiniboin, Plains Cree, and Plains Chippewa. René Jusseaume of the North West Company regularly visited the Knife River region to trade with the Mandan.

Spain, too, gained territory as a result of the French and Indian War. She received from France the Louisiana territory — roughly that land west of the Mississippi that was drained by the Mississippi and its tributaries. The Spanish soon developed an interest in trading with the Indians of the Upper Missouri. By 1790 Jacques d'Eglise, carrying the flag of Spain, had followed the Missouri as far

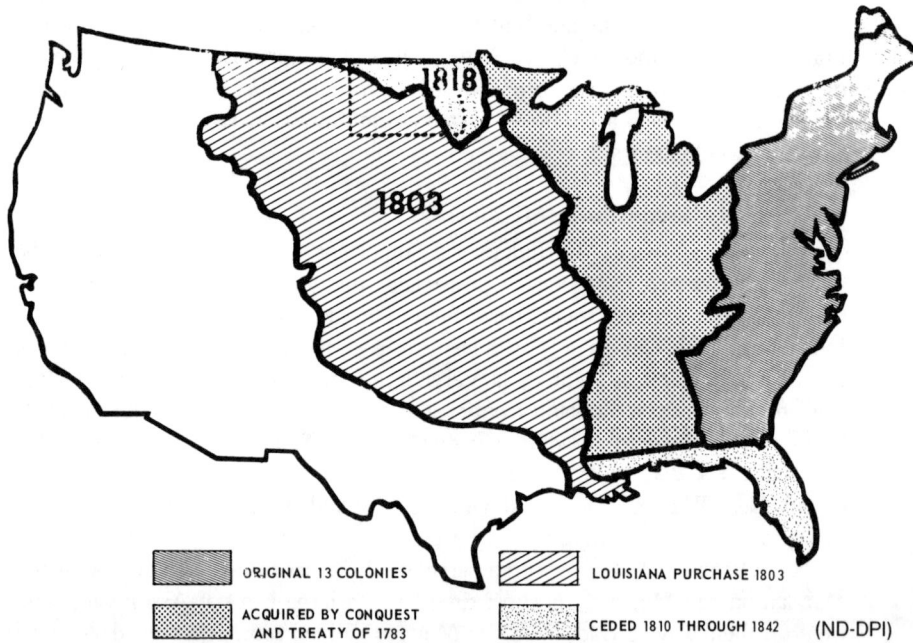

TERRITORIAL GROWTH OF CONTINENTAL U. S.

ORIGINAL 13 COLONIES

ACQUIRED BY CONQUEST AND TREATY OF 1783

LOUISIANA PURCHASE 1803

CEDED 1810 THROUGH 1842   (ND-DPI)

north as the Mandan villages. In 1794, St. Louis merchants organized the Commercial Company for the Discovery of the Nations of the Upper Missouri (called the Missouri Company) and soon began to establish trading posts. During 1794-1795, three Missouri Company expeditions tried to reach the Mandan country, but failed because angry Indians turned them back. In 1796 a fourth expedition led by John Evans succeeded in reaching Mandan country. Evans presented the Mandan chiefs with Spanish medals, raised the flag of Spain, and warned the Mandan not to trade with the English. The Mandan, however, preferred to trade with the English and drove Evans out, ending Spanish dreams of building trading posts on the Upper Missouri River. In 1801 Spain gave the Louisiana territory back to France.

In 1803 the United States purchased the Louisiana territory from France, opening up North Dakota to American adventurers. On May 14, 1804, a United States expedition led by Meriwether Lewis and William Clark headed north from St. Louis to follow the Missouri to the Pacific Ocean. Both Lewis, age 29, and Clark, age 33, were army officers who knew the ways of the wilderness. With a party of 42, Lewis and Clark began their journey in a 55-foot keelboat and two boat-like canoes called pirogues. The party carried gifts for the Indians, scientific equipment, arms, and medicine.

As the party made its way up the Missouri, Lewis and Clark held councils with the Indian tribes they met. They gave them presents and United States flags and told them that the country no longer belonged to Spain. They warned them to cooperate with the United States and threatened that, if they did not, the United States would cut off their supply of trade goods. In late October, after skirmishes with the Sioux, the Lewis and Clark expedition reached the Mandan and Hidatsa villages in North Dakota. Most of the Mandan and Hidatsa warmly greeted the American expedition. The Lewis and Clark party spent the winter of 1804-1805 in the region and built a heavily fortified post — Fort Mandan. They attempted to impress the Indians and raised the American flag. Lewis and Clark got along well with the Indians that winter. They made peace between the Arikara and the Mandan-Hidatsa and offered to punish some Teton Sioux who had killed and robbed a Mandan hunting party. The most important chief of the Hidatsa, "The One-Eyed," refused to meet with the Americans, but finally in March he did visit the fort. Lewis and Clark welcomed him with a two-gun salute and gave him many presents. This made the chief more friendly toward the newcomers.

The winter passed pleasantly. The Mandan visited the Americans often and on Christmas enjoyed rum at the fort. Lewis and Clark were told about Sakakawea, a 17-year-old Shoshoni who was the wife of Toussaint Charbonneau, a French trader. They hired him as an interpreter and Sakakawea as guide. This was a great stroke of luck, since Sakakawea knew the country through which they would go as they finished their journey to the Pacific.

The success of the Lewis and Clark expedition brought a steady flow of American traders up the Missouri. In 1807 two large parties left St. Louis for the Upper Missouri. The first, led by Ensign Nathanial Pryor and Pierre Chouteau,

William Clark

Meriwether Lewis

hoped to trade with the Mandan, but they were stopped by the Sioux and Arikara. Leaving several dead behind, the party returned to St. Louis. The second trading expedition, led by Manuel Lisa, was successful. He and his party avoided the Arikara and passed safely through North Dakota. They built a fort at the mouth of the Big Horn River in present-day Montana and spent the winter trading with the Crow. The success of Lisa's trading venture resulted in the organization of the Missouri Fur Company by St. Louis fur traders. The new company began an all-out effort to gain control of the Missouri River Indian trade. In 1809 the company sent a party of 350 men with enough merchandise for many trading posts to be located upriver. The company established several trading forts, and Manuel Lisa himself supervised the construction of Fort Lisa, about 12 miles above the mouth of the Knife River. After the Blackfeet drove the traders out of Montana in 1811, Fort Lisa was the northernmost company post and an important trade center. Indians traded furs for tools, weapons, ammunition, and whiskey at $10.00 a bottle.

The War of 1812 temporarily ended the Upper Missouri trade of the St. Louis merchants. The tribes of the Upper Missouri were sympathetic toward the British and discontinued their trade with the Americans. The long journey from St. Louis to the posts on the Upper Missouri discouraged trade. Unfriendly Indians and lack of United States military protection made the trip extremely difficult.

II. The Heyday of the Upper Missouri Trade

The day soon came, however, when the Missouri River became an open trade highway: the steamboat and the advancing military arm of the government made this possible. After the War of 1812 the government began to take an interest in protecting the western expansion of American trade. In the summer of 1819, Colonel Henry Atkinson, commanding 1,000 men, began a northward trip on the Missouri using steamboats. Because of low water, however, the expedition was forced to stop just north of present-day Omaha, where in 1821 Atkinson built a military post, which was named Fort Atkinson. The fort advanced the American military frontier several hundred miles. That same year William H. Ashley and Joshua Pilcher began fur-trading activities on the Upper Missouri at the mouth of the Yellowstone River. In 1823 the Blackfeet killed several of their men and drove the fur trappers out. While they retreated down the Missouri, they were attacked by the Arikara, who killed several more and many horses. Ashley and the survivors reported the attack to Colonel Henry Leavenworth at Fort Atkinson. He convinced 500 Teton Sioux to join his attack against the Arikara in return for plundering privileges. The Sioux attacked and plundered, but Leavenworth and his men fired only a few shots at the Arikara villages. This disgusted both the Sioux, who left, and the trappers, who believed that a military show of force would keep away the Indians. Leavenworth, however, did make a treaty with the Arikara to return Ashley's stolen property.

In 1825 the American government acted to protect the traders and trappers from the Indians. General Henry Atkinson and Benjamin O'Fallon, an Indian agent, signed treaties with 16 Indian tribes living between Fort Atkinson and the Knife River. The Indians agreed not to interfere with traders who were licensed by the government and to turn over any Indians who harmed white men. Both the Mandan and the Hidatsa entered into the treaties.

Although the army did not build forts north of Fort Atkinson, fur-trade activity on the Upper Missouri flourished from the mid-1820s until the 1850s. The Columbia Fur Company moved into the valley in 1822 and established several posts, two of which were in North Dakota near the Mandan villages and at the mouth of the White Earth River. John Jacob Astor's American Fur Company was the main competitor of the Columbia Fur Company. In 1827 Astor bought out the Columbia Fur Company, giving his American Fur Company a monopoly of the Missouri trade. Kenneth McKenzie, Daniel Lamont, and William Laidlaw headed the Upper Missouri activities for Astor. All three had worked for British fur companies and were experienced and energetic traders.

Fort Union at the mouth of the Yellowstone River became the center of activity as the company sought the fine beaver furs of the region. The company built a chain of forts along the Missouri: in 1832, Fort McKenzie near the mouth of the Marias; in 1831, Fort Clark at the Knife River villages, and Fort Pierre to serve the Teton Sioux. These forts of the American Fur Company had stockades for protection. Most forts had several residences, storage buildings, a blacksmith

Assiniboin trading goods at Fort Union. (SHSND)

shop, and a trading building. Fort Union had a still for making liquor that would be traded to the Indians. To take full advantage of the new field, the company built a steamboat, the *Yellowstone*, which could carry 144 tons of goods. Each year the *Yellowstone* made trips as far north as Fort Union, bringing English woolen goods, blankets, guns, powder, tobacco, utensils, and other goods to trade with the Indians. It always returned laden with beaver pelts and buffalo robes.

The American Fur Company did well in the Upper Missouri trade. John Jacob Astor became one of the wealthiest men in the country. Few, however, who actually did the trading and took the risks in the wilderness ended their careers as wealthy men.

The fur trade on the Upper Missouri reached its height during the late 1830s. The story of the American Fur Company after 1840 is one of decline. Several developments brought this about. First, smallpox epidemics reduced the Indian population. Second, buffalo and other game were becoming less abundant. Third, the increased use of steamboats on the Missouri made it easier for smaller trading operators to cut into the business of the American Fur Company. Fourth, by the late 1860s the army forts began to replace the old trading posts as centers of trading activity, and the government prohibited more than one trader at each post. These developments worked against a profitable fur trade.

III. Fur Trading on the Red River

During the latter part of the 1700s, the trading activity in the Red River Valley was dominated by English companies — the Hudson's Bay Company and the North West Company. Small, independent traders, however, made their way up the Minnesota River to the Red River region. In 1789 Robert Dickson took a canoe load of goods up the river. In 1800 he built a small fortification on Lake

Manuel Lisa. (SHSND)

Norman Kittson. (SHSND)

Traverse, which became his home base. He learned the Indian languages and married a sister of Red Thunder, a Sioux chief. The independent traders realized that they could not compete with the big companies, so in 1805 Dickson and the others formed the Michilimackinac Company. While the other companies traded mostly with the Indians in northeastern North Dakota, the Michilimackinac Company concentrated on the southern Red River Valley.

The first fur-trading post in North Dakota was built at Pembina in 1797 by Charles Jean Baptiste Chaboillez of the North West Company. Alexander Henry of the North West Company, however, was responsible for opening up that part of the valley after he built a permanent post at Pembina in 1801. His men built a high stockade around a storehouse, stable, blacksmith shop, and a cluster of small dwellings. From his base at Pembina, Henry sent out his goods with traders who wintered at such places as Grand Forks and Red Lake (Minnesota). In one winter, 1804-1805, he took in almost 3,000 beaver pelts. His work was dangerous. Often, Indian war parties would sweep down on his trading parties, and in one raid his Indian wife's mother and father were killed.

Two developments in Canada stimulated the growth of Pembina: the formation of the Selkirk Colony, also referred to as the Red River Settlement, at present-day Winnipeg, and the coming of Roman Catholic missionaries. In 1812 Thomas Douglas, the fifth Earl of Selkirk, founded an agricultural colony of Scots and Irish at the junction of the Red and Assiniboine rivers. Selkirk wanted a colony in America where landless peasants could settle. The Selkirk Colony faced many difficulties: distance, uncertain food supply, and the hostility of the fur traders, who feared that a farming settlement would destroy the natural habitat of the buffalo and beavers. Many colonists spent the winters near Pembina, hunting buffalo. The years 1812 to 1821 were difficult ones for the colony, but with the

A Red River cart train carrying trade items to St. Paul. (SHSND)

decline of hostility on the part of the fur traders and the arrival of more settlers, it survived and grew. The success of the Selkirk Colony meant that the Pembina outpost would become a significant trading and stop-over point between it and the growing American settlements on the Mississippi.

The coming of missionaries also promoted the growth of the Pembina settlement. In 1818 two Roman Catholic priests were sent to the Red River region. Father Joseph Norbert Provencher served the Selkirk settlement; Father Severe Dumoulin worked at Pembina. There he built a chapel, home, and store, and conducted an active ministry. In 1818, however, the United States and Great Britain signed a treaty which set the 49th parallel as the boundary between the United States and Canada. In 1823 a boundary survey indicated that Pembina belonged to the United States. The American flag was raised, and the Hudson's Bay Company ordered all whites and métis, who were the offspring of Indian mothers and French fathers, to move north of the 49th parallel. Although some stayed for a while, Pembina was soon deserted. Pembina would be the scene of various trading activities, but it did not grow as a community until the 1870s. The success of the Selkirk Colony, however, did mean that the Red River would become an important trade highway.

The withdrawal of English traders from the Mississippi Valley after the War of 1812 stimulated the growth of American fur-trade activity in the region. John Jacob Astor's American Fur Company purchased English fur-trade interests and was soon actively engaged in the Mississippi Valley trade. Although at first smaller operations such as the Columbia Fur Company competed with Astor, the American Fur Company controlled most of the Mississippi trade. By the mid-1820s the company had ten posts stretching from Mendota on the Mississippi into the tributary valleys such as the Minnesota. Because of Hudson's Bay Company opposition, Astor was not successful in establishing a post at Pembina until 1829.

By the 1820s the largest part of the Red River population was métis. The métis (French for mixed breed) were the offspring of white traders and trappers who had taken Indian women as wives. The métis played an important role in the development of the Red River fur trade.

The métis farmed small 15 to 20-acre plots and did some trapping. The buffalo, however, became their main source of food and trade items. The fur companies needed buffalo robes and a long-lasting food called pemmican, made from buffalo meat. Pemmican was an ideal food for traders and trappers because it did not easily spoil. To make pemmican one dried buffalo meat over a fire or in the sun. When the meat was dried, it was pounded until it became a powder. This powder was mixed with melted fat and put into a buffalo-hide bag that would hold 90 pounds. For both the métis and the Plains Chippewa, pemmican became important as a trade item. The métis furnished much of the pemmican and many of the buffalo robes which the fur companies wanted. As late as the 1840s, the métis would obtain as many as 2,000 buffalo on a single hunt.

By the 1840s two developments worked to increase trading operations on the Red River. First, St. Paul at the junction of the Mississippi and Minnesota rivers grew rapidly, and in 1849 Congress created Minnesota Territory, which included that part of North Dakota east of the Missouri River. Steamboats began to bring supplies on a regular basis to the growing St. Paul region. Second, the settlers in the Red River Valley were becoming hostile to the trade monopoly of the Hudson's Bay Company and were eager for American traders to give the English company competition. They began to enter into illegal trade with smugglers.

Henry Hastings Sibley and Norman Kittson played the key roles in expanding American trade activity at Pembina and the Selkirk settlement. Sibley had been in charge of the Minnesota and Red River valleys for the American Fur Company. In 1842 he agreed to supply another fur trader, Norman Kittson, with goods to trade with the Sioux on the James and Sheyenne rivers. The two became partners. Two years later, Kittson moved his operation to Pembina. With Sibley's support and secret agreements with independent traders at the Selkirk settlement, Kittson's operation flourished. He bought furs smuggled out of Hudson's Bay territory and gave trade goods in return for them. The Hudson's Bay Company, however, waged a bitter campaign to drive Kittson out of the region. The company began to pay more for furs and to offer its goods at lower prices. They even began trading rum for furs — something which Kittson could not do legally. In 1854 Kittson gave up and returned to St. Paul, leaving the post operations in the hands of Joseph Rolette. Kittson had built the St. Paul-Pembina trade business, but it would never flourish as it had during the late 1840s.

*   *   *   *   *   *

The fur trade chapter of North Dakota history is one marked by both triumph and tragedy. The shrewd business mind of John Jacob Astor earned him a fortune in the furs of the West. Indians obtained items in trade that they needed to maintain their way of life: horses, guns, powder, axes, and woolen fabrics. But the price was high, and the fur trade was not equally good to all traders or Indians. Manuel Lisa, like many traders, died very poor. Indians killed many trappers and traders; traders also killed Indians. The white man's disease, smallpox, took the lives of thousands of Indians. For example, the smallpox epidemic of 1837 reduced the Mandan from 1,800 to only 125; half the Assiniboin also died. For many Indians and traders, the fur-trade era was a time of tragedy.

7 Conflict on the Plains

The fur-trade frontier brought the whites and the Indians into conflict, but it did not promote white settlement. By the early 1860s, however, settlers began to look toward the prairies of northern Dakota. As they moved west, the United States army came with them. Naturally, the American Indians resisted the advancing tide of the settlers and the army. North Dakota was their land, and they — especially the Teton Sioux — fought to hold that land.

I. Soldiers to Dakota

For three decades the army had been content to limit its control of the Missouri to Fort Atkinson, located several hundred miles down river from the Upper Missouri trade operations. During the 1850s, however, white settlements were established in the southeastern part of what in 1861 would become Dakota Territory. During the same year that Congress created Dakota Territory, gold was discovered in Montana; hundreds of people began to cross the plains of Dakota on their way to the new gold fields. With these developments, the army saw the need to build forts in areas where travelers and new settlements needed protection.

Between 1855 and 1857 the army built three new forts: Fort Pierre in 1855; Fort Randall in 1857 on the Missouri in present-day South Dakota; and Fort Abercrombie in 1857 on the Red River, 12 miles north of present-day Wahpeton. Fort Abercrombie became the starting point for wagon trains headed for the Montana gold fields and for those going north to Pembina or Fort Garry in

Canada. Troops escorted the wagon trains on their journeys. Fort Abercrombie was manned by three companies of infantry and one of cavalry. Besides troop quarters, the fort had a hospital, workshops, powder storehouses, a blacksmith shop, and stables. Although the fort was not originally built with a stockade, increased Indian activity in the 1860s prompted the building of one. The soldiers at the fort depended on supplies which came from St. Paul, 250 miles away. The soldier who served at Abercrombie was indeed in the wilderness.

With the steady flow of white settlers to the West, the demand to push the Indians off their lands increased. By the 1860s the Santee Sioux in Minnesota had had enough. A treaty in 1851 had confined them to a 20 by 150 mile strip of land along the Minnesota River. The Santee were to receive $3,000,000 in gold for the land. As settlement moved up the Minnesota River, a new treaty in 1858 took away half their remaining land for 30¢ an acre. Although many Santee Sioux farmed, some, who preferred to hunt for their food, often went outside their territory. In 1862, drought struck down their crops, and many Santee faced starvation. When the United States, which was in the middle of the Civil War, did not make its payments for their land to them in gold, the Santee revolted. On August 18, 1862, led by Little Crow, the Santee began plundering and burning the homes and stores of the whites. Perhaps seeing this as their last chance to drive the white intruders out, the Santee killed over 350 settlers.

In the weeks following the uprising, the army capured over 300 Santee Sioux, but some fled westward across Minnesota. The white population demanded that all captives be executed. President Abraham Lincoln, however, ordered the army to hang only those who were guilty of killing the settlers. Guilt was difficult to determine, but on December 26, 1862, at Mankato, the army hanged 38 "guilty" Indians.

The army decided that hanging 38 Sioux was not enough punishment for the uprising. The following summer, General Henry H. Sibley and General Alfred Sully began a campaign into Dakota Territory to find and punish the Sioux who had escaped. In June 1863, Sibley, with almost 4,000 men, set out from Minnesota, while Sully with 2,000 cavalry planned to come up the Missouri on steamboats. The two armies would trap the fleeing Sioux between them. Because most of his men were on foot, Sibley moved slowly into Dakota during early July. Traveling northward, he set up Camp Atchison about three miles south of present-day Binford. He left some of his men at the camp and then moved on toward the southwest with 1,400 infantry and 500 cavalry. At Big Mounds, near present-day Tappen, he caught up with a group of Sioux who were hunting with bows and arrows and few guns. Again, however, the Sioux escaped the army's fire and moved toward the Missouri River. At Stoney Lake, near present-day Driscoll, the Indians attempted to slow down Sibley's advance in order to allow their women and children to escape across the Missouri. Sioux efforts failed, and Sibley reached the Missouri on July 9, just as many of the Sioux, mostly women and children, were crossing the river on rafts and small boats.

Sibley's fire did not kill many Sioux, but women and children drowned when their boats capsized in the river. His forces destroyed many carts and the Indian's food supply. Sibley claimed that his troops had killed 150 Sioux; few, if any, of these Indians had been involved in the Minnesota affair. He lost nine men. Weary from the pursuit across the plains, Sibley decided to return to Minnesota.

Sully had not been able to join forces with Sibley as planned because low water on the Missouri had made the advance of his steamboats extremely slow. Sully, however, upon learning that the Sioux had recrossed the Missouri and were hunting in the James River Valley, immediately set out to capture them. On September 3, 1863, Sully caught up with the Sioux and launched an attack. The Battle of Whitestone Hill was fierce and bloody; Sully's men killed about 150 men, women, and children; the army lost 17 men. The troops burned the Indian lodges, destroyed a half-million pounds of dried buffalo meat, and took 156 prisoners.

The following summer (1864), Sully again marched against the Sioux. On July 28, he discovered a Sioux encampment in the Killdeer Mountains and fired upon it with cannons. The Sioux quickly scattered, and Sully's men burned 1,600 tepees and about 200 tons of food. Sully, not wishing to chase the Sioux through the rough terrain, returned to Fort Rice, the first military fort built on the Upper Missouri in North Dakota.

Parade ground scene at Fort Yates, 1880s. (SHSND)

II. The Chain of Defense: Forts

The resistance of the Sioux convinced the army that it was time to move the military frontier into northern Dakota. Between 1864 and 1872, the army erected eight forts to protect the white population and to control the Sioux, especially the Teton. In 1864, prior to his expedition against the Sioux, Sully had established Fort Rice, about 25 miles downriver from Mandan. Fort Rice served as Sully's headquarters and as a supply base for his expeditions. Linda Warfel Slaughter, wife of the fort surgeon, became a well-known writer and lecturer about the early west. In 1877 Fort Rice was abandoned and replaced by Fort Yates, located near the Standing Rock Indian Reservation. In 1866 the army built Fort Buford on the Missouri near the mouth of the Yellowstone River. The fort was located in the heart of the remaining fur-trade area, and one of its main purposes was to keep the white traders from giving liquor to the Indians. Ex-Confederate soldiers manned the fort. In 1867 three more forts — Stevenson, Totten, and Ransom — were added to the chain of defense. Fort Stevenson, a two-company post located on the Missouri 12 miles north of Berthold, was commanded for several years by General Régis de Trobriand, who left a journal describing military life in early Dakota. Fort Totten was built on Devils Lake. Although most of the Indians in the region were peaceful, the army was there in case of disturbance and to protect railroad workers and surveyors laying out the boundary between the United States and Canada. Fort Ransom, on the Sheyenne River south of present-day Lisbon, was established to guard overland parties traveling from Fort Abercrombie to the Missouri.

Commanding Officer's home at Fort Abraham Lincoln. (SHSND)

Officers and their wives at Fort Buford. (SHSND)

In 1870 the army built Fort Pembina on the Red River. The fort was small, since the Chippewa in the area were generally peaceful. Two years later, two more forts were built on the plains: Fort Seward, which replaced Fort Ransom at Jamestown; and Fort McKeen on the Missouri, five miles south of Mandan. In 1873, Fort McKeen was enlarged and renamed Fort Abraham Lincoln. Fort Abraham Lincoln was the largest and best fortified installation on the Missouri. General George Armstrong Custer commanded the fort, which was called "Custer's Post" because of his dominant personality. The troops at Abraham Lincoln, like those at the other frontier military posts, protected the men who were building the railroad, escorted pioneers across the territory, and attempted to control the Indian population.

The new show of force by the United States military angered the Indians, who saw this as a further infringement of their rights. While the Chippewa and the smaller tribes — the Mandan, Arikara, and Hidatsa — caused little trouble, the Teton Sioux, who had been masters of the plains for over a hundred years, refused to give in to the military. They continually harrassed the forts. Direct confrontations were few, but the Teton often ran off with horses and cattle from the forts. The Hunkpapa, led by Sitting Bull, fought against the new military establishment. His bands attacked steamboats, mail carriers, and unprotected whites who were crossing the plains. When the soldiers could not control the Sioux, the United States began a series of treaty negotiations in the hope that this would end the continual skirmishes.

III. Treaties and Reservations

The United States government hoped to establish peace with the Indians by means of treaties which would set up reservations on which the Indians would live and become farmers. The government had no difficulty in dealing with the Three Tribes (the Mandan, Hidatsa, and Arikara). Ravaged by disease, poverty, and the Sioux, the Three Tribes were eager to have government protection. Under the terms of the treaty of 1851, they settled on land that was west and south of the Missouri between the Heart and Yellowstone rivers. In 1870 they lost most of the land south of Fort Berthold. The government set up an agency for them at Berthold, which became the home for over 2,000 of them. In 1867 the Sisseton, the Wahpeton, and the Cuthead Band of the Yanktonnai Sioux signed a treaty which gave them the Fort Totten Reservation south of Devils Lake. Since buffalo were becoming scarce in the eastern part of northern Dakota, these Sioux accepted farming as a way of life. By the 1870s a thousand Sioux lived on the Fort Totten Reservation.

The Teton (western) Sioux, however, did not give into the whites so easily. In 1865 many of the Teton tribes agreed to withdraw from the established travel routes in exchange for payments of money. Through 1865, 1866, and 1867, the Sioux met with government officials at Fort Rice to iron out the terms of a treaty. In late 1868, many of the Teton groups signed the Laramie Treaty. The Indians accepted a 22,000,000-acre reservation west of the Missouri from the North Platte River in Nebraska to the 46th parallel in the north. In return, the government agreed to help the Sioux begin a new way of life. Each family would receive equipment, a cow, a team of oxen, and a daily ration of a pound of meat and a pound of flour per person. Teachers, doctors, and blacksmiths were also provided for them. The Sioux were permitted to hunt off the reservation to the west if the buffalo herds were large enough. The United States promised that white men would not be allowed to enter the reservation "as long as the streams flowed to the sea." By 1870, almost 5,000 Sioux were living at the Grand River Agency on the Missouri River. About 3,500 were at the Standing Rock Agency.

The Laramie Treaty, however, was soon violated by the whites. In 1871 and 1872, army expeditions, accompanying railroad surveyors, went through the Sioux lands. In 1874 General Custer led an expedition into the Black Hills and announced to the world that the Hills were rich in gold. Custer's announcement brought pressure from the whites to open the Hills to gold prospectors. When the Teton refused to sell the Black Hills to the government, the army let in the flood of prospectors. By 1876, 25,000 whites had made the mad scramble for gold. The Sioux were justifiably angry at the violation of the treaty of 1868. They were also unhappy with the haphazard way in which they received, or did not receive, their daily meat and flour rations. Not all Indian agents were honest, and some made fortunes selling goods that were intended for the Indians. At some agencies the food rations seldom appeared. Facing starvation, many Sioux began leaving the reservations to hunt and gather food.

Left, a Fort Buford soldier. Right, Seventh Cavalry band leader who was killed at the Little Big Horn, 1876. (SHSND)

The Indians at Fort Totten and at Fort Berthold adjusted to the reservations. The reservation system was designed to turn the Indian into a white with the values of white civilization. Up to the 1880s, each reservation was assigned to a religious group that was to work with the Indians: Roman Catholics at Standing Rock and Fort Totten, Congregationalists at Berthold. The church groups attempted to convert the Indians to Christianity, and they built schools to teach them about white civilization. By 1890 over 8,000 Indians filled the state's reservations, and 1,200 children attended the religious schools.

Although some small bands continued to follow their traditional ways, most Indians were on the reservations, learning the ways of the white man. It was a difficult adjustment, but many were making it. By the 1890s at Fort Totten, all the adult Indians were making their own living. At Fort Berthold the Three Tribes were earning 70 percent of their living, but at Standing Rock, home of the Teton Sioux, only 30 percent were self-supporting. Their land was marginal.

In 1881, Gall and Sitting Bull, along with their 1,300 followers, returned to the United States and settled on the Standing Rock Reservation. Sitting Bull became the symbol of the old days of Indian power. Unlike Gall and the other leaders, he refused to accept Christianity and would not give land to the government without a fair price. The Indian agents branded him as a troublemaker.

Sitting Bull. (SHSND)

Gall. (SHSND)

IV. The Little Big Horn and Wounded Knee: Victory and Defeat

The treaty violations caused unrest among the Western Sioux. Sitting Bull, of the Hunkpapa Sioux, had not signed the treaty of 1868; and he, along with Crazy Horse and Gall, led a large band of Sioux into Montana, where the buffalo were more abundant. As conditions on some of the reservations became worse, many Indians joined Sitting Bull's band. In 1875 the government ordered all the Sioux who had left the reservations to return or be considered "hostiles." When few returned, the army set out to capture them. Believing that this was their last chance to hold back the advancing tide of white settlement, the non-reservation Sioux, led by Crazy Horse, Sitting Bull, and Gall, struck with full fury. They defeated General George Crook on the Rosebud and wiped out General Custer and his men at the Little Big Horn. But the government quickly flooded the region with troops, and by the fall of 1876 the Sioux were beaten. The defeated Indians were forced back to the reservations, and Sitting Bull and his people fled to Canada.

The price of victory at the Little Big Horn was high. The Sioux lost the Black Hills. The government tightened its control on all the reservations, and Indians could not leave without a pass. Indian agents cut off food rations to Indians who would not do what they were told.

Sioux Ghost Dancers in 1890. (SHSND)

In 1890 a new religion arose among the Sioux. It taught that a Messiah would soon come to restore all their lands to the Indians. This gave the Sioux new hope for a brighter future. The Ghost Dance, which was to hasten the coming of the Messiah, became the new ritual, and the Sioux danced it with a frenzy. Although Sitting Bull did not accept the new belief and even warned his people against it, he received much of the blame for the movement. The agent at Standing Rock ordered Sitting Bull arrested. Just before dawn on December 15, 1890, the Indian police, who were friendly toward the agent, broke into Sitting Bull's house and seized him while he slept. The aging leader did not resist, but some of his friends became angry and fired at the police, wounding one of them in the leg. The police responded by firing two bullets into Sitting Bull's back. He was dead. Conflict continued as troops tried to capture the Ghost Dancers. At Wounded Knee Creek in South Dakota, the cavalry killed 300 Sioux. The Ghost Dance days were over, and Wounded Knee became the symbol of the defeat of the Sioux Nation.

*   *   *   *   *   *

In less than a generation, North Dakota was turned from the land of the Indian into the land of the white settler. The buffalo were gone and the Indians had been placed on reservations to learn how to farm and about the white man's ways. Not all Indians resisted this new life, but many did. The tepee no longer dotted the North Dakota landscape; now it was the sod house or the small, white frame building. The dust of the settler breaking the sod replaced the dust of the buffalo hunt.

8 Carts, Stages, and Steamers

The plains of Dakota were a long distance from the settled part of the United States. This made it difficult for settlers to reach the area. A transportation system was the key to settlement. The transportation that would bring settlers to Dakota went through three stages. The Red River carts led the way in the development of trade between St. Paul and the Red River country. Then came the stagecoaches and steamboats, carrying freight and passengers to remote places. The railroads, however, would be responsible for bringing the great waves of settlers to the Dakota prairie.

I. The Red River Cart

The opening of trade between St. Paul and the settlement on the Red River at Fort Garry in Canada resulted in the development of the first transportation system in the Red River Valley. Before this, trade goods had arrived at Fort Garry by way of Hudson Bay and York Factory. When it became quicker and cheaper for Canadians to obtain merchandise from St. Paul by way of the Red River Valley, they began trading in the American markets.

Norman W. Kittson pioneered the trade between St. Paul and the Red River community north of Pembina. Kittson realized that St. Paul was not only a good place to obtain goods that people in the Red River Valley wanted, but also a good market in which to sell buffalo robes and pemmican. The Red River cart would carry this trade. The métis had developed the Red River cart to use on their buffalo hunts. It was a unique vehicle for overland hauling. Made entirely of

Red River carts from Pembina, 1858. (SHSND)

wood, the two-wheel carts were constructed without the use of iron parts or nails. The cart was made of oak, and the wheels were about five feet in diameter. The rims of the wheels were covered with buffalo rawhide so they would not sink into wet ground. The body of the cart rode high on the axle, making the fording of streams an easier task. Because no lubrication was used on the axles, they made a squeaking sound that could be heard several miles away. Pulled by an animal, usually an ox but sometimes a horse or mule, the cart could carry loads up to 1,000 pounds. One man could drive up to six carts with each cart linked to the other by a strap. The cart trains traveled up to 20 miles a day.

In 1844 only six carts made the journey from Fort Garry to St. Paul, but by 1850 hundreds made the trip each summer. The Red River cart made trade possible between the outposts on the Red River and the population center at St. Paul. The cart trains leaving Pembina in early June could travel one of three principal trails. The earliest was called Kittson's Trail and ran along either side of the Red River to Lake Traverse, then followed the Minnesota River to Traverse de Sioux, near present-day St. Peter, Minnesota. There the goods were transferred to river boats for the trip to St. Paul. The cart trains would be reloaded at Traverse de Sioux with merchandise for the trip back to Pembina. Later, two other trails were used.

The plains trail route, which went directly to St. Paul, followed Kittson's trail and then a good road which ran from St. Cloud to St. Paul. A third trail, known as the woods trail, branched off from Kittson's trail near Moorhead and went on to St. Paul by way of Crow Wing.

The cart trains, covering nearly 500 miles in six weeks, arrived at St. Paul amid much excitement. The St. Paul merchants realized the value of the new trade routes and the prosperity they would bring to the growing community. People were beginning to hear about the Red River country.

II. Steamboat 'round the Bend: The Red River

Kittson operated a trading post at Pembina until 1854, supplying the people of the Red River settlement with grocery items and agricultural implements which he bought from merchants in St. Paul. Kittson pioneered the development of trade by cart between the settlement and St. Paul. But the steamboat would bring the era of large-scale trade activity.

In 1857 the Hudson's Bay Company got permission from the United States to import English goods, duty-free, by way of St. Paul; this resulted in sizable savings for the company. Soon, the Fort Garry settlement (present-day Winnipeg) would become tied economically to St. Paul, and hundreds of tons of goods would be transported yearly between the two communities. The carts could not handle this increase in hauling, so in 1858 Russell Blakely, who operated steamboats on the upper Mississippi, investigated the possibility of using steamboats on the Red River. When he reported that the Red was navigable, the St. Paul Chamber of Commerce offered a prize of $1,000 to the first person to put a steamboat on the Red River.

Anson Northrup dismantled his steamboat, the *North Star*, at Crow Wing, placed it on sleighs pulled by oxen, and set out on the 150-mile journey to the Red River. In the spring of 1859 the *North Star*, rebuilt and renamed the *Anson Northrup*, was launched on the Red. This was the beginning of the use of steamboats on the Red River.

After one trip to Fort Garry, Northrup sold his boat to the Minnesota Stage Company. The company renamed the boat the *Pioneer*. The Minnesota Stage Company built a 152-mile road, complete with bridges, between St. Cloud and Fort Abercrombie in the fall of 1859. Now, the Red River and St. Paul were connected by roads over which wagon trains and stagecoaches made regular runs and brought trade goods to the steamboats on the Red.

The stagecoach service improved in 1862, when twice-weekly service was provided between St. Paul and Fort Abercrombie. By 1871 the stage line was extended northward to Fort Garry and carried mail and passengers in addition to freight. The stagecoaches, pulled by four horses, ran on regular schedules through the Valley after 1871.

In 1862 the *Pioneer* was replaced with a new steamer, the *International*, a much larger boat which could carry up to 135 tons. The *International* served the freighters well and earned them good money. When the Chippewa objected to the use of the steamboats on the Red River, Norman Kittson, who had known the Indians in his years as a trader, was placed in command of the *International*. Trouble with both the Sioux and the Chippewa hurt the company, and it finally sold the *International* to Kittson, who acted as an agent for the Hudson's Bay Company.

James J. Hill and Chauncy Griggs began flatboat business on the Red River and by 1870 were very successful. Flatboats were barges that used only the

Red River boating activity. Top, the *Dakota*, 1873. Middle, Grand Forks sawmill and flat boats. Bottom, the *Selkirk*, 1882. (SHSND)

CARTS, STAGES, AND STEAMERS

current of the river for power. When a flatboat reached Fort Garry, it was dismantled and sold for lumber. Hill, an emigrant from Canada, later became famous as a railroad builder, and Griggs, who had operated steamboats on the Ohio River, saw the future of transportation on the Red. Since no rail service connected Winnipeg (chartered as a city in 1873) with the Canadian east, the Red River became that settlement's highway of commerce.

In 1871 Hill and his associates built the *Selkirk*. With the introduction of the *Selkirk*, the monopoly of the steamboat business by Kittson and the Hudson's Bay Company came to an end. Kittson tried to compete successfully with Hill, but he could not. Therefore, he joined forces with Hill and together they formed the Red River Tranportation Company. New Boats, the *Alpha* and *Cheyenne*, were added to their fleet. Attempts by other companies to compete with Hill and Kittson ended in failure.

The steamboats on the Red River did a tremendous business and aided settlement in the Valley. They carried thousands of tons of freight and hundreds of passengers. The steamers, for example, were responsible for the establishment of Grand Forks. Captain Alexander Griggs plotted the town and became a leading figure in the city's early growth and development. He organized several new businesses and served as an early mayor of Grand Forks.

The 1870s were the heyday of Red River steamboating. But in 1878, when railroad lines connected Winnipeg and St. Paul, the steamboat era was coming to an end. Even though two new boats, the *Grandin* and the *Grand Forks*, built to haul grain, were launched in 1895, the railroad would soon become the principal means of transportation. When in 1912 the *Fram* broke its moorings at Grand Forks and sank, the last riverboat was gone.

A stagecoach in front of the Griggs House at Grand Forks, 1882. (SHSND)

III. Steamboats on the "Big Muddy"

The Missouri River, known as the "Big Muddy," was an early highway for fur traders and the army. Steamboats were used on the Upper Missouri long before any appeared on the Red River, and they remained in use there for many years after steamboats had left the Red. Kenneth McKenzie and Pierre Chouteau, Jr., prominent fur traders, were the first to navigate the Upper Missouri successfully. In 1831 they placed the *Yellowstone* on the river, but it got only as far north as Fort Tecumseh at Pierre, South Dakota. In later years, however, it regularly ran as far north as Fort Union. In 1833 the American Fur Company launched the *Assiniboin*. In 1850 Chouteau chartered the steamer *El Paso*, which reached the mouth of the Yellowstone River. In 1864 Pierre Chouteau and Company and the Montana-Idaho Transportation Company hauled passengers and mining equipment to the gold fields in Montana. As more boats entered the trade, Sioux City became the principal port on the Upper Missouri and held a monopoly over the river's operations. The completion of the Northern Pacific Railroad to Bismarck in 1873 finally broke the monopoly.

In the years 1873 to 1879, Yankton and Bismarck became the principal centers of Upper Missouri steamboat operations. The two cities were able to operate as major ports because they were supplied by the railroads. Four companies dominated the trade during these years. The Missouri Transportation Company, known as the Coulson line, was the most successful. Headed by Sanford B. Coulson, "the Napoleon of the Big Muddy," the Company had seven

The steamer *Rosebud* on the Missouri. (SHSND)

boats on the River. The best known of these boats was the *Far West*. The *Far West* made history in 1876 when it raced from the Little Bighorn River to Bismarck, bringing the news of Custer's defeat. The 900-mile run was made in a record 54 hours, a feat that was unrivaled by any other boat on the Upper Missouri.

The other three companies included the Kountz line, the Peck line, and the Fort Benton Transportation Company. The Fort Benton Transportation Company, known as the Power line, eventually became the last to use steamboats on the Upper Missouri. Several small independent operators also entered the steamboat business. For example, I.P. Baker ran his boat, the *Red Cloud*, between Bismarck and Fort Benton. He was in the merchandising business himself, and mostly carried his own goods.

The Panic of 1873 caused a temporary halt in railroad construction and stimulated the steamboat business. Mining operations in Montana and the opening of western Canada for settlement also helped steamboating. The steamboat business relied heavily on federal contracts to carry military supplies along the river. By the mid-1870s about 35 boats were doing business on the Upper Missouri.

The dining room on the Missouri steamer, *Montana*, 1870s. (SHSND)

After 1880, Bismarck became the principal river port. The Coulson line, which originally had its offices in Yankton, now moved to Bismarck. Expecting future business to be good, the Coulson line, the Fort Benton Transportation Company, and the Northern Pacific Railroad constructed large warehouses on the levee at Bismarck in 1881. After 1885 the Fort Benton company, headed by Issac P. Baker and Thomas Power, held a monopoly of the steamboat business out of Bismarck. Baker, who had served as an agent for several lines in St. Louis, came to Bismarck in 1881. He worked for the Coulson and Fort Benton companies and in 1883 purchased an interest in the Fort Benton Transportation Company. From 1885 to 1936, commercial boating from the port of Bismarck was under the direction of Baker and his sons.

The completion of the Manitoba Railroad (later the Great Northern Railroad) to Great Falls, Montana, in 1888 dealt a serious blow to the Fort Benton company. The railroad could now carry supplies to the settlers in the Montana area. With the disappearance of trade opportunities on the Upper Missouri, Baker reduced the number of boats in his fleet to six. Throughout the early 1890s, most business on the river was between Pierre and Bismarck, and after 1896 the boats went no farther south than Fort Yates.

In 1900, Baker bought a new type of river boat, called the packet boat. This kind of boat was less than 100 feet long and was powered by a gasoline engine. The packet boats replaced the steamers, which were much larger boats, having an average length of 200 feet, a 35-foot beam, and an average capacity of 400 tons. During the last years of the Fort Benton Transportation Company, packet boats were used to haul grain. The last effort to increase the use of boats occurred in 1910 when Baker, thinking that areas in Montana could be better served by boat than rail, extended his line to Glendive on the Yellowstone River. The company continued to run packet boats until 1937. Boat traffic on the Missouri ended for the same reason it ended on the Red — the coming of railroads.

Not all steamboats in North Dakota plied the rivers. For example, the *Minnie H* was the pride of Devils Lake. Constructed in 1883, the *Minnie H,* 110 feet long and 20 feet wide, carried mail, freight, and passengers from the town of Devils Lake to Fort Totten and Minnewauken. Low water levels on the lake and lack of business ended her colorful career in 1908.

Stage lines provided an early means of transportation in western Dakota as they had in the Red River Valley. They could go where steamboats could not, carrying people and goods to out-of-the-way places. When gold was discovered in the Black Hills, a flood of gold seekers rushed to make their fortunes. The Northern Pacific Railroad and Bismarck businessmen saw an opportunity to start a stage line connecting Bismarck with Deadwood.

In 1877 the Northwestern Express and Transportation Company began freight, mail, and passenger service from Bismarck to the Black Hills. The company constructed a stable and large corral at Bismarck, developed a 210-mile trail to Deadwood, and built ten stations along the route. Business was good; on June 26, Concord coaches and 200 teams of wagons rumbled along the route. As

The *Minnie H* docked on Devils Lake. (SHSND)

the railroad built west, other stage routes were developed from Dickinson, Belfield, and Medora to Deadwood. As railroads pushed across South Dakota, however, the long journey from the North Dakota towns on the Northern Pacific was no longer the best way to get to Deadwood. By the end of the 1800s, the days of the stagecoach were numbered.

* * * * * *

The steamboat era on both the Red and Missouri rivers was a romantic one. Many a small boy found the lure of the river irresistible. The bustling activity on the dock, the marvelous tales told by deckhands, and the excitement when boats arrived were delightful experiences to those who lived in the river port towns. Like Mark Twain, the youngsters found excitement in the river traffic: the huge boats with their paddle wheels thrashing the water to a foamy broth, great smokestacks belching smoke, the shrill sound of the whistle, the thumping and humming of the engine. The Captain, symbol of authority and conqueror of the mysteries of the river, stood as an awe-inspiring figure. Many boys wished that when they grew up they could command their own river steamers.

Like the river boats, the stage lines colored the legend of the West. Thundering hooves and the stirring call of "stagecoach coming" brought a quickened heartbeat for those who waited for news from back East or for the arrival of long-awaited friends and relatives. The coming of the railroads, however, ended the need for steamboats and stagecoaches.

9 The Iron Horse

Railroad building in the northern part of the United States after the Civil War involved bold financing, get-rich schemes, mismanagement, and bankruptcies that led to eventual success. Not until the emergence of new leadership and major reorganization of the railroad companies would North Dakota be served with adequate rail transportation.

Building a railroad took a huge amount of money and large tracts of land for the right-of-way. The money was supplied by the wealthy of the eastern states and foreign investors; the United States Congress supplied the land. The construction of railroads out of St. Paul and their westward expansion across Minnesota furthered the influence of the Twin Cities and provided incentive for settlement of remote northern Dakota. The railroad was the most important factor in the settlement of the state.

I. The Northern Pacific Railroad

As early as 1848, some Congressmen were interested in building a railroad from the settled eastern region of the United States to the west coast. Various interests had proposed three routes: a northern route through the upper part of the United States, a middle route, and a southern route. When Isaac Stevens returned from an expedition that led him from Fort Union to the Pacific coast, he reported that it would be possible to build a railroad from Minnesota to the Pacific Ocean. Congress passed a bill for a northern route, and President Lincoln signed the charter of the Northern Pacific Railroad in 1864.

A Northern Pacific construction crew working in Morton County, 1879. (SHSND)

As incentive to build, the Northern Pacific received a generous tract of land — the biggest grant that Congress ever gave a railroad. Over 50,000,000 acres — 20 sections per mile in Minnesota and Oregon and 40 sections per mile in Dakota, Montana, Idaho, and Washington — went to the Northern Pacific. The railroad received alternate sections on each side of the right-of-way. The company, however, did not begin construction for five years. In the meantime, the completion of the Union Pacific Railroad linked the east and west coasts through the center of the country.

Although the northern road attempted to attract investors, none showed interest until 1869, when the famous banking house of Jay Cooke and Company of Philadelphia offered to promote the financing. Cooke signed a contract to sell $100,000,000 worth of bonds that paid 7.3 percent interest. In return, he was to receive a twelve-percent commission and about three fifths of the company's stock.

The financing of the Northern Pacific Railroad was the largest single business venture ever undertaken in the United States up to that time. Plans called for the building of a 2,000-mile railroad from the head of the Great Lakes at Duluth to the Pacific Ocean through the yet unsettled northern country.

Jay Cooke had sold the bonds that financed the Union government during the Civil War. He knew the value of advertising and began an extensive campaign to sell the new railroad bonds. Calling the area through which the right-of-way would pass the "fertile belt," Cooke waged an all-out advertising campaign. He raised $5,000,000 to start construction of a road that was to run from Thompson Junction near Duluth to the Red River. After that, the company was to continue construction only as fast as he could sell the bonds.

Troubles hindered the whole effort. After raising only a part of the required money, Cooke had great difficulty in interesting large banks and foreign investors in bonds. Eventually, he had to turn to smaller banks and investors. To add to the problem, the company officials did not turn their full attention to the road and spent money recklessly. They entered into construction contracts before Cooke had a chance to sell enough bonds to meet the payments. Finally, Cooke's firm had to advance its own money or give up construction. After spending more than $5,000,000 of its own money to cover the costs, Jay Cooke and Company went bankrupt in 1873. This helped to bring about the "Panic of '73," and Cooke lost his personal fortune.

The Northern Pacific, however, was under construction and pushing toward the Red River. It reached Moorhead in 1871; by the summer of 1872 it had crossed the Red River, and by 1873 it was completed to Bismarck. On the west coast, 150 miles of track had been laid from Tacoma, Washington, to the Columbia River.

A Northern Pacific train at the Wahpeton depot, 1884. (SHSND)

THE IRON HORSE

In 1875 Frederick Billings became president of the Northern Pacific. The company, reorganized under his management skills, made its first profit in 1876. With ledgers in the black, the railroad was able to secure the money it needed for completion. By 1881 the Northern Pacific went through the Badlands and moved on to the Pacific. A million-dollar bridge had been constructed across the Missouri at Bismarck, and branch-line construction was under way. From 1880 to 1887 the Northern Pacific built several branch lines. In 1882-1883 it ran tracks from Fargo to La Moure along the James River. Other lines were constructed north and south of Jamestown in 1883-1885, and by 1887 a line that entered the state at Grand Forks was completed to the Canadian border.

Although the Northern Pacific was the first railroad to enter North Dakota, it would soon have to compete with another. A young shipping clerk, James J. Hill, in St. Paul would put together a rival road that would run across the northern part of the state and make his name important in the settlement and development of early North Dakota.

II. The Great Northern Railroad

The Great Northern Railroad had its beginning as the St. Paul and Pacific Railroad. In 1857 Congress authorized a grant of 6,000,000 acres in Minnesota for railroad construction. Four companies were chartered to build the roads and receive the land grant. The Minnesota and Pacific Railroad, which received the

James J. Hill.

largest grant, did not start construction, and the St. Paul and Pacific, chartered in 1862, took its place. It was to build a road from St. Paul to St. Cloud and then on to the Red River at Breckenridge. Also included in the plans was a branch line to St. Vincent near the Canadian border. By 1871 the St. Paul and Pacific had built a line from St. Paul to the Red River; by 1872 the company had also constructed 35 miles of track from St. Cloud to Melrose, a short four-mile line north of St. Cloud, and a section running from south of Glyndon to north of Crookston. This section, which could be used as a feeder line to the Northern Pacific, was a little over 100 miles long and was not connected to the rest of the system.

The St. Paul and Pacific, like the Northern Pacific, experienced financial difficulties. The railroad eventually went into bankruptcy. Railroad building in Minnesota by the end of 1872 had been a very disappointing experience.

It was James J. Hill who finally completed what the St. Paul and Pacific had set out to do. Hill was a Canadian emigrant who, in 1857, at the age of 18, began working as a shipping clerk in St. Paul. Like many of the early Scottish settlers, Hill was ambitious and farsighted. By 1856 he had gone into business for himself. He became a shipping agent for the Winnipeg merchants, and he later entered the river-transportation business and in 1874 formed the Red River Transportation Company. On his travels to Winnipeg, by dog sled in the winter and steamboat in the summer, Hill came to realize the importance of the Valley and plains of North Dakota. His iron will and determination brought the railroad to the northern part of the state and eventually to the Pacific coast. The Red River Valley and North Dakota would become known as "Hill country."

After the depression which began with the Panic of 1873, railroad building began again. The Northern Pacific constructed a line from Brainerd to Sauk Rapids, which met with the St. Paul and Pacific by 1878, thus giving the road a St. Paul connection. In March 1878 Hill and three associates signed an agreement with the investors of the St. Paul and Pacific to take control of that company. Hill and his men had to find money to complete the lines from Crookston to St. Vincent and from Melrose to Alexandria. With his own personal zeal, Hill secured the money, materials, and labor. Under his personal direction, the line to St. Vincent was completed by December 1878. This line met the Canadian Pacific, providing a direct connection between Winnipeg and St. Paul. The Melrose-to-Alexandria line was finished the same year.

In May 1879 the St. Paul and Pacific was taken over by a new company, the St. Paul, Minneapolis, and Manitoba, which was also known as the Manitoba. Hill organized and managed the new company, which had 657 miles of track and nearly 2,000,000 acres of land in the state of Minnesota.

Under Hill's brilliant management, the railroad progressed. The old line was extended west of Crookston to the Fisher's Landing (present-day Fisher, Minnesota). Here, supplies were loaded on the steamers for the trip north. By the spring of 1880, tracks linked Fisher and Grand Forks. From 1880 to 1884 the Manitoba made great strides in constructing branch lines. Running north and south through the Valley, lines connected Fargo, Grand Forks, St. Thomas, and

The Great Northern Railroad trestle over Gassman Coulee west of Minot, 1887.(SHSND)

Neche on the Canadian border. Farther west, the Manitoba built from Wahpeton through Casselton, Mayville, Larimore, Park River, and finally to Langdon in 1887. Two lines in 1883 went west, one from Wahpeton and one, which would be the main line, from Grand Forks to Devils Lake. Later, two branch lines, one to Cando and the other to Bottineau, would connect those towns with the main line at Devils Lake. Hill's road reached Minot in 1886 and Great Falls, Montana, in 1887. This was a tremendous feat; road construction averaged three and a quarter miles per day.

In the early 1890s the Manitoba had almost a thousand miles of track in North Dakota; it had overtaken the Northern Pacific in track mileage and serviced the Red River Valley, the most settled part of the state. In the next years, the line would reach the Pacific coast, and its name would be changed to the Great Northern Railroad.

The two major railroads did not compete directly for business. In 1882 the Northern Pacific and the Manitoba entered into an agreement to divide business in the state. In general, the deal involved branch lines. The Northern Pacific built branch lines north from Jamestown, which would serve the Drift Prairie west of the Red River Valley, The line extending north from Casselton to Mayville was sold to the Manitoba. The Northern Pacific, however, did build a line which paralleled the Manitoba from Grand Forks to Winnipeg. The agreement between the two lines divided the traffic and raised freight rates.

The Great Northern depot at Grand Forks. (SHSND)

Three other major railroads were also built in North Dakota. The Chicago and Northwestern ran a line from the southern part of the state to Oakes. The Soo Line had track in the southeastern part of the state, and the Chicago-Milwaukee and St. Paul ran from Ortonville, Minnesota, to Fargo, with a branch line to Edgeley, North Dakota.

With the completion of railroads, North Dakota was tied to the grain markets of Minneapolis and St. Paul. Settlement progressed as rail lines extended through the state. As Minneapolis became a chief milling center, more and more wheat would be needed. The railroads provided the means of transporting wheat from the Red River Valley, and brought supplies to the pioneer settlers. The settlers would pay a price for railroad development. The lives and fortunes of the people of the state would be tied to the interests of those who controlled the railroads and their allies, those who controlled the grain trade.

*   *   *   *   *   *

The construction of railroads excited all North Dakotans. The crews worked to level the gound and build the gradings to carry the rails. Depots became centers of activity with arrivals and departures of trains. In the larger towns such as Fargo, Grand Forks, and Bismarck, the depot was a prominent building. The mighty chugging steam engine with its red-glowing fire box, trailing a long column of smoke, was a friendly sight to tired field hands as it moved across the darkened prairie. The long, low moan of the train whistle in the night moved many to dream of adventure in far-off places. To some, the railroads meant a way to leave the hard life of farming. They saw the brightly lit passenger trains, their elegant dining cars filled with well-dressed people, and imagined the day when they would travel in style. Eric Sevareid once wrote that as a boy he would stand looking down the tracks from his home town of Velva, knowing that somewhere at the end of those tracks there was a great big world awaiting him. Other boys dreamed of working on the railroad, becoming engineers who could run the engines and wave to people who stopped at the crossings. The railroad symbolized adventure, but more important, it made possible the settlement of North Dakota.

10 Day of the Bonanza

A spirit of excitement gripped America during the years following the Civil War. Railroads began to stretch like fingers across the continent; men such as John D. Rockefeller and Andrew Carnegie were building business empires. Cities groaned under the strain of population growth as thousands of immigrants poured into the country. Almost over night the United States had become the world's industrial giant and a symbol of opportunity. Men with capital looked for new schemes which would turn an investment into a fortune; and those with little money, many of whom were immigrants, were looking for a place to make a living. The West offered much to both.

I. The Land Lies Open

Ever since Horace Greeley told Americans to go west in pursuit of a better life, travelers and promoters had written about the West as a land of hope and opportunity. The farm lands of the East were filled or exhausted; the lands of the West were open. Minnesota became a state in 1858, and its population grew rapidly. As railroads pushed toward Dakota Territory, interest in the new region increased. By 1870 the army had control over most of the Indians, and the Northern Pacific entered the Red River Valley. Northern Dakota was open to settlement. But many people had serious questions about settling in northern Dakota: Could the land produce enough to support the people? Was it a fit place to live? Could people thrive and make a living in such a climate?

Many believed that Dakota could produce spring wheat as Minnesota did. Yet, spring wheat was inferior, and prices for it were lower because of milling problems. Spring wheat had one characteristic which made it less desirable than winter wheat, which was grown farther south. The bran (the outside covering of the kernel) of spring wheat was very brittle. In the grinding process, the bran broke into fine pieces, making it difficult to separate it from the flour. This caused the flour to have a yellowish color; it would not keep as well as the higher-priced flour made from winter wheat.

By 1870 two southern Minnesota millers discovered that milling spring wheat with a slow, loose, grinding produced a much better flour. This process was adopted by George C. Christian, who had won the friendship of one of the millers and had learned their secret. Christian began using the new process in Minneapolis. Christian's mill had a purifier which separated the bran from the flour between grindings. Using rollers instead of mill stones, the new process produced a new flour, called "Minnesota Patent," which equaled winter wheat flour in color and quality. The new flour sold at a higher price and became the best on the market. The development of this new process opened a tremendous market for the product. Minneapolis soon became the nation's milling center.

As Christian was promoting his new product, the Northern Pacific tracks were entering the Red River Valley. The mills needed new supplies of spring wheat, and the railroads needed to carry wheat and supplies to make money. If it could be demonstrated that Dakota was well suited for the growing of spring wheat, settlers would come to the state and take up farming. The railroads, the millers, and the newly formed Minneapolis grain exchange stimulated great interest in farm land in the Red River Valley and began the Great Dakota Boom.

II. The Great Bonanza Farms

The word "bonanza" implies a big fortune, hitting it lucky, making a spectacular windfall. In Dakota, bonanza farming meant huge farms to grow the profitable spring wheat crop. Because the farms were run in a factory-like operation, they were unique.

After the Northern Pacific went bankrupt in 1873, investors who held securities (bonds or preferred stock) could either sell them on the open market for only a small fraction of their original cost or exchange them at face value for land which the railroad had received in its grant. Most investors preferred to trade their securities to the company and acquire large sections of railroad land. James B. Power, land agent for the Northern Pacific, recognized that such a condition could lead to speculation; a speculator would acquire land and hold it until he could sell it for a profit. This might not bring settlement. Power persuaded George W. Cass, president of the Northern Pacific, to start a large farm that would demonstrate to the nation the wonderful and profitable opportunity for farming in Dakota. If the bonanzas could prove to be a financial success, they would attract settlers to the area. Power became the father of bonanza farming.

The residence on the Hughes and Hersy bonanza farm near Arvilla. (SHSND)

The railroad expected to profit by the settlement of northern Dakota. This would mean that it could dispose of its land and also transport goods to Dakota and grain to Minneapolis. The bonanza farm accomplished these aims.

By 1885, 90 bonanza farms of over 3,000 acres each flourished in the Red River Valley. Cass and Benjamin Cheney, one of the directors of the Northern Pacific, established the first. In 1874 they purchased 13,440 acres of Northern Pacific land near present-day Casselton. This well-publicized farm became the model for bonanza farming. The Grandin brothers from Pennsylvania made one of the largest purchases of land, 26,000 acres, near Mayville. The Sharon and Amenia Land Company farmed over 28,000 acres north of Casselton; in Richland County the Antelope farm was 13,300 acres. The Spiritwood spread in Stutsman County was 19,700 acres. The Carrington and Casey purchases of 35,700 acres lay within Wells and Foster counties. Outside the Northern Pacific land grant in Grand Forks County, the Elk Valley, Emery, Larimore, and McCanna bonanza farms thrived.

Although the bonanza farms were operated in different ways to suit different managers, the general operation of the farms fit a standard pattern. The farms were huge investments for the owners and, therefore, were regarded as a business enterprise intended to produce a profit. Because of this, owners of the farms relied on professional management. They knew that good management was essential to a successful operation. The manager was hired for his managerial skills, not his knowledge of farm work or agriculture.

Harvest time on the Dalrymple bonanza farm using mule power. (SHSND)

The first and perhaps best-known manager was Oliver Dalrymple, who was hired as manager of the Cass-Cheney bonanza. Dalrymple came from Pennsylvania and had attended Yale Law School. He went to Minnesota in 1856 to practice law and later entered farming with a 3,000-acre spread. An extremely able man, Dalrymple used the latest farming methods, which made his farm very successful and earned him the title of "Wheat King" of Minnesota.

Dalrymple received a generous contract from Cheney. He received a third of the profits and an option to buy one-third of the land at the original cost. This enabled Dalrymple to acquire land and increase his holdings. Bonanza farmers wanted an account of every penny spent and earned. The owners employed bookkeepers, one of the few year-round employees, and closely watched the books. Oliver Dalrymple set the pattern for the operations of the huge farms.

The bonanza farms were broken into divisions of 5,000 acres or less. Each division had a superintendent, and under him was a foreman for each of the subdivisions of 1,200 to 1,800 acres. Each division had the usual farm buildings: houses, shops, granaries, and machine sheds. The headquarters farm was the center of business operations. Contact between the divisions and headquarters farm was made by horse and buggy in the summertime. When the telephone came into use, lines connected the divisions and headquarters, and the foreman called in each morning. The foreman also received a written schedule of operations for each day.

Migrant workers who followed the seasons provided the labor for the bonanzas. In the spring, ground was broken and seeded. When the crop was in, more new land was broken for the next year. In the summer, usually July, hay was put up for the winter months. Harvest on the bonanza was a time of great activity. Gangs of binders (machinery that tied wheat into bundles), as many as 53 at a time, would move across the field under the supervision of a foreman. A mechanic and wagons which carried twine, water, and spare parts followed the binders. The threshing crew of over 20 men harvested a section (620 acres) in about a week. A steam engine supplied the power for the machinery, and as many as ten teams of horses and wagons would haul the bundles. When threshing was done, many of the workers would be dismissed, and only a small crew would remain to do fall plowing and other chores.

Many of the farms had dormitories in which as many as 50 men were housed. Cooks fed work crews of as many as 100 men in mess halls. The meals served on the bonanza farms were generally good and nourishing. A standard fare might include meat, potatoes, fresh cakes and pies, and tea or coffee. The men received from $15 to $20 a month and room and board for their work. During the planting and harvest times, when work had to be done in a rush, the wages varied from $1.75 to $2.50 a day. Many of those who came to work on the bonanza farms were entranced by the plains of Dakota and saw a chance to get into the farming business themselves. They realized that here was a new land where opportunity awaited the man who was willing to take the risk and acquire land.

The bonanza farms were profitable enterprises. They grew one crop — wheat. Because of this, they did not use the land to grow food for their own use; most of what was consumed had to be shipped in by rail. Bonanza farms bought great quantities of lumber, food, and farm machinery at wholesale prices, and the railroad gave them special lower freight rates. By the middle and late 1880s, however, wheat prices had declined and were threatening to erase bonanza profits. At the same time, demand for small farms increased as immigrants began moving into Dakota. The bonanza farms were eventually broken into smaller parcels and rented or sold to individuals who could earn a living on a half-section of land. The bonanzas did, however, prove that North Dakota was a productive land and advertised this fact to the rest of the world.

III. The Cattle Bonanza and The Marquis de Morès

When the bonanza farms in the Red River Valley were in their heyday, a book appeared which stirred the imaginations of many. In 1881 General James E. Brisben published *The Beef Bonanza; or How to Get Rich on the Plains*. With chapter titles such as "Millions in Beef" and "The Money to Be Made," he showed that investment in cattle could bring large profits. Others agreed. Dakota Territory's immigrant guides promoted "splendid natural meadows" and "nutritious grasses." They claimed that "Dakota is the finest field in the world for stock growers."

American and European investors poured millions of dollars into the cattle business during the 1870s. And as the grasses of Colorado, Nebraska, and Wyoming began to wear out, cattlemen looked toward Dakota. During the 1880s many of the West's large cattle outfits moved north into Dakota. Soon, over a half million head of cattle were grazing in the region from the Black Hills to the Badlands of the Little Missouri country.

With the coming of the Northern Pacific into the Badlands in 1881, the rugged country became a favorite hunting spot for men like Howard and Eldon Eaton of Pittsburgh and A.C. Huidekoper of Meadville, Pennsylvania. The Eaton brothers, who had first visited the Badlands on a hunting expedition in 1880, returned the following year and made their living as hunting promoters and guides. In 1881 Huidekoper met the Eatons while hunting buffalo, and they became convinced that the Badlands would be excellent for grazing. Huidekoper and the Eatons formed the Custer Trail Cattle Company, with headquarters a few miles south of the point at which the railroad crossed the Little Missouri River. Huidekoper furnished the capital, and the Eatons managed the range. Howard Eaton purchased 1,000 cattle in Minnesota, and Huidekoper secured a carload of shorthorn bulls in the East. In 1882 the company purchased 23,000 acres of railroad land on the Little Missouri and the following year moved its herd to the new range. The Custer Trail Cattle Company had one of the finest herds in the West.

Cowboy camp on a bonanza ranch, 1880s. (SHSND)

Theodore Roosevelt (left) and the Marquis de Morès (right) in their western outfits. (SHSND)

Shortly after Huidekoper and the Eatons began their effort, the Continental Land and Cattle Company, a $3,000,000 business, started ranching on the Little Missouri. By 1884 it had 35,000 cattle. The year 1882 also saw the organization of the Badlands Cattle Company by two Minnesotans, H.B. Wadsworth and W.L. Hawley. Managed by A.W. Merrifield and Sylvane and Joseph Ferris, all of whom had come to the Badlands to hunt in 1881, the company brought 200 head from Minnesota to its Maltese Cross Ranch on the Little Missouri near the mouth of the Cannonball River.

By 1883 the Badlands had a nationwide reputation as a land of the beef bonanza. It was a challenging country that attracted colorful people. Of those who came to the Little Missouri country, two especially stand out: Theodore Roosevelt and the Marquis de Morès.

Roosevelt, a young Harvard graduate and New York legislator, at age 25 came to the Badlands, hoping to bag a buffalo. He found not only buffalo but also a place to regain his health and a country in which to invest. He was not in Dakota long before he was caught up in the spirit of the new country. He bought out the Wadsworth and Hawley ranching interests for $12,000, and Merrifield and

The Marquis de Morès' packing plant at Medora. (SHSND)

Ferris ran the operation for him. Roosevelt split the profit with his managers. Roosevelt hunted, chased thieves, and wrote books during his months in the Badlands. He would later say that his Badlands experience contributed to his becoming President.

Antoine Amédée Marie Vincent Amat Manca de Vallombrosa, the Marquis de Morès, was an adventuresome young Frenchman who married Medora von Hoffman, the daughter of a Wall Street banker, and came to America in 1882. On April 1, 1883, the tall, handsome, dashing Frenchman stepped off the train at Little Missouri to begin his career in Dakota. He had a bold scheme to build a packing plant on the plains where the cattle fed. Instead of shipping live cattle to Chicago, cattlemen could sell their cattle to the Marquis, and he would slaughter the cattle and ship the beef by refrigerated railroad car to the market — both in Dakota and the East. On the east bank of the Little Missouri River, he founded the village of Medora and built his packing plant. The Marquis built a hotel, and his wife provided funds for a church.

Viewing Dakota as a place to make a fortune, the Marquis entered many business deals. He organized a stageline to the Black Hills, raised sheep, shipped salmon from the Pacific to New York City, speculated in land, and became involved in gold mining. His restless energy and boundless optimism forced him into businesses about which he knew very little. He was determined, however, to make a name for himself in the American business world. The Marquis led an active life: attempting to oversee his business empire, hunting wild game, vacationing in Paris, and traveling around the United States. While in Medora, he and his family lived in a 25-room ranch house perched on a bluff overlooking the village of Medora. Here he lived in old-world comfort with servants, cooks, and gardeners to keep up his "chateau." He even had a custom-made tin bathtub and a wine cellar.

DAY OF THE BONANZA

The Eaton brothers' ranch house south of Medora, 1880s. (SHSND)

From 1883 to 1887 the village of Medora bristled with the activity of the Marquis' business ventures. From 1885 to 1887, however, the Marquis began to face both personal and business difficulties. In 1883 he had been involved in a shoot-out between his men and a trio of buffalo hunters who were angry because the Marquis had fenced their trails. One of the hunters was killed, and in 1885 the Marquis was tried for the murder. Although he was acquitted, many people remained hostile toward him. After 1885 his business ventures were losing money. In 1887 his business empire collapsed, and the Marquis returned to France with a loss of over a million dollars. He had wanted to become a business success, but he failed because he lacked business ability. So, he returned to France, where he became involved in French politics and was a leader of the anti-Semitic movement. In 1896, at age 37, he was killed in North Africa while leading a personal expedition which he hoped would increase French influence among the Moslem tribes. In Medora he left behind his chateau and packing plant. Today the chateau stands as an historical monument to an adventuresome young Frenchman who in 1883 had seen Dakota as a land of unlimited opportunity.

* * * * * *

By the 1890s the day of the bonanza was over. Smaller operators were moving into North Dakota. Bonanza farming and bonanza ranching, however, had served useful purposes in the settlement of the state. They were big ideas in a big land. Both demonstrated that the land was productive and that it could support a sizable population. Few episodes in North Dakota history created more attention than bonanza farming, cattle bonanzas, and the Marquis de Mores. Eastern newspapers and magazines often wrote about them, giving Dakota a reputation as an exciting and good land.

11 Dakotaland, Sweet Dakotaland

To the world, Dakota was a distant and unknown land. Many people had heard about the bloody conflicts between the army and the Indians, but few knew much about the land itself. The creation of Dakota Territory in 1861 did not excite many people to leave their homes and head for the new country. Population grew slowly. Bonanza farming helped to stir up interest in Dakota. The acres and acres of golden wheat proved that the land could be productive. People, however, had to be convinced that northern Dakota was a good place to live.

I. Going to Northern Dakota

The railroad, which had entered northern Dakota in the 1870s, became the most important agent in "selling" people on Dakota. The Northern Pacific had much to gain from settlement — selling land, carrying people to and from the new frontier, and hauling goods. The Northern Pacific began a massive advertising campaign in 1879 to attract settlers. Under the direction of James B. Power, head of the land department of the railroad, the Northern Pacific promoted Dakota in the eastern states as well as in many foreign lands. Railroad agents spread the word in the British Isles, Denmark, Sweden, Holland, and Norway. Promotional advertising was published in American, Canadian, Scandinavian, and German newspapers. The Territory, too, began to promote itself. It published a 500-page book to tell the world about Dakota. Entitled *Resources of Dakota,* it painted a glowing picture of the Territory, pointing out the healthful climate, fertile soil, and free land. It appealed to those who wanted to start anew and build a better life for themselves.

Promotion paid off; settlers rushed to northern Dakota. Between 1878 and 1890, population increased from 16,000 to 191,000. Most of the settlement was in the Red River Valley, and there the largest towns were located. By 1890 Grand Forks had a population of almost 5,000, while Fargo was the largest with 5,664. The Drift Prairie had less settlement; Jamestown grew to 2,296 during the boom years. The Missouri Plateau had the least number of settlers; the settlement pattern there was six to 18 inhabitants per square mile, and Bismarck had 2,186 people.

During the population boom, the railroad brought most of the pioneers to Dakota. The railroads operated emigrant trains, and sometimes whole colonies of settlers would come to the Territory. The usual method was for some influential men of a community in the eastern states or Europe to organize an association for colonization made up of those who wanted to pioneer. The association would then send a committee to the Territory to choose a suitable place to settle. When the site was chosen and the transportation arrangements made, usually with the help of the railroad, the colony of a hundred or more families would move to the new location. A colony from Lansing, Michigan, established itself in McIntosh County. In Morton County a colony of German-Russians settled during the boom years. Not all who came to Dakota could afford a train ticket. Pulling up stakes where they lived, they would pile their belongings in a wagon, hitch up a horse or ox, and set out for the prairie.

Breaking the sod in Pembina County. (SHSND)

The rush of settlers produced a whirlwind of settlement and new towns. Almost overnight a community would spring up and become a hub of activity. As the new settlers began to dot the prairies with their homes, railroad centers became trading centers. Minot grew to a town of 1,000 in five weeks after the Manitoba railroad reached there in 1886. Devils Lake's population grew to 1,000 in 18 months. Buildings in the early towns were mainly canvas tents and shacks. As time went on, they would be replaced by frame buildings and eventually some brick structures.

A great many of the pioneers who came were foreign-born. In 1890, 43 percent of North Dakota's population had come from other lands. The largest numbers had come from Norway and Canada. Others were from England, Ireland, Germany, Sweden, and Russia. Before settling in Dakota, many of the immigrants had spent time in other states such as Minnesota, Wisconsin, and Iowa. American-born settlers came from many states. Many came from the older states of Minnesota, Wisconsin, New York, Michigan, and Ohio.

II. Hard Work on the Prairie

When pioneers came to the Territory, they had to face a new way of living on the prairie. Many hardships and discouragements awaited the newcomers. Making a go of it would mean fighting disease, weather, and loneliness. But the first problem was land.

An ox-drawn binder in the Red River Valley, 1877. (SHSND)

Most of the early settlers came to acquire land—a stake in the future. There were four ways by which land could be acquired. It could be bought from the Northern Pacific Railroad or the Federal Government, or it could be obtained free under the terms of the Homestead Act and the Timber Culture Act.

In 1889 the Northern Pacific sold its land at prices ranging from $2.50 to $6.00 an acre. If the land were cultivated within a two-year period, the railroad gave a 25 percent discount. The agreements also gave the purchaser five or ten years to pay, with a seven percent interest charge on the unpaid balance. Under the Preemption Act, the federal government sold its lands at $1.25 an acre. If a person did not already own 320 acres in any state or territory, he could buy 160 acres at the quoted price, provided that he had lived on the land six months and had made certain improvements.

The prospective settler could get land free under the Homestead Act. He could acquire 160 acres of land, provided that he lived on the land for a period of five years and cultivated a portion of it during that time. The homesteader had to pay $14.00 to $18.00 when he filed for the land to homestead, and $4.00 to $8.00 when he applied for the title after five years. If a settler could afford it, he could, under an 1880 law, buy his homestead without living on the land five

NORTHERN PACIFIC

RAILROAD

LANDS FOR SALE

The Northern Pacific Railroad Company has a large quantity of Agricultural and Grazing Lands for sale at low rates and on 5 and 10 years' credit.

OVER 1,000,000 ACRES IN MINNESOTA.
OVER 8,000,000 ACRES IN NORTH DAKOTA.
OVER 19,000,000 ACRES IN MONTANA.
OVER 1,750,000 ACRES IN IDAHO.
OVER 13,000,000 ACRES IN WASHINGTON AND OREGON.

Over **40,000,000 Acres For Sale** at prices ranging chiefly from **$2 to $6** per acre for the best **Wheat Lands**, the best diversified **Farming Lands** and the best **Grazing Lands** now open for settlement.

These extremely productive lands stretch out for 50 miles on each side of the Northern Pacific Railroad, and reach from the Great Lakes to the Pacific Ocean and Puget Sound, through Minnesota, North Dakota, Montana, Northern Idaho, Washington and Oregon—the new and prosperous Northern Pacific Country.

years. This process, called commuting, allowed the settler to pay for his land after living on it only six months. The price he had to pay for commuting was the same as if he had bought land under the Preemption Act.

The Timber Culture Act of 1873 allowed the pioneer a fourth way to gain land. This law, intended to place trees on the prairie, had terms similar to the Homestead Act. A settler could acquire 160 acres of land by planting ten acres in trees. At the end of eight years, the land became his when he proved that he had 675 living trees on the land and paid a fee of $14.00. People of North Dakota referred to land acquired in this manner as tree claims. Many acquired 480 acres by using a combination of the Preemption, Homestead, and Timber Culture acts. Although this could not be done at the same time, a settler might first file a preemption claim; then, after acquiring title, one could file a homestead claim and then a tree claim.

Once having acquired land and started farming, the pioneer probably found life to be quite different from what he thought it would be when he first read the promotional literature about Dakota. The new unsettled land required adaptation to frontier life. The broad, treeless prairies were quite different from the places from which most had come. The long winters and the sparseness of the population caused feelings of isolation and loneliness.

A Cavalier County sod house, 1890s. (SHSND)

When people came to North Dakota, one of their first necessities was a place to live. The earlier settlers built several types of dwellings. If they had settled near the rivers where the trees grew, they could build log cabins of one or two rooms with an earthen roof laid across long pole beams. This type of cabin had few windows and usually only one door. Along the rivers and coulees, if the banks were steep enough, settlers could dig out a place to live in the bank itself. The dugout required only a front wall and earthern roof and made a dark but warm home.

Sod houses were built on the prairies where wood was not available. The house had walls of sod strips, sometimes two feet thick. Often the walls were covered with boards and then whitewashed. Although rough looking, the sod house proved to be warm and comfortable during the North Dakota winter. Some settlers made two and three room homes of sun-dried bricks which were plastered inside and out and whitewashed. Some hauled lumber from a railroad station and built tarpaper shacks. Often sod would be piled around the outside for greater warmth.

To come to a virgin land and start anew meant long hours of hard work and many hardships. The work was always there. In the spring, the settler had to break the sod with an ox- or horse-drawn plow. The rough sod was difficult to break, and plow shares had to be sharpened almost every day. In the second year, the land was plowed again and seeding started in the spring. The labor was extremely difficult. Children were expected to do a day's work as soon as they were strong enough for the farm tasks. For the early pioneer, a day's work stretched from sun-up to sun-down. The men rose early, prepared the horses for the day, and were in the field when it was light enough to see. Quitting time came when it became too dark to work. At home, the women did the chores, milking cows, churning butter, and cooking meals to feed the hungry family.

Perhaps the pioneer farm life was hardest on the women. Theirs was a lonely life filled with endless tasks. They cared for the children, did the house chores, and helped the men in times of emergency. They often bore babies with only a neighbor woman present, and sometimes all alone. When sickness came, medical help was miles away, and home remedies had to do. Many times the woman of the house was left alone to tend the farm when her husband went for needed supplies. Sitting in the home, listening to the howling winter wind, with only the children for comfort, took a special quality. Some women homesteaded alone.

All faced the hardships of living on the prairie. The winters would bring the blizzards, freezing the cattle and making homes icy and cold. In the spring, floods could sweep away a year's work. If rain did not come, the crops would wither away, and feed for the animals would be short. In dry years, prairie fire became a threat. Whipped by the wind, the wall of fire moved with tremendous speed across open, dry grainland. Farmers would plow strips of land as fire breaks; families would fight the fire with wet sacks and blankets. Sometimes a homestead would be completely burned out. The Dakota prairie could break the spirit.

Quilting parties brightened pioneer life. (SHSND)

III. The Bright Side of Pioneer Life

Not all of life in Dakota was just a matter of survival. A trip to town in the 1870s or 1880 brought a refreshing change to the routine of the farm work. Many towns that sprang up became thriving trade centers with many types of businesses. Many merchants would let the farmer charge his supplies, waiting until he had received his money for the crops before paying the bill. For those who lived on the farm, a trip to town was an adventure. For the women, the stores offered fashions from the East. Ice cream and candy delighted the children. Also, there was entertainment. The larger towns had baseball teams. In the spring, track and field events were held, as well as boat races at Fourth of July celebrations. Fargo, Grand Forks, and other larger communities held fairs in late summer. The whole family would come to town and spend a day at the fair. In the fall, a farmer journeyed to town to lay in the winter's supplies of sugar, coffee, flour, and some canned goods. A trip to town in the wintertime could be a hazardous event if the weather turned bad.

The pioneer home was the center for entertainment and learning. Families would visit each other and organize card parties, play chess and checkers, or while away the time with stories and news of the area. Getting together with the neighbors helped overcome the loneliness. Often there would be sleighing and ice skating on the frozen ponds.

Learning to read and write started at home. Families often read to each other on the long winter nights. Many brought their collections of books with them when they came to Dakota. Formal schooling, if it could be had, was obtained in the one-room school that was built by a community of neighbors.

Religion was an important part of life and, like learning, religious instruction began in the home. Strong religious beliefs sustained many who at times found frontier life unbearable. When deaths occurred or crops failed, it was comforting to have a strong belief in one's religion. Most families had Bibles and would read passages to their children. If a home had a piano or reed organ, neighbors would gather at holidays to sing hymns and hold prayer meetings. The prairie frontier was not without the word of God.

IV. City Lights

During the 1870s and 1880s, early towns in Dakota were typical of those on the frontier. At first, they were a collection of tents and tarpaper shacks; the streets were muddy when it rained, and there were no trees or lawns. Life could be harsh for the inhabitants. Saloons and gambling were common. Many railworkers, drifters, speculators, and adventurers were part of early populations. As settlement increased, the towns began to acquire the essentials of civilization and became law-abiding places. The settlers needed supplies and services. Soon blacksmith shops, stores, hotels, implement dealers, and banks became well established businesses. Wooden frame and brick structures replaced the temporary buildings. Doctors, dentists, lawyers, teachers, and other professional people took up residence. Newspapers were started in almost every town; in 1873 the *Bismarck Tribune* became the first. At one time, Fargo and Grand Forks each had three dailies. Early congregations constructed churches and held regular services. Many leading businessmen built themselves large, fine homes.

Racing at Grand Forks brought town and farm folk together. (SHSND)

By the turn of the century, the larger towns had acquired a cosmopolitan look. Police and fire departments were organized in Fargo, Grand Forks, Bismarck, and Jamestown. Although sanitary conditions were very poor in the early years, cities began to install water and sewer lines. The water, however, was untreated and contained harmful materials. Grand Forks had a gas plant which provided gas lighting for streets and homes. Fargo and Grand Forks had street cars which ran on the main thoroughfares.

Hotels, which provided lodgings for visitors and traveling salesmen, were places of much activity. Their lobbies were elegant and teeming with guests. The restaurants in some of the better ones — the Dacotah in Grand Forks, the Headquarters in Fargo, and the Patterson in Bismarck — could boast of sumptuous meals. The Christmas Day menu of 1886 for the Headquarters Hotel in Fargo included raw oysters, green turtle soup, roast loin of beef, roast young lamb, boiled sugar cured ham, Roman punch, rabbit a L'Italienne, chocolate ice cream, and other mouth-watering foods. Almost every town had a livery stable; larger towns had from two to five, where farmers could leave their teams during their visit in town. Town life provided entertainment. People could attend plays and musical shows at local theaters. Grand Forks had the Metropolitan Opera House, which hosted popular traveling shows and artists of the day. Athletics were also important. There were baseball games and track and field events in the summer, especially at Fourth of July celebrations. Those interested in keeping fit formed athletic clubs, such as the YMCA, for exercise and fellowship. Life on the Dakota prairie was not all drudgery and work.

A steam-powered merry-go-round at Dickinson. (SHSND)

DAKOTALAND, SWEET DAKOTALAND

Fargo, 1878.
(SHSND)

Grand Forks, 1884.
(SHSND)

Tower City, 1880.
(SHSND)

Kirkwood House, Carrington, 1880s. (SHSND)

Bismarck Theater, 1880s. (SHSND)

Sheridan House, Bismarck, 1890. (SHSND)

The sitting room of a Bismarck home, 1890. (SHSND)

V. End of the Boom

Between the late 1870s and 1890 the population increased 1,000 percent. By the 1890s the pace of settlement slowed down. Some of the cities lost population. People were still coming to North Dakota, but during the depression of the 1890s some left. Not all who came to the new country ever intended to stay. Many were land speculators who hoped to reap a good profit by purchasing land, holding it until prices rose, and then selling out. Real estate values rose spectacularly, especially in the towns, where the price of lots in some cases went from $25.00 to $2,000.00 in four years. During these years, many got the urge to speculate — doctors, lawyers, teachers, businessmen, and others. All wanted to acquire land in the hopes that the price would rise.

By 1890, people in North Dakota had purchased more land than had acquired it from the United States government. Eight million acres were purchased, while only 3,600,000 acres were earned under the free-land programs. The boom brought a tremendous transformation of the prairie. The countryside was dotted with settlers' homes. The grain elevator, a distinctive feature of the North Dakota landscape, was to be found in most communities. The state had over 50 towns and villages; there were eight communities with populations of over a thousand.

*   *   *   *   *   *

Many of those who stayed in Dakota after the boom were successful and prospered; some became rich. They had conquered the frontier with all of its hardships and had overcome the temptation to leave when things were tough. It took strength to tame a raw country. Courage, energy, ambition, and optimism were the traits that characterized those who stayed in frontier North Dakota. Those who came to the barren prairie and overcame its hardships created a new society.

12 Now It's North Dakota

By the 1860s enough folks had come to Dakota country, mostly to the southern part, so that Congress could give the people their own government. In 1861 Congress passed legislation creating Dakota Territory. From 1861 to 1889 the people in Dakota Territory lived under a governmental system that was intended to prepare them for statehood. The territorial system, however, did not give the people a strong voice in government. Soon, the residents wanted the Territory to become a state. Statehood would give the people more power and, they thought, more of a chance to control their own lives.

I. The Territorial System

The Constitution of the United States, in Article IV, Section 3, states that "Congress shall have power to dispose of and make all needful rules and regulations respecting the territory or other property belonging to the United States." This same article gives Congress the authority to admit new states into the Union. In order to provide "rules and regulations" for the people who were coming to Dakota country in larger and larger numbers, Congress in 1861 created Dakota Territory (which consisted of present-day North Dakota and South Dakota) and provided a government for the Territory.

Government officials in Dakota received their offices in two ways: some were appointed by the President, and others were elected by the people. The President, with the consent of the United States Senate, appointed the territorial governor, secretary, and judges. The people elected a territorial delegate to Congress, and the members of the territorial legislature. The President appointed the territorial governor for a term of four years, but he could remove him at any time. The governor served as commander-in-chief of the militia and, until 1871, as superintendent of Indian affairs. He had the power to veto bills passed by the legislature, but the legislature could override his veto by a two-thirds vote. The governor, with the consent of the legislature, could appoint territorial officials such as the auditor, the treasurer, and the superintendent of public instruction.

Most Dakota governors were easterners who gained their positions through political pull. William Jayne (1861-1863), Andrew J. Faulk (1866-1869), John A. Burbank (1869-1873), John L. Pennington (1874-1878), William A. Howard (1878-1880), Nehemiah G. Ordway (1880-1884), and Gilbert Pierce (1884-1886) came to the Territory only after they had been appointed to the governorship. Newton Edmunds (1863-1866) had come to Dakota in 1861 as chief clerk in the surveyor general's office, and Louis K. Church (1887-1889) had served on the Dakota Supreme Court. Only Governor Arthur C. Mellette (1889), who practiced law in Watertown, was a "Dakotan."

Most of the Dakota governors had been faithful Republican party workers in the East. Jayne had been Lincoln's family physician and campaign manager in Illinois. Faulk was the father-in-law of Territorial Delegate Walter A. Burleigh, and Burbank was the brother-in-law of a prominent Republican senator. Howard had supported Rutherford B. Hayes for President in the Republican convention of 1876. Ordway, Pennington, and Church were party workers in their home states.

The governors of Dakota brought a variety of experiences to the office. Faulk, Pennington, and Pierce had been newspapermen. Church and Mellette were attorneys. Jayne was a physician. Only Burbank, Howard, and Ordway were politicians.

Most of the Dakota governors were men with adequate training who worked for the best interests of the Territory and its people. Judged in terms of the difficulties of the frontier, they did a good job. Only three of the governors left the Territory when they left office. The governors did, of course, have different capabilities and motivations. While most were honest and sincere, a few did use the office for their personal benefit. John Burbank (1869-1873) is an example of a governor who used his position for personal gain. He disliked life in Dakota and spent much of his time in Washington, D.C., or campaigning around the country for the Republican party. This ambitious governor lobbied on behalf of railroad interests, and as reward for his efforts he was made a director of a railroad. These activities forced his resignation.

Another key official was the territorial secretary, who was also appointed by the President for a term of four years. In the case of the death, removal, or absence from the Territory of the governor, the secretary served as acting governor. Secretaries could use the governor's powers when the governor was out of the territory. Twice each year the secretary reported to the President on territorial affairs.

William Jayne, First Governor of Dakota. (SHSND)

The territorial judicial system was headed by three judges who were appointed by the President for four-year terms. The three made up the Supreme Court; individually, each acted as a district judge. Because of population growth and more court cases, Congress increased the number of territorial judges in 1879 to four, in 1884 to five, and 1887 to eight. The great size of the Territory made the administration of justice very difficult because district judges had to spend much of their time traveling from place to place.

Every two years, the voters of Dakota Territory went to the polls to elect their delegate to Congress, and the members of the territorial legislature. The territorial delegate did not have the same rights as members of Congress who represented states; he could take part in congressional debates, but he could not vote. Nevertheless, the people considered their delegate to be a politically powerful person; he served in Congress as the spokesman for territorial officials, the legislature, and the people. Many candidates eagerly sought this position, and much political blood was spilled at election time.

Voters also elected the members of the territorial legislature every two years. The legislature was bicameral, which means that it had two houses. The upper house was called the Council, and the lower house was called the House of Representatives. The original Dakota legislature had nine Council members and 12 House members. By 1887 Congress had increased membership in the Council to 24 and membership in the House to 48. Congress specifically prohibited territorial legislatures from passing laws that would interfere with "primary disposal of the soil," tax the property of the United States, tax the land and property of non-residents at a higher rate than residents, or interfere with the right of private property. After 1886, Congress prevented territorial legislatures from passing local or special laws which changed county seats, regulated county affairs, or granted divorces. Although the governor had veto power, the legislature could override his veto with a two-thirds vote.

Dakota Territory was the creation of Congress, and Congress claimed full authority over it. Although the President appointed significant officials, Congress had the power to control territorial matters. Because Congress, however, was so involved with what it considered to be more important affairs, Washington officials did little to interfere with territorial questions. Dakota officials ran the territory pretty much as they pleased.

II. The Statehood Movement

As early as the 1870s, many Dakotans were becoming dissatisfied with their territorial status. They were growing tired of having the President appoint the major government officials, and they wanted to gain control of the political process. They could do this only if Dakota became a state. Since most of the territorial population lived in southern Dakota, the movement for statehood was born in that section of the Territory. The leaders of the statehood movement came from Yankton, the territorial capital. They represented Republican, conservative, business-professional interests. The Yankton group, which was opposed to federal control and disgusted with what they considered to be the corrupt governorship of Nehemiah G. Ordway, had developed a well-organized

Nehemiah G. Ordway.
(SHSND)

movement for statehood by the early 1880s. Ordway's actions as governor furthered the statehood movement. Ordway had built a powerful political machine. He used his political influence and his friendship with Alexander McKenzie, the Northern Pacific Railroad's political agent in northern Dakota at Bismarck, to promote the transfer of the capital from Yankton to Bismarck. The territorial legislature appointed a commission of nine members to select a new site for the capital. After visiting many communities that wished to have the capital, they voted five to four to select Bismarck, even though it was in a sparsely settled region.

Embittered by this, the Yankton group launched a full-scale attack on Ordway, accusing him of incompetence. Although President Chester Arthur removed Ordway in 1884, Bismarck remained the territorial capital. Yankton's leaders now began a furious campaign to have Dakota Territory admitted into the Union as a state. In 1883, territorial residents approved constitutions, but the vote was small and there was not much grassroot support for statehood. Congress, too, was not enthusiastic about statehood for Dakota. Democrats, who always controlled at least one house of Congress during the 1880s, opposed admitting states that might send Republican congressmen to Washington. Railroads also opposed statehood, preferring weaker territorial control over their operations to what might be stricter state control.

In spite of this opposition, sentiment for statehood was growing as the 1880s ended. By the late 1880s, northern Dakota had 190,000 residents and southern Dakota had over 348,000 — populations which justified statehood. Dakota Democrats supported a bill which would admit Dakota as one state. On February 22, 1889, however, Republicans and Democrats in Congress voted for the Omnibus Bill, which authorized the framing of constitutions for North Dakota, South Dakota, Montana, and Washington.

III. Making a Constitution

Throughout the Territory, Dakotans celebrated the long awaited advent of statehood. In May, North Dakota voters elected 75 delegates to a constitutional convention which was to meet in Bismarck on July 4. When Independence Day came, Bismarck was decked out with colorful banners, and the people were in a festive mood. Hundreds marched in a memorable parade which included 500 Sioux led by Sitting Bull carrying an American flag.

Of the delegates who arrived at Bismarck for the convention, over 40 percent came from the more populated six counties of the Red River Valley. Only nine delegates were over 50 years of age, and some were in their twenties. A majority were Republicans. Twenty-nine were farmers, the largest occupational group represented at the convention; lawyers came in a close second.

When the convention convened, Erastus A. Williams from Bismarck introduced a model constitution which had been drafted by a Harvard Law School professor. The constitution which the convention finally approved followed this

Parade through Bismarck opening the Constitutional Convention, July 4, 1889. (SHSND)

model in many respects. The delegates, however, made many changes which they believed to be good for their new state. The delegates were especially afraid that the governor and the legislature might be influenced by out-of-state interests; therefore, they limited the power of both and created many independent boards and commissions that had the responsibility for controlling such things as railroads and school lands.

The delegates had their most bitter debate over the question of where to place state institutions. Every community wanted such an institution because its residents believed that this would promote its growth. The territorial legislature had already located the capital and penitentiary at Bismarck, the hospital for the "insane" at Jamestown, and the university at Grand Forks. Article XIX of the state Constitution, which provided for the location of state institutions, was designed to please almost everyone. It left the capital at Bismarck, the university at Grand Forks, and the hospital at Jamestown. In addition, Fargo received the agricultural college; Mayville and Valley City were given normal schools (teachers colleges); Pembina County got a school for the blind; Devils Lake, a

Dakota's territorial capitol building became the state's capitol in 1889. (SHSND)

school for the deaf and dumb; Lisbon, an old soldiers home; and a forestry school was to be located some place in Bottineau, McHenry, Ward, or Rollette counties. Overnight, North Dakota had 11 new institutions. On August 17, after a 45-day session, the convention adjourned; it had written a lengthy document, almost six times as long as the United States Constitution. On October 1, the voters approved the Constitution 27,441 to 8,107. A prohibition article in the Constitution, which was voted on separately by the people, narrowly passed 18,552 to 17,393. North Dakotans celebrated their new Constitution without the aid of alcoholic beverages.

IV. The Constitution

The writers of the Constitution did not want either the governor or the legislature to be too powerful. They restricted the power of both — especially the governor. The Constitution divided the executive power among several offices: Secretary of State, Auditor, Attorney General, Treasurer, Superintendent of Public Instruction, Commissioner of Agriculture and Labor, and the Railroad

Commission. These offices acted independently of the governor's office. The governor could call the legislature into special session and make recommendations to it. He could veto a bill or any part of an appropriation bill. The legislature could override the governor's veto by a two-thirds vote. The governor could not try to influence legislation by threatening to use his veto power or his appointive or removal power. If a governor violated this part of the Constitution, he would have to forfeit all right to hold any office of trust in the state.

The Constitution provided for a Senate with 30 to 50 members elected for four-year terms, and a House of Representatives with 60 to 140 members elected for two-year terms. The Constitution also prohibited "log rolling." This means that a legislator could not promise to vote for a measure in return for someone else's vote on another measure. If a legislator did this, he was considered to be guilty of accepting a bribe and was expelled from the legislature. The Constitution listed 35 subjects on which the legislature was forbidden to pass special or local laws. The Constitution also required that the first legislative assembly establish a system of free public education from the first grade through college. The legislature could not put the state into debt for more than $200,000, except when the people voted to authorize the additional debt for special purposes. Thus, the makers of the Constitution limited the power of both the governor and the legislature. Such limits, however, could not be placed upon the judicial branch of government. Judicial power rested with the State Supreme Court, District and County courts, Justices of the Peace, and Police Magistrates. The Supreme Court was made up of three justices elected for six-year terms; it handled mostly appeals cases and supervised the lower courts. The Constitution established a lower court system made up of six district courts and a court in each county.

The Constitution gave all males who were 21 years old, were citizens, or had declared their intentions of becoming citizens, the right to vote. All Indians who had severed tribal relations two years before the election could also vote. Women could vote in school elections only.

V. Now It's North Dakota

North Dakotans busied themselves with preparations for their first complete experience at democratic government, hoping that they could control their own fortunes. In November 1889, residents of the state went to the polls to elect their state officials. Republicans easily won all state offices and a sizeable majority in the legislature. John Miller, a native of New York and a successful farmer in Richland County, became North Dakota's first governor. Henry C. Hansbrough, a newspaper editor from Devils Lake, was elected to the United States House of Representatives.

The first North Dakota legislature had much routine work to do. It defined the duties of state officials, organized the structure of county and city government, and established schools and other institutions called for by the Constitution. Because of pressure from farmers who believed that the railroad and grain businesses had too much control over North Dakota, the legislature passed several laws regulating these businesses. It also gave the Board of Railroad Commissioners authority to regulate railroads and grain elevators, to reduce unreasonable railroad rates, and to establish wheat-grading standards. It required railroads to furnish elevator sites, to build loading platforms, to equalize rates for long and short hauls, and to give no special rates to certain companies. The legislature also fixed the legal rate of interest that could be charged on loans at seven percent, but this could be increased up to twelve percent by mutual consent of the lender and borrower.

Since United States senators were not elected by the people until 1913, the first legislature spent much of its 120-day session selecting senators. After a heated contest, the legislature elected Gilbert Pierce, former governor of Dakota Territory, and Lyman R. Casey, a rancher. The most controversial issue in the first session was the Louisiana lottery. The lottery was run by a company in Louisiana that sold tickets throughout the nation and gave away nearly a million dollars in prizes at each drawing. The company was due to lose its charter in 1893, and it was looking for a new home state. It asked North Dakota for a charter and offered in return to pay the state $100,000 during the first year and $75,000 each year thereafter. Bismarck stirred with activity during the days that the legislature considered the lottery proposal. Some legislators thought that the income from the lottery would help the new state, but others believed that selling lottery tickets was an immoral activity. The lottery bill was finally defeated. After 120 hectic days during which the legislature put the wheels of North Dakota government into motion, it adjourned.

The 1895 legislature faces the question of drastic budget cuts. (SHSND)

VI. The First Decade: The 1890s

North Dakota was born during difficult times. By the late 1880s the price of wheat was declining, and many who had gone into debt to begin their new lives in North Dakota found themselves in economic trouble. The bright glow of the new land began to dim. By the early 1890s the price of wheat had dropped to below 40 cents a bushel; a depression had hit. The farmers complained bitterly about their plight; they argued that railroads charged outrageous rates, bankers expected too high interest rates, merchants — especially implement dealers — made too much profit, and the grain buyers cheated at the scales.

In 1884 a group of farmers as well as city folk met at Huron to discuss the farmer's situation. The group organized the Dakota Farmers Alliance. The Alliance hoped to elect farmers to office in order to get laws passed that would control the grain trade and railroads. Within six years the Alliance had 30,000 members in South and North Dakota. It waged an aggressive campaign to improve farm conditions. It elected men who were sympathetic to farm legislation; it held social events to brighten farm life; it spoke out against monopoly and high railroad rates; it developed its own banking, warehouse, insurance, and elevator businesses. But it failed. The businesses lost money, and the Alliance had little success in either the territorial or North Dakota legislatures.

The most influential man who opposed the reform which the Alliance demanded was Alexander McKenzie. McKenzie had settled in Bismarck in 1873 when the Northern Pacific Railroad, for whom he worked, reached that city. At age 24 he became sheriff of Burleigh County and soon thereafter was appointed as the Northern Pacific's territorial agent. By 1883 he had become a powerful force; he was the one mainly responsible for moving the capital from Yankton to Bismarck in 1883. McKenzie was a friendly fellow who knew how to manage people. As a representative of the Northern Pacific, he opposed regulation which would impose restrictions on railroads. By the 1890s McKenzie was the boss of North Dakota politics. The Republican party, which McKenzie controlled, and congressmen were very close to McKenzie. Although he never held a state political office, he called the shots and planned Republican strategy from the backroom. Because of McKenzie's influence on legislatures and governors, political change came slowly.

With one exception, North Dakota's governors in the 1890s were Republicans who agreed with Alexander McKenzie. John Miller, 1889-1890; Andrew Burke, 1891-1892; Roger Allin, 1895-1896; Frank Briggs, 1897-1898; and Fred Francher, 1899-1900, were all loyal to the McKenzie political machine. They were not dishonest men; they worked hard to promote what they thought was best for the state. None, however, believed that reform was needed.

The only successful challenge to McKenzie's political power came in 1892 when Democrats, independents, and some reform-minded Republicans banded together to give Eli C.D. Shortridge, who ran as an Independent, a narrow victory

Alexander McKenzie.
(SHSND)

for the governorship. The anti-McKenzie administration, however, became so involved in patronage (appointing people to office) and politics, that it achieved very little. The legislature did make significantly larger appropriations to state institutions and did enact radical legislation which called for the construction of a state-owned terminal elevator at Duluth. Because the depression of 1893 forced the next governor, Roger Allin, to cut spending drastically, neither came to be.

* * * * * *

Great excitement accompanied the opening of the constitutional convention, and after days and days of hard work, the Constitution was ready. The people went to the polls with great enthusiasm to approve the new Constitution. Most believed that statehood would bring independence; North Dakotans would be their own masters. Soon, however, most realized that this was a myth; McKenzie controlled the political machinery within, and the Northern Pacific and Minneapolis grain-trade market controlled the economy from without. Many were disillusioned. The economic hard times of the decade added to the feeling of helplessness. Still, more and more people came to North Dakota. During the 1890s the population increased from 191,000 to 319,000. Beneath the surface of discontent, there remained a confidence that the new state would prosper.

13 The People at the Turn of the Century

By the year 1900, 319,146 people were making their homes in North Dakota. Of this population, about one third had been born outside the United States; and many, many more had one or both parents who had come to North Dakota from Canada or Europe. Only about two percent of the population consisted of native American Indians. In less than 50 years the settlers had turned North Dakota from a land of buffalo hunting into a land of farms and towns. From Pembina to Beach and from Crosby to Wahpeton, the horizon was broken with churches, elevators, and farm houses. By 1900, North Dakotans had built 63,000 dwellings to house the state's 64,500 families. Of those dwellings, 44,000 stood on farmsteads. In little more than a generation, North Dakotans had developed over 15,000,000 acres as farm property worth over $225,000,000. Over 60 percent of the people lived on farms that averaged 343 acres. North Dakota was a farm state, and wheat determined the welfare of the whole population. The towns that sprang up along the rivers and railroads were farm-trading centers that depended as much on a good crop as did the farmer himself.

I. "The Melting Pot" — The Immigrant

The Norwegians were the largest immigrant group in North Dakota. They settled mostly in the eastern counties. Norwegians began migrating to the United States as early as 1825, but the main flow began after the Civil War. Over 100,000 came between 1866 and 1873; between 1879 and 1889, over 250,000 arrived in the United States. They had many reasons for leaving Norway; most hoped for a better economic life.

Norwegians in the United States began to move westward as the tide of immigration increased. With the expansion of the railroad and the removal of the Indian menace, they moved west from states such as Wisconsin and Illinois. By the 1870s they pushed across Minnesota into the Red River Valley. And by the middle of the 1880s, Norwegians lived throughout the eastern third of North Dakota. They seemed to choose the state for their own.

Another large immigrant group in North Dakota was German. There were two distinct national groups of Germanic origin — the "Reich" German and the "Ruzlands" or German-Russians. Together, they made up about a third of the state's immigrant population. The "Reich" Germans were those Germans who migrated to the United States directly from Germany. The primary cause of their emigration was economic; however, political conditions in western Europe provided another reason for leaving the fatherland. The first Germans to move west settled in Wisconsin and southern Minnesota. As more and more came into the area, their frontier was extended into parts of North Dakota. In North Dakota the "Reich" Germans were scattered over the entire state, but the greatest concentration was in the southwest in the area west of the Missouri River and on the extreme southeastern counties.

The German-Russians were not Russian in origin, but German. These people left Germany and went to the area around the Balck Sea during the years of war and unrest in Europe. Catherine II and Alexander I of Russia offered them religious freedom, tax exemption, loans, self-government, tariff-free trade, and exemption from military service if they would settle in Russia. Alexander II, however, cancelled their military exemption in 1874. Soon, thousands of men and their families left Russia for America, where they found new homes in the agricultural states of the West. In North Dakota the German-Russians settled mostly in the southern and central part of the state.

Long before the Europeans began to find homes in North Dakota, French and English Canadians had crossed the international boundary and settled in the northern counties. The Canadian population reached its peak in 1900 with 25,000 people or nine percent of the state's total population. They settled mostly in those counties bordering Canada — Walsh, Cavalier, Pembina, Rolette, Towner, and Bottineau. Europeans also came from many other countries: Sweden, Denmark, Ireland, Austria, Poland, and Hungary.

Those who came to North Dakota had given up homes, churches, schools, and even families to make a new life in a new land. This took courage and optimism. They had a determined spirit to make good on the North Dakota frontier. Of the men who journeyed thousands of miles to the new land, Ole Flom was typical. Ole had left Norway with his wife and two children in the early 1880s. He spoke no English, and he had been lured to the new country by literature printed in Norwegian by American railroads. He had little in the old country — a few acres near the foot of a mountain. His brother, a fish merchant,

A German immigrant family at Carrington, 1895. (SHSND)

helped him with a loan, and he set out on his bold venture to America: the country of opportunity and free land. When he arrived in New York, he had little money and worked on the dock to earn railroad-ticket money to Wisconsin, where his cousin owned a small farm. The trip was difficult, and the family had almost nothing to eat.

They were overjoyed to reach Wisconsin, where they could talk with people and worship in Norwegian. With help from the cousin, the Floms continued their journey to Dakota, where they settled in Nelson County. Here they felt comfortable among other Norwegians who lived in the region. There were complaints, of course: no seafood, no mountains, no fjords. North Dakota was nothing like the old country. The Floms knew that this would be the case, but they missed the land they had left behind.

Like others who came to North Dakota, the Floms were caught between two worlds, the old and the new. Because they could not completely cut their ties with the old world, they found comfort and security in the Norwegian-language services at the Lutheran Church, in reading American newspapers printed in Norwegian, in conversing with neighbors who spoke the old tongue, and in celebrating the great Norwegian festivals. At the same time, they knew the value of a school which would teach their children English and the ways of the new country. By 1900 the Floms were successful farmers, and the Fourth of July had become as important to them as Norwegian holidays.

To the Norwegian immigrants — and to all who had to adjust to the new environment on the prairies and plains — the church and the school were important in making the adjustment. Whether people had come to North Dakota from Vermont, Wisconsin, Poland, or Sweden, they had to make a dramatic change that required support and strength. The church and the school helped give both.

II. **The Church**

The church came to Dakota as the fur trade opened the West. As early as 1818, Roman Catholic priests made their way to the Red River Valley. Fathers Sévère Joseph Dumoulin and Joseph Norbert Provencher began working among the white settlers, métis, and Indians. Father Dumoulin stayed at Pembina for five years, carrying on an active ministry and operating an educational mission. After the decline of Pembina, priests from St. Boniface worked among the people in Dakota. In 1848, Father George A. Belcourt established missions at Pembina and near Walhalla. During his years on the plains, he converted many Indians to Christianity and conducted an aggressive preaching and teaching ministry.

Father Pierre Jean DeSmet began the Roman Catholic missionary activity in the Missouri Valley. Between 1839 and the late 1860s, he often traveled up the Missouri to visit the Indian villages. In 1876, Abbot Martin Marty set up the first permanent mission at Fort Yates, from which priests served new communities along the Northern Pacific tracks. Four years later, in 1880, the Roman Catholic

A Dutch immigrant family near Mott, 1905. (SHSND)

St. Stephen's Episcopal Church, built of stone, at Casselton, 1890s. (SHSND)

Church appointed Marty as Bishop of Dakota Territory. By this time, the church had 13 priests throughout the Territory. Although in some places mass was celebrated only now and then, the Roman Catholic church did minister to its people's spiritual needs. In 1889 the creation of the Diocese of Jamestown gave North Dakota its own Roman Catholic organization. John Shanley became its first Bishop. Since almost half of the state's church membership was Roman Catholic, Bishop Shanley faced a tough task of ministering to so many people spread across the state. By 1900, almost 200 Roman Catholic churches had been built in North Dakota and served about 50,000 members.

Protestants, unlike the Roman Catholics, did not carry on a vigorous missionary effort among the Indians. During the 1850s, several of their missions failed because of Indian opposition. Protestant clergy came with the railroad and white settlement. Although Lutheran ministers organized congregations throughout the Red River Valley and along the Northern Pacific route during the early 1870s, the Protestant groups did not begin fully to organize in the state until the 1880s. One fourth of church membership in the state was Lutheran — mostly Scandinavians and Germans. Each of the Scandinavian nationalities had its own national church organization; the Norwegians even had five. All these organizations, called synods, established churches in North Dakota to serve their

Quale Lutheran Church, built of wood, in rural Walsh County, 1900. (SHSND)

specific Scandinavian members. German Lutherans had their own synod — the Missouri. In 1900 the 30,000 Lutherans were served by pastors who spoke the tongues of the old country and conducted services in German, Norwegian, Swedish, Danish, and Icelandic.

The other quarter of North Dakota's church membership was divided among over 30 denominations, of which the larger were the Methodists, Presbyterians, and Baptists. With great optimism over future population growth, the church groups fervishly labored to provide every town with their message. By 1916, North Dakota had 1,352 churches to serve a membership of just over 140,000 people. Many congregations were very small, and in their desire to serve the people, denominations built more churches than could be served by their ministers. One Norwegian pastor served 16 congregations at once; another traveled by horse and buggy to conduct seven services each Sunday. Those who worked for the church did so at considerable hardship and sacrifice.

The church played an important part in developing the new land. Facing adversity and hardship, many people needed the spiritual courage which the church provided. Those churches which ministered to the immigrants in their native tongue made the adjustment to a new country and life easier.

III. The Schools

Those who choose to settle in North Dakota were a literate people. Only six percent of those over age 10 in 1900 could not read and write. And by 1900, 84 percent of the children between the ages of 10 and 14 were attending school. Almost 80,000 students filled the state's classrooms, learning the basics of education from 4,000 teachers.

The Territorial legislature had established a school system which provided the vast territory with school districts. When North Dakota became a state in 1889, the Constitution made sure that education would be an important part of North Dakota's life. It guaranteed a system which would provide education from the grades through college with a superintendent in each county. The legislature required teachers to meet certain requirements, and children between the ages of 8 and 14 had to attend school. The legislature and the people supported their schools, and, by 1912, North Dakota ranked second in the nation in per capita expenditures for schooling.

Over half of the state's children attended small, one-room, rural schools in which one teacher taught all eight grades. Because many of the students had to help on the farm, attendance was often low and the school year short. The average one-room schoolhouse pupil spent less than 90 days a year in the classroom. Teachers in these schools were dedicated, but they generally had little teacher training. Many were only eighth grade graduates. Very few who attended the one-room schoolhouses went on to high school.

Town schools were of better quality. Not tied to the chores of the farm, town children were able to attend for the standard nine months. Most teachers in town schools held college diplomas and were able to teach more specialized courses. By 1890 only about 600 students were enrolled in high school.

Although in 1900 very few North Dakotans had finished high school or were prepared for college work, the state set up an extensive system of higher education. With confidence in the future, the makers of the Constitution made sure that the opportunity for education would be available for the young. The territorial legislature had already provided for the university at Grand Forks. The Constitution reaffirmed this and added an agricultural college for Fargo, a school of science at Wahpeton, an industrial school at Ellendale, normal (teachers) colleges at Valley City and Mayville, and a school of forestry. Since most of the population was in the eastern counties, the framers of the Constitution put the colleges there. As people moved westward, the legislature provided for normal schools at Minot and Dickinson. By 1900 the agricultural college, the normal

Opposite page: Top, town schools, Grand Forks. Middle, Nelson County rural school. Note the consolidation of two school buildings. Bottom, high school German class at Buffalo. (SHSND)

schools at Mayville and Valley City, and the school at Ellendale had joined the university as growing institutions. The state's schools of higher education, hampered by the lack of qualified students as well as state funds, developed very slowly. Prior to 1900 only 278 students had earned their degrees. Both the leadership and faculties of the pioneer schools, however, were strong, and North Dakotans received a sound education.

The school became an agency of Americanization. Here the immigrant boy learned about George Washington and Abraham Lincoln. He soon could read Edgar Allen Poe and recite the poems of Walt Whitman. The one-room schoolhouse became a symbol of progress.

IV. "Americanizing" the Indian

By 1900 just under 7,000 Indians, about two percent of the population, remained in North Dakota. They lived on four reservations: the Teton Sioux at Standing Rock, a mixture of Santee and Yankton Sioux at Fort Totten, the Three Tribes at Fort Berthold, and the Plains Chippewa in the Turtle Mountains. A series of treaties had set up the reservations, and gradually a series of new treaties reduced the land owned by the Indians. For example, in 1889, the Government took away half (11,000,000 acres) of the Great Sioux Reservation and set up six smaller reservations. In 1880 and 1891 the Three Tribes lost over half of their land. The government opened up the former reservation lands to settlement and paid the Three Tribes $800,000. The Turtle Mountain Reservation of the Plains Chippewa lost 90 percent of its land without consultation or payment. The buffalo were gone, and little of the Turtle Mountain Reservation land was fit for farming. It could not support the people, and during the winter of 1887-1888 more than 150 died of starvation. Finally, in 1892 the government paid the Plains Chippewa — Little Shell's Band — a million dollars to give up all rights to their 10,000,000 acres in North Dakota — about 10c per acre.

On the reservations the Indian was treated as a ward of the government. The Bureau of Indian Affairs looked after the reservations. The Indian was expected to give up his Indian ways. He was supposed to become a farmer who would fit into white society. In reservations schools he learned about white civilization, and in the churches he was taught about Christianity. He was told that the Sun Dance was heathen and that the vision quest was a waste of time. Government authorities, most white people, and some Indians believed that the Indian should be brought into the main stream of American life as soon as possible.

Individual Indians did not own land; land was held by the tribe. In the 1880s many reform-minded whites began to call for a change. They argued that each Indian should own his own land — private ownership. Private land ownership had been basic to the American way of life, and they believed that individual land ownership would hurry Indian people toward giving up their old ways. Others who supported this idea had selfish motives. They knew that there would be land left over after each Indian was given a parcel; they urged that this surplus land be opened to white settlement.

Above, the Fort Totten Indian School band, 1890s. Below, the Sioux children at the Standing Rock School celebrate Columbus Day, 1892. (SHSND)

THE PEOPLE AT THE TURN OF THE CENTURY

In 1887, Congress responded to the growing pressure for change and passed the Dawes Allotment Act. The head of each Indian family received 160 acres, and each child, 40 acres. An unmarried Indian over 18 got 80 acres. Indian land owners were given United States citizenship. To keep dishonest whites from cheating Indians out of land, the Indian could not sell his land for 25 years.

By 1900, reservation farms averaged only 29 acres of crop land. Much reservation land was poor farm land, and most farmers did not prosper. Drought in the western part of the state hurt farming at Berthold and Standing Rock. Only at Fort Totten did the Indian farms do reasonably well. There, most Indian farmers were becoming self-sufficient.

The allotment system did not accomplish what many hoped it would. Although the law protected the Indian from land-hungry whites, almost two thirds of the Indian land was sold to whites during the years that followed. Conditions at Berthold, Standing Rock, and especially in the Turtle Mountains deteriorated. The Indian was caught in a web of federal bureaucracy. The government continued to force the Indian into white society: soon, native worship was forbidden; government officials replaced tribal leadership; children were required to leave their home to attend government boarding schools. The government — and whites in general — believed this to be the proper course of action. Like Norwegian or Polish immigrants, the Indian had to be Americanized. Some Indians agreed; some resisted; all wept as their children left for boarding schools.

* * * * * *

The people of North Dakota were a mixture of many kinds. A teacher who came from Missouri to North Dakota in 1895 was amazed at the variety: "Half my class barely speaks English. I have four Norwegians, three Poles, three Irish, two Swedes, two Danes, and an assortment of other children. I must say they are eager to learn." The church and especially the school brought this mixture together and made something called North Dakotans. And they were eager to learn.

14 The Golden Age

The period from 1898 to 1915 was a time of progress for the young state of North Dakota — progress in farming and in democracy. The depression of the 1890s was over, and King Wheat was healthy. These were years of good rainfalls, good crops, and good prices. More and more people were coming to North Dakota, and those who were already here found life better. Reform in politics gave the people still more voice in the decisions which affected their lives. This was an age of optimism.

I. More and More: Railroads and People

From 1898 to World War One, the railroads expanded their lines in North Dakota, doubling the miles of tracks. The Northern Pacific and the Great Northern laid new tracks to new places, and other roads entered the state. Most of the construction involved building branch lines from the main lines to serve more out-of-the-way places. The Minneapolis-St. Paul and the Sault Ste. Marie (the "Soo") began to compete with the Northern Pacific and Great Northern, forcing them to build branch lines. In 1905 the "Soo" built the "Wheat Line," parallel to the Great Northern, from Oslo, Minnesota, to Kenmare, North Dakota.

The Great Northern began running tracks out across the Drift Prairie to towns such as Walhalla, Hannah, Souris, and Mohall. In 1912 it opened a direct line from Fargo to Surrey. The Northern Pacific added lines that reached Oakes, Esmond, and Linton. In 1911 it began to extend its lines north and south from Mandan.

The Chicago, Milwaukee, and St. Paul and Pacific Railroad, known as the Milwaukee, entered the state from the south and extended a line from South Dakota to Linton. In 1907 it laid tracks on the Missouri slope, the first since the main line of the Northern Pacific had been built in 1880. By 1911 the Milwaukee line stretched from McLaughlin to Mott.

At the beginning of the railroad-branch expansion, new roads were built within North Dakota. In 1902 the Farmers Grain and Shipping Company organized and built a railroad from Devils Lake to Starkweather, and extended the line to Hansboro in 1905. William D. Washburn, a Minneapolis miller and a director of the "Soo," started the Bismarck, Washburn, and Fort Buford Railroad. By 1900 this line had been built to Wilton and began hauling lignite. Washburn's aim was to haul coal from the beds which he controlled. The rails were extended to Washburn by 1901, but in 1904 the road was sold to the Soo. The Midland Continental Railroad, which hoped to build a north-south road from Winnipeg to Galveston, Texas, only completed a line from Edgely to Wimbledon.

The railroads greatly improved their equipment and operation. The tracks were of heavier steel, and the road beds were better. Many old bridges were replaced, and curves and grades were improved. First-class passenger trains, such as the Northern Pacific's North Coast Limited, served the state. The Great Northern, interested in passengers going to the Orient, had first-class trains which connected with two steamships on the Pacific Ocean. The Empire Builder and the Oriental Limited became known around the world. The construction of more track ended with World War One. The completion of branch lines tied the state together and boomed the settlement of out-of-the-way places.

NORTH DAKOTA RAILWAY SYSTEMS

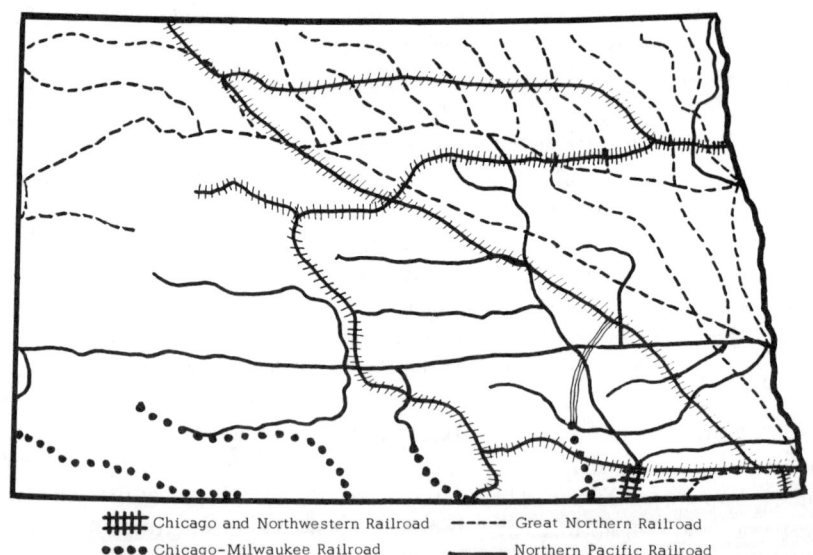

(ND-DPI)

The federal government had changed its homestead policies in 1891 and passed an expanded Homestead Act in 1909 which applied to North Dakota by 1912. This law reduced the number of years required for residence in order to claim a homestead. It had been five; now it was three. A settler was required to live on the land only seven months of each of the three years. To commute a homestead, one had to be a resident for fourteen months and pay $1.25 an acre, or $2.50 if the land were within the railroad grant. By doing this the settler could acquire title to the land immediately and use it as security for loans.

The state experienced its largest growth during these years. From 1900 to 1915, population increased 135 percent. The population in 1915 was 637,000, compared to 319,000 in 1890. Much of the increase occurred in the Missouri Plateau area, but many towns on the Drift Prairie also grew in size. Although some of the older counties along the eastern edge of the state declined slightly in population, the towns there grew tremendously. Fargo jumped from 9,589 to 14,331; Grand Forks from 7,652 to 12,478; and Jamestown from 2,853 to 4,358. Bismarck, the state capital, gained 2,124 people, reaching 5,442. Minot, Devils Lake, and Williston also grew rapidly.

When the railroad arrived, small towns boomed overnight, Mott, 1910. (SHSND)

THE GOLDEN AGE

The railroads and land agents brought thousands of settlers to beautiful and bountiful North Dakota. (SHSND)

II. "Wheat is King!"

The speculator — one who purchased large amounts of land and hoped to make a profit by re-selling it in small tracts to actual settlers — represented both large and small investors. Large investors such as the D.S.B. Johnson Land Company purchased all of the Northern Pacific land in five counties. W.H. Brown and Company of Chicago opened an office in Richardton and began dealing in its 200,000 acres. Individuals, too, invested in large holdings. James C. Young of Minneapolis had over 900,000 acres around Dickinson. Alexander McKenzie invested in 300,000 acres and may have made a million dollars as a result of rising land prices. All the large holdings were advertised in surrounding states in order to attract people to the state. Settlers came in droves to purchase land.

Small land speculators continued to be of every occupation and profession. They also bought land because they believed that prices would rise sharply.

Whether they purchased land from a company or homesteaded public lands, many of these speculators left the state without attempting to farm. Some tried farming for a while and then gave up and sold out. Some moved to the towns and became tradesmen or professional people. The size of farms increased as speculators and those who gave up farming sold their land to those who planned to stay and make a go of it.

The farmer, not the speculator, was the solid base of population. Farmers had much to be optimistic about. Farm prices were rising, and rainfall was adequate. As the nation's population increased, the demand for food rose. It was the "Golden Age of Agriculture." Yields and prices were good; farmers were recovering from the depression of the 1890s.

Wheat was king. North Dakota was the "Land of the Number One Hard Wheat." New varieties of wheat gave wheat growers more diversity. Red Fife, sometimes called Scotch Fife, a Canadian import, was the number one hard variety. By the time of World War One, most farmers were growing a variety called Marquis. This wheat was superior because it could tolerate heat, ripened easily, and was rust resistant.

Durum, a wheat from Russia, became an excellent producer in terms of bushels per acre, but its flour was suited more for macaroni products than for baking. Most of this variety was grown in the eastern part of North Dakota, outside the Red River Valley. North Dakota soon produced three fourths of the nation's durum wheat. The state's farmers also grew flax, oats, barley, and hay; they raised cattle, sheep, and pigs; some had dairy cows. But wheat was king, and farmers put their faith in the golden harvest.

Breaking the sod near Hettinger during the Second Boom, 1910. (SHSND)

101— NINE OF THESE GIRLS WILL HAVE NO HUSBANDS. If the 12 boys in the picture marry their school mates, there will be 9 girls left for young men from other states. No wonder the teacher looks anxious. This is a recess scene at the Public School in Flasher North Dakota, one of the hundreds of graded schools supported out of t enormous School Funds of this State. From a series of photographs by WM. H. BROWN COMPANY, REAL ESTATE DEALERS, Mandan and Richardton, North Dakota or 131 LaSalle St., Chicago, Ill.

This photograph and description is from a real estate company's promotion book. (SHSND)

Many businessmen, whose well-being depended on a healthy farm economy, and agriculture experts began to call for diversification on the state's farms. They thought that placing one's future just on the price and productivity of wheat was risky business. They believed that if the wheat crop were to fail, the farmer needed some other source of income. The Agricultural College at Fargo organized the Tri-State Grain and Stock Growers Association for the purpose of educating farmers about better farming methods and the advantages of diversification. The Great Northern and the Northern Pacific railroads backed this program. James J. Hill of the Great Northern warned against one-crop farming and helped farmers start beef herds.

Minneapolis businessmen and North Dakota bankers supplied money and support for the North Dakota Better Farming Association, which was organized to promote diversification and improved farming methods. Thomas Cooper of the Minnesota Agricultural College became the Association's director. He developed the county agent system. In 1911 he hired a field worker, and by 1913 he had 18 agents working with farmers. In 1913 the state legislature passed a county agent law, and the Association was merged with the North Dakota Agricultural Experiment Station. Farmers could now find new avenues of education and information about farming methods and operations. Better-farming enthusiasts continually advocated diversification, especially dairy farming. Some farmers moved toward this, but most did not. The farmer preferred his sure profit from wheat.

III. The Reform Spirit

During the years after 1900, the United States was swept up in a reform spirit. People became unhappy with the growth of business monopoly, the concentration of wealth in the hands of a few, and corruption in both private companies and public offices. Many believed that the people needed to have a larger part in directing the course which the country was taking. The people, not the corporations or political machines, should decide what laws should govern society. People such as Theodore Roosevelt, Woodrow Wilson, and Jane Addams who wanted reform were called "progressives" because they believed that progress would come only by increasing democracy. This would give the people control over corporations and government. The progressives attacked boss-rule and monopoly. They demanded laws that would give the people more voice: direct election of senators; the initiative, which would allow the public to make their own laws; the recall, by which voters could throw elected officials out of office; and the direct primary, which would give the voter, not the bosses, a chance to select party candidates.

North Dakota was very much a part of the national reform spirit. For a long time people had believed that they were controlled by the corporations, such as the railroads, and by political bosses, such as Alexander McKenzie. The time was ripe for change.

The railroads were vital to the farmer. They moved the farmer's crop to market and brought the supplies which he needed. Because railroads were supposed to make money for their investors, they fought any increase in state taxes which they would have to pay. This brought them into conflict with the people. The railroads had considerable track mileage in the state, much more in relation to the size of the population than in any other state. They had actually spent $100,000,000 in building railroads in North Dakota, but they had sold stock to investors for almost three times that amount. By claiming that high freight rates were necessary to make a profit on their huge investment, the railroads seemed to earn money on false investments. Besides this, train service was not always adequate. In 1905 much of the grain crop was unable to move out of the state because of a shortage of cars.

The legislature tried to force the railroads to improve service; it passed laws that required improvements in passenger service, depots, and road crossings. The state had steadily increased the taxes on the railroads. In 1900, taxes had been $187 per mile of track; by 1915 this had risen to $371. The legislature set up a schedule which lowered rates for hauling lignite. The North Dakota Supreme Court upheld the legality of the rates, but in 1915 the United States Supreme Court ruled in favor of the railroads.

The outside interests which dominated much of North Dakota's economic life continued to have the support of Alexander McKenzie and his political machine. McKenzie, still associated with the railroads, could secure free passes for state legislators and other public officials. The railroads contributed heavily to the political campaigns of the men whom he supported for office. McKenzie had the friendship of many well-known national Republican figures, including Mark Hanna, a "boss" of the Republican party. This gave him an inside track for getting federal jobs for his friends.

The McKenzie machine achieved success in its opposition to reform. Frank White and Elmore Y. Sarles, McKenzie men, held the governorship from 1901 to 1906. Playing the political game, the machine at times appeared to favor reform when that suited its purpose. The machine opposed legislation that would expand democracy: woman suffrage, the initiative, the referendum, and the direct primary. The direct primary, which would allow the people to choose candidates, would have robbed McKenzie of much power. The McKenzie forces continually fought restrictions on railroads.

The progressive reform spirit finally brought an end to the McKenzie machine in 1906. The progressives, led by Republican George Winship, crusading editor of the *Grand Forks Herald*, formed the "Good Government League." The league appealed to those of both parties who were reform-minded and tired of McKenzie control.

The anti-McKenzie movement was strengthened in early 1906, when author Rex Beach wrote articles about McKenzie's shady dealings in Alaska. His widely published book, *The Spoilers*, added fuel to the fire. Beach told how McKenzie had obtained an appointment for Arthur H. Noyes, a former North Dakotan, to be judge of the Second Judicial District of Alaska. Judge Noyes then used his influence to get mining claims for McKenzie in Alaska. All of this was investigated by the Federal Court of Appeals in California. The court issued an injunction that prohibited McKenzie from working the claims; he defied this and took the gold anyway. The court removed Noyes as judge and sentenced McKenzie to a year in jail. Beach's accounts of this were printed in many newspapers, and McKenzie lost popularity with many people.

Despite this, the McKenzie machine controlled the Republican state convention in 1906 and nominated Sarles for a second term as governor and Judge John Knauf of Stutsman County for the North Dakota Supreme Court. The Democrats, in order to attract reform progressives, nominated Charles J. Fisk, a respected judge from Grand Forks, for the court, and John Burke for governor. Burke, nicknamed "Honest John," was a Devils Lake lawyer with a reputation for honesty and fairness. The son of an Irish immigrant, he had served in the state legislature.

Burke waged a vigorous campaign. Speaking several times a day, he attacked McKenzieism and the control of North Dakota by the grain trade and the railroads. With the support of reform Republican newspapers such as the *Grand Forks Herald*, and the growing number of those unhappy with McKenzieism,

Governor John Burke (standing) and a group of citizens at the capitol. (SHSND)

both Burke and Fisk won. This defeat of McKenzie and his followers was called the revolution of 1906.

In the 1907 legislature, the progressive Republicans and Democrats controlled the House, and conservatives controlled the Senate. In spite of heavy lobbying against reform, the legislature passed a direct primary law and proposed a constitutional amendment to permit the initiative and referendum. The direct primary law attacked the very heart of machine politics.

In 1908, Burke won another victory, and Alexander McKenzie resigned as national committeeman for the Republican party. In 1910, Burke ran for a third term as governor. Calling the election "McKenzie's last stand," Burke faced an all-out bitter attack by the machine. Using large out-of-state contributions and directed by McKenzie himself, the machine campaigned hard and tried to picture the McKenzie candidates as more progressive than the Democrats and Burke.

Again, John Burke won, making him a three-term governor. He was able to win because of Republican dissatisfaction with McKenzie. The progressive reformers, both Democrats and Republicans, won control of the legislature. The 1911 legislature had a progressive outlook. It produced many laws dealing with railroad passes, juvenile courts, a presidential primary, workman's compensation, and corrupt practices in elections. Reform had carried the day; the McKenzie hold on state politics had ended.

Progressive reform in North Dakota was not restricted to the activities of the governor and legislature in Bismarck. In Fargo at the Agricultural Experiment Station, chemist Edwin F. Ladd crusaded against the adulteration of foods, paints, and fertilizers by producers and processors. His research and leadership led to state laws prohibiting adulteration and calling for food inspection. Ladd, who later became president of the Agricultural College and a United States Senator, was

The interior of a jewelry store at McVille, 1913. (SHSND)

influential in bringing about the Pure Food and Drug Act of 1906, passed by Congress. In Grand Forks at the University, John M. Gillette, eminent rural sociologist, studied farm conditions, child labor, and the state's jails and worked for reforms in these areas. Charles F. Amidon of Fargo became a recognized leader of progressivism as a federal judge. In Washington, the North Dakota congressional delegation reflected some of the same reform spirit. Senator Porter J. McCumber, a McKenzie man and a conservative, sponsored the Pure Food and Drug Act of 1906. Senator Asle J. Gronna broke with McKenzie and joined the ranks of Senate reformers.

*   *   *   *   *   *

The years between 1900 and World War One were years of progress for North Dakota. Population increased rapidly; farmers had good crops and prices; boss rule was killed; the progressive reform spirit had created legislation that gave the people more voice in state affairs. This was the Golden Age. Not all problems had been solved, however, by prosperity on the farm and the defeat of the McKenzie machine. But, when "King Wheat" was healthy, so was North Dakota. People were beginning to believe the slogan, "Nothing was ever lost by an abiding faith in North Dakota."

15 Political Prairie Fire: The NPL

During the years 1900 to 1915, North Dakota farmers were much better off than they had been during the 1890s. Many, however, continued to believe that things should be even better. Although prices and harvests were good, the farmer was certain that he was not getting a fair return on his crops. He was still concerned about high freight charges and was becoming more disturbed about the grain market and problems related to it. Although the boss rule of Alexander McKenzie was over, the influence of the railroads and the grain interests was very strong. Since North Dakota depended heavily on both, the problem touched the lives of most North Dakotans. Farmers wanted more control over their own destinies. They wanted change, and change came. The Nonpartisan League swept across the state like a prairie fire.

I. The Roots of Discontent

The farmer had limited opportunities to market his crop. He could sell to an elevator owned by a milling company, to an independent elevator, or to a track buyer who had no storage space. The milling-company elevators received daily price quotations from Minneapolis. This was the price the farmer would get — nothing more.

Profit made on "reselling" the grain angered many farmers. Some of the wheat purchased by the elevators went directly to the mills, but much of it was sold by commission men in Minneapolis or Duluth grain exchanges. In these exchanges, the grain was resold for a profit. The farmers believed that this practice was unjust.

Besides the exchanges, the practice of grain grading, storage fees, and payment for screenings angered the North Dakota farmers. Grain grading was subject to much abuse. When the farmer sold his grain in the fall, the grain inspectors graded with rigid standards. When the grain went to the terminal markets to be sold by the grain dealers, the grain was graded by less rigid standards. The farmer lost money when he did not receive payment for the screenings. The screenings, the less than whole kernels of grain, were worth money, yet the farmer received nothing for it. The suction draft used to remove dirt from the grain also removed wheat. When the grain was weighed after such cleaning, the farmers lost money. Within ten years, the elevators on Lake Superior shipped out almost 27,000,000 bushels more than they had paid for. What could the farmers and the people of the state do to correct such abuses?

One solution was co-operative elevators. A co-op elevator is one that is owned by the farmers who sell their grain to it. It was hoped that the co-ops would give the farmer a fairer price and honest grading and dockage. The co-ops faced rough competition. No sooner were they organized than the milling-company elevators began paying higher prices for wheat. The farmer was tempted to sell to these elevators because they were paying more than his co-op. In the bitter battle to compete, the co-ops succeeded in lowering the difference in price paid at the elevator and the terminal markets. By 1920 the co-op elevators shipped over thirty percent of the state's grain to Minneapolis.

The co-op movement also tried to end exploitations by the grain trade. In 1908 the Equity Co-operative Exchange was organized and set up a marketing exchange in Minneapolis. The Exchange grew under the leadership of George S. Loftus when he became its sales manager in 1912. It opened a terminal elevator in St. Paul in 1917. The Exchange organized a livestock commission company, built elevators, and began to offer supplies at reduced prices to its members. The Exchange did not have an easy time, but it became the first successful farmer-controlled exchange.

The elevator became the state's symbol of progress. Carpio, 1900. (SHSND)

William Lemke. (SHSND)

This organization helped some farmers, but many did not belong to the exchange. Sentiment to have state-owned terminal elevators grew. These elevators would purchase and store the wheat that had been grown in North Dakota. In 1912 the voters approved an amendment to the Constitution allowing the state to establish a terminal elevator in Minnesota or Wisconsin. In 1914 they approved another amendment to build a state-owned terminal elevator within North Dakota.

The belief that such an elevator would remedy the wrongs of the wheat market gained widespread popularity among farmers. Common problems involved in selling wheat united farmers and made them aware of their economic situation. Many wanted immediate political action to solve these problems.

State ownership of a terminal elevator was socialistic. The Socialist party had been organized in North Dakota in 1902 by Arthur Basset and Arthur Le Sueur. It adopted a platform that called for an end to the abuses of out-of-state interests. The Socialist party demanded state-owned terminal elevators and flour mills, state-financed hail insurance, and state-owned banks that would loan money to farmers at reasonable interest rates. The party ran candidates for public office, and Arthur Le Sueur was elected president of the Minot city commission in 1911.

In 1913 the Socialist party hired Arthur C. Townley as an organizer. Townley, who had been born in Minnesota and had taught school there, moved to Beach in 1907. He started flax farming and had borrowed heavily, hoping to hit it big. He went bankrupt in 1912, when prices and weather conditions ruined his operation. Bitter over his $80,000 loss, Townley concluded that socialism was the answer to the economic plight of the farmer. He was a brilliant organizer and understood politics and economics. While working for the party, he devised a plan for organizing the farmers. Townley talked to farmers individually, persuading them to pay a dollar a month to join the party. He used this money to buy a Model-T Ford, which provided transportation for party organizers who continued the drive. The plan worked with a great deal of success; soon Townley had purchased four Model-T's and covered nine counties. The Socialist party, however, fired him because it disagreed with his methods.

At that time, the legislature was considering a proposal to build a state-owned terminal elevator. Even though previous legislatures had proposed a Constitutional amendment setting up such an elevator and had levied a one-eighth mill tax for it, a committee dominated by McKenzie men reported unfavorably on the plan. Farmers lobbied for the elevator and demanded action. The fight between farmers and legislators became bitter. Treadwell Twitchell, a House member, allegedly told the farmers that "running the state was none of their business" and to "go home and slop the hogs."

II. The Birth of the Nonpartisan League

A.C. Townley, who had observed the fight between the farmers and the legislature, saw the growing mood of anger and frustration. At that point, Townley decided to start his own farm organization. He discussed his ideas with some Socialist party members. Fred B. Wood, a successful farmer in McHenry County, seemed interested. Wood, who was a Socialist and a farm leader, listened to Townley and liked the idea. They worked out a brief statement of what the organization would hope to accomplish. This meeting marked the beginning of the Nonpartisan League.

The Platform of the League called for state ownership of terminal elevators, flour mills, cold storage plants, and packing plants. The state would have a hail insurance program based on a three-cent-per-acre tax, and state-owned banks would provide low-interest loans. The state would inspect grain, using uniform and rigid standards; farm improvements would be exempt from taxation. By the time the League started to form a national party in 1917, its platform included a call for democratic world government, public works for the unemployed, graduated income tax, inheritance tax, and federal ownership of public transportation and communication.

The original ideas of the League found fertile ground in the old resentments of the farmer against the grain trade and the railroads. It would, however, take an organization of united members to achieve the League's goals. Once organized, the League would have to enter politics and get its candidates into office.

Townley employed the same organization methods that he had used when he was working for the Socialist party. The very next morning after Townley and Wood had met, Townley and Wood's son, Howard, visited neighbors to whom

A.C. Townley. (SHSND)

William Langer. (UND-LC)

they gave the sales pitch. If the farmer decided to join, he would in turn introduce the League organizers to his neighbor. This method of having "converts" introduce league organizers to their neighbors became standard.

League dues were $6.00 a year and later $18.00 for two years. Townley bought Model-T Fords and hired a staff of organizers. The organizers, many of them Socialists and Townley's old friends, swarmed over the state, talking the language that most farmers wanted to hear. Preaching against big business, they played on the complaints of the farmer. They stressed that the grain buyer, the banker, and other farm-produce buyers were agents of eastern interests who had always controlled the state and exploited the farmer. Townley himself was a brilliant agitator. Wherever he spoke, he could stir emotions and bring out old antagonisms.

The plan worked. The League grew rapidly. It spread like a political prairie fire. By 1916 it had 40,000 members. If the farmers who joined could not pay their dues in cash, the organizers accepted a post-dated check. The Model-T and the post-dated check became the symbols of the Nonpartisan League.

In September 1916 the League began publishing its own newspaper, *The Nonpartisan Leader.* The paper carried political cartoons by John M. Baer and was under the direction of a well-known socialist writer, Charles Edward Russell. *The Leader* kept members informed about political strategy and helped many understand the political processes and the importance of voting for League candidates at election time.

The growth and expansion of the League were not the result of Townley's efforts alone. Others joined the League and emerged as leaders. Among the more prominent leaders was William Lemke. Lemke was raised on his father's farm in Towner County. Growing up on a farm, he knew the struggles and hardships of farming and the lonely life on the prairie. Lemke attended the University of North Dakota, where he participated in debate, played football, and did well academically. After leaving the University, Lemke studied law at Yale and Georgetown University and in 1906 began the practice of law in Fargo.

Lemke became an attorney for the Equity Co-operative Exchange in 1911. His background on the farm and the prevailing spirit of reform instilled in him a hatred of special interest groups such as the railroads and grain exchange. He became a tough, intense fighter for the interests of the common man. He was a powerful speaker both in the courtroom and at the political rally. His determination, energy, and convictions made him a fighter for a better life for the farmer. The League and what it stood for became his life's work.

The League also attracted another man who became a prominent political leader — William Langer. Born on a farm near Casselton in 1886, Langer had gone to the University of North Dakota and been graduated from the Law School in 1906. While at the University, he and Lemke had become friends. Langer enrolled in Columbia University in New York and received his B.A. degree. In 1914, at the age of 28, he became state's attorney of Morton County, where he sued the Northern Pacific Railroad for back taxes and won. The decision was upheld by the State Supreme Court, and the railroad paid $1,250,000. A brilliant attorney, Langer had a talent for friendship and an instinct for appealing to the emotions of the farmers. He had a reputation as one who would fight against the corporations.

To gain control of the political machinery of the state, the League had to get its candidates nominated in the primary election, a process instituted during the governorship of John Burke to break control of party bosses. The League had to control the legislature. To achieve this, it began to publish its program and develop a political strategy. Meetings were held in each precinct on February 22, 1916. At these meetings delegates to legislative districts were selected; and, during March, candidates for the legislature were chosen. A legislative candidate from each district then attended the state convention in Fargo. The strategy worked. Meetings were held in almost every precinct. The Nonpartisan League was organized at the grass-roots and ready for action.

The League planned to run its candidates on the Republican ticket, since most farmers had been loyal to that party. At the state convention, the League endorsed Lynn Frazier for governor and William Langer for attorney general. Frazier campaigned throughout the state, speaking to crowds in most towns. The League held picnics at which Townley spoke against big business and the evils of the corporations.

In the primary election of June 28, 1916, the League carried all but one state office. The victory was sweet. In the November general election, the League won again. All of its candidates for state offices were elected. In the House of Representatives the League held 81 of the 113 seats. Because of the staggered terms in the Senate, however, only 18 of the 44 seats were gained by the League. The election was a great victory for the Nonpartisan League.

A cartoon from the *Nonpartisan Leader*, 1916. (UND-LC)

III. The League in Action

The legislature of 1917 did not adopt the League program because the Senate was controlled by conservatives. The main concern of the League during this session was a controversial bill, a bold attempt to rewrite the state Constitution. In order for the League program (with the exception of a state owned elevator) to be enacted, the Constitution had to be amended. The bill would have changed the Constitution to allow the state to engage in any business or industry. It passed the House but was killed in the Senate.

In spite of the bill's failure, the 1917 legislature did pass many progressive reforms. It set up a better grain grading system, established a state highway commission, prohibited rate discrimination by the railroads, increased aid to primary education, and proposed constitutional amendments for woman suffrage and the exemption of farm improvements from taxation. Hoping to show that state-ownership would not work, League opponents introduced a bill to build a small, state-owned terminal elevator at a cost of $300,000; it passed both houses, but Governor Frazier vetoed it because he believed that one small elevator would not help the farmers much.

In the election of 1918 the League swept to total victory. Frazier and the entire League ticket were elected. Now the League controlled all but one of the state offices, both houses of the legislature, and four out of five supreme court judges. All that remained to be done to achieve total success was to amend the

Governor Lynn J. Frazier signs the woman's suffrage bill, 1917. (SHSND)

Constitution to allow state-owned businesses. The League had initiated seven amendments to the Constitution to be voted on by the people in the 1918 election. All seven received a majority vote; some, however, did not receive a majority of the highest vote total in the election — a requirement of the Constitution. The North Dakota Supreme Court, dominated by Leaguers, ruled that all the amendments had passed. The ruling gave the League what it needed to enact its program.

The 1918 election was an astonishing victory for the young political movement. Although its victory was complete, the opponents of the League began to stir. Prior to the election, the Independent Voters Association (the IVA) was organized to fight the League, its candidates, and its proposals. The IVA appealed to townspeople and farmers who desired farmer-controlled co-ops. The IVA could do little to put out the political prairie fire in 1918. It did, however, reflect a growing suspicion of the League's activities.

In 1919 the League-controlled legislature established "state socialism." To oversee the state's new businesses, it created a three-man Industrial Commission, composed of the governor, the attorney general, and the commissioner of agriculture. The legislature set up the Bank of North Dakota with a capital of $2,000,000. The Bank was to provide farm loans at low costs, finance the state enterprises, and serve as a clearing house for the banks throughout North Dakota. In order to do this, the law required that all state and local government funds be deposited in the Bank to supply it with money. The North Dakota Mill and Elevator Association was another state business. The Association was to engage in the manufacture and marketing of farm products and in the establishment of elevators and warehouses. The League set up a Home Building Association to finance houses which could be purchased with a 20-percent down payment and installment payments that could run for 20 years. It revised the state hail insurance program to provide a three-cents-an-acre tax to pay for the cost of the system.

Other reform measures also became law during the session. A state printing commission was formed to select one newspaper in each county in which the official proceedings of county officials would have to be published; the newspaper would be paid for this service from public funds. At the next election and thereafter, the voters themselves would choose which county newspaper would print the proceedings. This law would provide a source of income for small, weekly newspapers which supported the League. The Legislature provided for a workmen's compensation law, set maximum hours for working women, and provided for inspections of and working standards in the coal mines. It also proposed a constitutional amendment for the recall of public officials. To get labor support, it limited the use of injunctions in labor disputes. The League had won the battle. It controlled the law-making process and set the wheels of state socialism in motion.

IV. The End of League Power

The schemes of the League did not begin smoothly. The North Dakota Mill and Elevator Association had a great deal of trouble. In 1919 it had purchased a small mill at Drake, but the mill did not make a profit and closed in 1927 with losses. In 1919 the League announced that a state mill and elevator would be built in Grand Forks. Businessmen had agreed to purchase $1,000,000 worth of bonds and furnish a building site. Construction started, but stopped in the fall of 1920. The first unit of the Mill was not completed until 1922 and the second in 1923.

The Bank of North Dakota also had difficulty getting under way. It could not find investors willing to purchase the $2,000,000 in bonds which were to supply its capital. Eastern investors were suspicious of state socialism, and the opponents of the League worked against the Bank. The Bank, however, did open in July 1919, and, according to the law, the treasurers of the state, counties, townships, and school districts began to deposit their funds in the Bank, giving it deposits totaling $28,700,000 by 1920. Banks throughout the state also deposited money. The Bank made some farm loans, but it could not offer a competitive interest rate.

The Home Building Association had management problems. Disregarding the law which created it, the Association started to build homes on contracts that consisted mostly of oral agreements with less than the 20-percent down payment.

By 1919 the League had troubles. Three of the League-elected state officials left the party. William Langer, the attorney general; Karl Kositsky, the state auditor; and Thomas Hall, the secretary of state, began to attack the League leadership. They claimed that the leadership had become corrupt and was running state enterprises for its own benefit. Langer charged that the Bank was mismanaged and was being used for selfish ends. Langer and Kositsky began to publish the *Red Flame*, which was distributed throughout the state. This free pamphlet attacked the League leadership and referred to Townley and Frazier as "comrade." Many began to doubt the League and its leaders. Langer ran against

President Woodrow Wilson visits Bismarck in 1919. (SHSND)

Frazier in the 1920 primary and was defeated by a narrow vote. By the fall elections, the appeal of the League was decreasing.

The IVA initiated five measures meant to cripple the League program. For example, one of them would have removed the requirement that public funds had to be deposited in the Bank of North Dakota. In 1920, voters approved all the measures. Anti-League candidates gained control of the House of Representatives, even though Frazier won the governorship. The approval of the anti-League initiated measures in the fall elections brought the state industries to a standstill; the Home Building Association stopped building homes; the Bank of North Dakota could not make farm loans; construction on the State Mill at Grand Forks was halted.

Confident after its victories in 1920, the IVA stepped up its attack on the League. The voters in 1920 had approved a League-sponsored constitutional amendment by which petitions could be circulated for an election to recall state officials. Now this amendment would be used against the League. The IVA asked for the recall of the members of the Industrial Commission. Three IVA candidates would run against the League elected members: Lynn Frazier, governor; William Lemke, attorney general; and John N. Hagen, commissioner of agriculture. The IVA supported Rangvold A. Nestos for governor, Sveinbjorn Johnson for attorney general, and Joseph A. Kitchen for commissioner of agriculture. The election centered on two issues, the membership of the Industrial Commission and whether or not the state should continue the industries.

The IVA was successful. For the first time in the history of the United States, the people of a state recalled their governor, attorney general, and commissioner of agriculture from office. The IVA candidates won by narrow margins. Six measures on the ballot to halt or limit the state businesses, however, did not win. The people of the state had lost confidence in the leadership of the League, but they were not ready to give up its program.

Near the end of 1921, the League began to fall apart. Memberships lapsed. Townley, who had earlier been convicted of trying to discourage army enlistments in Minnesota, began serving a 90-day jail sentence. The heyday of the League was over.

V. The Great War

In 1914 war erupted in Europe. The people of North Dakota generally opposed the war. The North Dakota press waged an attack on the war and warned the country not to become involved in the affairs of Europe. The state's congressmen opposed any actions that might draw the country into war. Senator Porter J. McCumber summarized it best when he declared that the United States should be "so everlastingly neutral in this war that not one of the nations engaged in the conflict can make any complaint against us." In 1915 Governor Louis B. Hanna was the only American elected official to join Henry Ford on his peace ship mission — an attempt to restore European peace. In 1916 North Dakotans voted for Democrat Woodrow Wilson because "he kept us out of war." The Nonpartisan League took a strong stand against the war. North Dakotans feared that this was a war designed to bring profits into the pockets of munitions makers and bankers. The people thought that this was a war from which only eastern interests would benefit. North Dakota public opinion was clearly against American entry into the war. And, when Congress voted to declare war in April 1917, North Dakota's Senator Asle J. Gronna cast one of the six votes against the declaration.

A patriotic float in Bismarck during World War One. (SHSND)

Once the nation was at war, however, North Dakotans rallied to the cause. North Dakota's war effort was a credit to the people of the state. They bought more bonds, called liberty bonds, than the prescribed quota on all five bond drives — in all, $65,500,000 worth. In addition to buying bonds, North Dakotans did their part on the home front. Red Cross membership drives brought hundreds of members. The Sioux gave over $2,000 to the Red Cross. Women helped make surgical dressings, socks, sweaters, and other needed items for the troops. Housewives canned vegetables and followed wartime restrictions on the consumption of food. War gardens sprouted all over the state.

North Dakota men did their patriotic share; 31,269 officers and enlisted men, almost 20,000 of them volunteers, served in the armed forces during the war. Two National Guard Units were organized in June 1917, and President Wilson called them into service in July. Both became a part of the Forty-first Division, known as the Sunset Division. Chateau Thierry, Saint Mihiel, and the Marne would be names remembered by the boys who were "over there." They knew first-hand the trenches, the artillery fire, and the charges over the top. Of those who went, 1,305 did not come home.

Although the Nonpartisan League pledged that its members would support the war effort, opponents of the League used the issue of patriotism and loyalty to discredit it. Some newspapers implied that Governor Frazier and other Leaguers were disloyal to the country. The Red Cross refused to accept League donations. In the eyes of many, the League was equated with socialism. When a socialist agitator spoke out against the war in North Dakota, many thought the Nonpartisan League was speaking. For example, after the United States had entered the war, Kate Richards O'Hare, an eastern socialist writer, delivered a violent attack on the war during a speech in Bowman. She called American mothers "brood sows" who were raising sons whose blood would "enrich or possibly fertilize the soil of France." The League supported the war, but its opponents identified the League with disloyalty.

* * * * * *

The Nonpartisan League fought hard to gain control of North Dakota. Its organizers worked day and night, and their strenuous effort paid off. In one legislative session — 1919 — the League achieved a revolution. Some League ideas failed; the Bank of North Dakota and the State Mill and Elevator succeeded, and railroad and grain trade laws curbed some abuses. Yet, the League could do little to solve the problem of the market. Farmers still had to sell at the going price; they were still victims of the grain trade.

The League continued as the liberal faction of the Republican party, but by the 1920s its radicalism and its hold on the state were gone. Some of the League's leaders had been thrown out of office; others such as Langer abandoned the League; A.C. Townley went to jail. The political prairie fire had been snuffed out.

16 Road to Depression: The 1920s

In 1920 North Dakotans went to the polls and three out of every four voted for Republican Warren G. Harding. Americans hoped that Harding would be the man to continue the prosperity which they had enjoyed during World War One. Harding represented what North Dakotans liked: optimism and prosperity. In the months before the election, crops had been good, and wheat prices were very high at $2.96 per bushel. Tied to a wheat economy, North Dakotans needed good crops and good prices, and they had generally enjoyed both since the turn of the century. The Twenties, however, would show North Dakota the danger of an economy based only on wheat.

I. The Economy: From Boom to Bust

During World War One, the national government encouraged expanded production from all Americans for the war effort, and North Dakotans responded. They bought tractors, trucks, and new kinds of equipment. Many bought additional land and put poorer land into production. This meant heavy indebtedness, and by 1920, 70 percent of the farmers in the state who owned their farms had mortgage debts totaling over $286,000,000. But the future was bright and times were good. A Divide County farmer summed it up when he recalled: "Those were good days. The future seemed bright. God provided, and we had faith that He always would."

The look of the 1920s.

The Twenties have been characterized as a decade of national prosperity, the Jazz Age, the years of flaming youth with bath-tub gin and hip flasks. Young people danced the wild Charleston and took part in marathon dancing contests. Girls wore their skirts above the knee, and boys drove around in flashy cars with rumble seats. And Republicans Warren Harding, Calvin Coolidge, and Herbert Hoover presided over a nation experiencing industrial expansion and good times.

The general prosperity which the businessmen in New York or the steel workers in Pittsburgh enjoyed, however, was not shared by the farmers of North Dakota or those in other states tied to the wheat economy. A year and a half after the election of Harding and $2.96 wheat, the bottom fell out of the wheat market; prices dropped to a low of 92¢. Throughout the Twenties, wheat prices fluctuated between 97¢ and $1.20. These low prices spelled trouble for farmers, especially those who had gone heavily into debt during the boom years of World War One. In 1920 a farmer could have bought a suit by producing ten bushels of wheat; by 1923 that same suit would cost him 31 bushels. He was getting much less for his product while he was paying about the same for the goods he had to buy. The North Dakota farmer found himself in a severe price squeeze.

The reasons for the economic difficulty which faced the farmer were overproduction and underconsumption. Rapid mechanization and an all-out war effort produced more wheat than a peacetime population needed. Foreign countries bought less; and Americans, who during the war had been persuaded to eat less, continued to eat less after the war. These conditions forced down the price of wheat — the foundation of the North Dakota economy.

Declining land values, which dropped about one third, also hurt North Dakotans. A farmer found himself in another difficult position: a piece of land which he had purchased for $10,000 in 1920 was valued at less than $7,000 in 1925 — yet his payments were based on the $10,000. His taxes did not decline much.

When the farmers suffered, the whole state felt the consequences. North Dakota banks began to fail. In 1920, 898 banks served the state — more banks per person than in any other state. Because North Dakota needed credit for agricultural expansion, the state did not impose strict regulations on banking. During the boom years of World War One, banks extended credit to farmers with little caution and often overextended themselves. When the farm depression of the Twenties came, banks attempted to call in loans, but they could not collect payments from farmers who could not pay. In 1923, 99 banks failed. And by 1933, 575 of the 898 banks in the state had closed. Depositors lost over $50,000,000. The plunge of wheat prices had brought disaster to the whole state: farmer, banker, merchant. All faced bleak times.

II. Politics: A Struggle for Power

During the Twenties, North Dakota remained faithful to the Republican party. The struggle for power between the liberal Nonpartisan League and the conservative Independent Voters Association for control of the Republican party continued. The Democratic party remained weak, and many Democrats joined with moderate Republicans to fight the League. Although the Nonpartisan League remained alive in politics, its more radical leadership, especially William Lemke and A.C. Townley, had been discredited, and the moderate Leaguers controlled the party.

In 1922 the IVA was successful in getting Rangvold A. Nestos, a Minot attorney, elected governor, and in controlling both houses of the legislature. The League was out. Nestos had been elected in the 1921 recall of Governor Lynn Frazier. Although the anti-League IVA had elected Nestos, he saw value in both the Bank of North Dakota and the State Mill and Elevator and worked to make them succeed. Nestos attempted to help farmers fight the collapse of the wheat market by encouraging a farm-loan program in the Bank and by hastening the completion of the State Mill at Grand Forks. Governor Nestos earned himself a reputation as a man of strong convictions. To cut state spending, he vetoed several money bills.

Nestos gained the support of farmers because of his support of the Bank and the State Mill, but he angered others with his vetoes. Nestos lost renomination in 1924 by a narrow margin to Arthur G. Sorlie, a well-to-do businessman from Grand Forks. Although Sorlie was not a Leaguer, he gained League endorsement because he had supported the State Mill. The League unexpectedly won, electing half the state officials, a majority in the House of Representatives, and nearly half of the Senate. The League of the Twenties, however, was much more moderate than the one which had introduced "state socialism."

Governor Sorlie faced opposition from radical Leaguers who wanted him to expand state businesses, and from conservatives who wished that he would close down and sell the "socialist" Bank and Mill and Elevator. In spite of this, he won re-election in 1926 with the support of moderate Leaguers and those IVAers who did not want to close the state industries. Even with Sorlie's business sense and support, the State Mill and Elevator lost money, giving his opponents grounds to attack him. The 1927 legislature, led by the strange coalition of radical Leaguers and conservatives, investigated the Mill's management. The investigating committee recommended that control of the Mill be removed from the governor because of poor management. During the summer of 1928, Governor Sorlie died, and his political opponent, Lt. Governor Walter Maddock, filled out the remaining months of his term.

In the 1928 election, the Nonpartisan League called for more "state socialism" and the expansion of state-owned industries. This return to radicalism did not appeal to most voters, and IVA candidate George F. Shafer defeated League candidate T.H.H. Thoresen, an attorney from Grand Forks, for governor. Shafer, who had been attorney general since 1923, was well-qualified for his new job and was able to make the State Mill and Elevator a profitable investment for North Dakotans. In the 1930 election, the voters dealt the Nonpartisan League a severe blow; Shafer won an easy second term, and the IVA took both houses of the legislature.

By the end of the Twenties, the anti-League IVA had taken control of the state away from the Nonpartisan League. The League, however, faired better in congressional races. Both United States Senate seats belonged to the League. Lynn J. Frazier, whom the voters had recalled in 1921, was elected to the Senate in 1922 and served for 18 years. E.F. Ladd, professor at the Agricultural College and crusader for pure food and drug legislation, had won election in 1920. Ladd,

Gas tractors and movie billboards became common by the 1920s, Bowman. (SHSND)

however, died in 1925, and Governor Sorlie appointed Gerald P. Nye, editor of a Cooperstown newspaper, to the Senate. He remained in office until 1944.

Of North Dakota's three members in the House of Representatives, two were anti-Leaguers. Olger B. Burtness, a Grand Forks attorney, represented the eastern First District from 1920 to 1932. George M. Young, an attorney at Valley City, held the central Second District position from 1913 to 1924. In 1924 another anti-League Republican, Thomas Hall, was elected and remained in Congress until 1932. The western Third District representative was James H. Sinclair, an educator, banker, farmer, and land dealer in Binford and Kenmare. Sinclair, a loyal Leaguer, served from 1919 until 1935.

III. "Farmers, organize!"

Farm-state congressmen, however, could do little to persuade President Coolidge that farmers needed some kind of federal help; the President vetoed farm programs that would have given the state's farmers a fair price for their crops. Farmers turned to self-help in an attempt to remedy the situation. Farmers of the state soon grew tired of low wheat prices, declining land values, and the high prices they had to pay for machinery, twine, and other goods. Many had put their faith in the Nonpartisan League. But with the decline of the League during the Twenties, farmers looked for new solutions to their problems.

The farm co-operative continued as one answer. The co-operative concept, which was based on co-operative marketing and buying of goods, was not new to North Dakota, but the troubles of the Twenties brought it new life. In 1920, the American Farm Bureau Federation began an all-out effort to bring the existing co-

The coming of the automobile meant new roads. A road crew in McLean County, 1920s. (SHSND)

ROAD TO DEPRESSION: THE 1920S

operatives in North Dakota under its control. Aided by federal legislation which exempted farm co-ops from anti-trust laws, the Farm Bureau launched a campaign to enroll the state's farmers. It would provide grain terminal facilities and reduced prices on items the farmer needed to buy. Although many local co-operatives succeeded, the efforts of the Farm Bureau failed by the mid-Twenties. Only control of his market could improve the situation of the farmer, and the Farm Bureau was unable to do this.

Many farmers were more optimistic about another organization which preached improved farm prices through monopoly of the market — the North Dakota Wheat Growers Association. Organized in 1922 at Grand Forks by George E. Duis, A.J. Scott, and R.L. Taft, the North Dakota Wheat Growers Association had as its objective a market monopoly of all the spring wheat. If North Dakota's wheat growers could band together, they could force buyers to pay their price. Under this plan, farmers would contract to pool their wheat with the Association. The Association would pay the farmer 70 percent of the market price at the time of delivery. It would then sell the wheat at the best market times and divide the profits among the pooling farmers. In spite of a well-organized campaign and a good idea, the Association was never able to persuade more than a third of the state's wheat growers to join. Independent-minded farmers were leary of the Association and continued to fight the market alone. By 1930 the Wheat Growers Association was dead.

Of the attempts to improve the lot of the farmer, only the North Dakota Farmer's Union succeeded. The Farmer's Union began in Texas in 1902, and its early efforts to organize North Dakota farmers were not very successful. By the mid-Twenties, however, the Farmer's Union, led by M.W. "Bill" Thatcher, succeeded in establishing a foothold. Charles C. Talbott, an aggressive and energetic man, became the first state president of the Union. Members could ship their grain and livestock to the Union's facilities in St. Paul and obtain insurance, lumber, oil products, and other items at reduced prices through the Farmer's Union Exchange. The Farmer's Union grew rapidly, and, although it could do little to raise the price of wheat, it did give its members strong leadership and a break at the marketplace.

IV. Overcoming Isolation

By 1930, North Dakotans were still growing wheat; and the IVA and the Nonpartisan League were still fighting it out at the ballot box, but beneath the economic and political struggles, North Dakota was changing. Two innovations made North Dakota a better place in which to live — the automobile and the radio. The automobile helped conquer the state's wide open spaces and the great distances between towns and farms. By 1930 there was one car for every four people in the state — considerably better than the national average. During the Twenties, the state spent millions of dollars constructing new roads and improving old ones. In 1930, one could travel about 8,000 miles on the state's

The automobile and radio helped end the isolation of living in a large remote state. (SHSND; FSA/UND-LC)

The burning of the capitol in 1930. (SHSND)

highway system. The Tin Lizzy represented North Dakota's growing freedom from isolation.

The automobile brought North Dakotans closer together; the radio brought them closer to the world. Two years after commercial broadcasting began in Pittsburgh in 1920, WDAY in Fargo went on the air. North Dakota had a radio station before Minneapolis did! Other stations soon went on the air in Bismarck, Grand Forks, Minot, Devils Lake, and Mandan. The music of Bach and Beethoven began floating into North Dakota homes; first-hand news reports of the world's happenings stirred the people, and many heard the World Series and heavyweight prize fights. As stations expanded and became more powerful, North Dakota began to enjoy a richer and less isolated life.

* * * * * *

The Twenties in North Dakota offered a sharp contrast to the decade before and during World War One, when the state had gained a new level of productivity and prosperity. With tractors to make farm work easier and more profitable, and with a State Bank and State Mill and Elevator to help him, the farmer dreamed of a bright and progressive future. The pioneers, who had sacrificed and lived through the ups and downs of the frontier, now thought that their hard work and faith in the soil had been rewarded. It was not to be so during the Twenties. North Dakota fell victim to the wheat market. As prices dropped during the decade, so did the spirit of the people. Listening to Amos 'n Andy on the radio did little to cheer up the North Dakota farmer who sat crouched by his radio set. Yet, comparing these times to what was in store for the state during the Thirties, many would later recall that the Twenties were not so bad.

17 Years of Despair: The 1930s and the War

A young minister who was serving a rural church near Minot captured the spirit of the 1930s when he commented: "Those were bad days for everyone; the spirits of the people were low. I spent most of the time assuring my people that things would get better and that God would answer their prayers." The 1930s were "bad days for everyone." The depression ripped across the country like an angry tornado, tossing people's lives around like matchsticks. Drought, hot dry winds, and grasshoppers made life in North Dakota more unbearable than in most other places.

I. The Economic Crisis

The nationwide depression dropped wheat prices as low as 36¢ per bushel and cattle to $3.60 per hundred weight. In 1925 a farmer could have paid off a $10,000 loan with 6,700 bushels of wheat; by 1933 it took 33,000 bushels. This was a difficult task. The people might have overcome low prices, but they could not win the fight against nature. Drought struck; rain was scarce; the heat was intense. In 1934, the average rainfall was a scant 9.5 inches. Temperatures in the 100s became common, and in 1936 the thermometer at Steele hit 121°. Winds whipped across the state, churning the soil into clouds of dust that turned noon into night. Grasshoppers added to the plague. In August 1933, the city of Mott had to turn on its street lights because swarms of grasshoppers blocked out the sun. At Killdeer, 'hoppers piled up four inches deep.

Drought ruined the crops. A farmer near Dickinson shows how tall his wheat should have been. (FSA/UND-LC)

On many farms the bugs ate those crops that the wind and heat had not destroyed. In 1934 and 1936, crop yields were extremely low; the 1936 wheat crop averaged only five bushels per acre, and many farmers had no crops at all.

Headlines such as "WIND, DUST STORMS DAMAGE CROPS AND MAKE LIFE DREARY" were common. North Dakotans were in the grip of depression, and stories of desperation filled the newspapers. Merchants resorted to barter; in Cando a grocery store owner accepted rabbit hides in exchange for goods. A sheep rancher near Berwich reported that he had shipped five sheep to St. Paul and waited for his check. Instead, he received a bill of $1.56 to meet the packer's expenses. Many counties abandoned juries because funds to pay them were gone. Yet, many retained a sense of humor; an Edgeley couple found that the depression made it impossible to buy Christmas cards, so they purchased penny postcards and wrote in red and green ink:

> Postage went up and wheat went down,
> Collections are punk all over town.
> The voters gave our salary a slash
> And we Republicans took an awful crash.
> We wondered HOW we'd send a greeting to you,
> And finally decided a postcard would do.
> But in a BIG WAY its full of good cheer
> For a Merry Christmas and a Happy New Year.

The drought and grasshoppers did not strike evenly. The western third of the state was devastated. The northwest around Divide County was the hardest hit. There, one in five farmers was forced off the land, and as a result of the 1934 drought, 89 percent of the population was forced onto federal relief projects in order to exist. Crops in the Red River Valley, however, were not wiped out. In Traill County only one in 52 farmers lost his farm, and none in Traill received federal relief in 1934. Nature spared the Valley from the total disaster that struck the western part of the state.

North Dakota was the hardest hit of the forty-eight states, and its citizens suffered immensely. Land values dropped 50 percent. One third of the farmers left the land between 1930 and 1944. Tied to the one-crop wheat economy, the state fell victim to drought. The depression was severe, but the drought delivered the knockout punch. Like other plains states hard-hit by drought, North Dakota could not have survived without help.

II. The Federal Government to the Rescue

The depression hurt all Americans. Although it struck North Dakota harder than other places, it was a national crisis. In 1932 Franklin D. Roosevelt became President, and traditionally Republican North Dakota joined the Roosevelt bandwagon. Roosevelt immediately developed programs called the New Deal to fight the depression.

Congress enacted the Agricultural Adjustment Act (AAA) to help farmers. The AAA set up a program under which farmers would be paid "benefit checks" for cutting production. Less production would raise farm prices. When the Supreme Court ruled the AAA unconstitutional in 1936, Congress enacted the second AAA, which established the idea "parity" — federal price supports that would bring farm prices into equality with the price of goods the farmer had to buy. These programs greatly benefitted North Dakota farmers. A 1934 Minot headline screamed the news that "WHEAT CHECKS WILL BRING OVER $6,000,000 TO NORTHWEST N.D." This was good news to a state on the verge of total economic collapse. Between 1933 and 1940, the government paid the state's farmers over $142,000,000.

The tragedy of the depression, however, called for more than just aid to the farmer. The Roosevelt New Deal responded to the deepening crisis with several programs. The immediate concern was to aid those who had no means of support with a work-relief program. The Federal Emergency Relief Administration (FERA) was created and given $500,000,000 to battle the depression. Although direct cash help was available through FERA, the program encouraged work. In 1935, FERA employed 190,000 North Dakotans to build such worthwhile things as roads, bridges, tennis courts, baseball fields, playgrounds, swimming pools, airports, and parks. FERA programs also provided surplus food for the hungry, employed teachers to keep the school open, gave college students part-time jobs, set up smallpox immunization clinics, and conducted historical surveys. FERA programs brought almost $35,000,000 into the state. In 1936 the work of FERA was taken over by the Works Progress Administration (WPA). Under WPA, workers received $40 a month, barely enough to live on in the depression. By 1938, WPA was still employing thousands of people and bringing $20,000,000 into North Dakotans' pockets.

Two programs were especially designed for younger people. The Civilian Conservation Corp (CCC) hired young men to improve forests and parks, help control soil erosion, work on flood control projects, and develop recreational areas. By 1940, over 30,000 youth had taken part in the state's CCC projects. The National Youth Administration (NYA) gave part-time employment to students in high school and college. About 2,500 received help each month, and the NYA spent over $2,000,000 in North Dakota.

These federal programs gave the people food, shelter, and, just as important, lifted their spirits and gave them courage to fight. Elwyn B. Robinson estimates that North Dakotans lost $1,340,000,000 during the depression. Almost 90,000 became discouraged and left the state. State government had almost no money to throw into the attack on depression. The Federal government, however, pumped $266,000,000 into the state. Citizens occasionally grumbled about red tape and bureaucracy, but they realized that these federal programs meant survival.

Government programs employed thousands of North Dakotans in projects such as road building. (FSA/UND-LC)

III. The William Langer Era

No man has ever dominated a decade of North Dakota history as William Langer did in the 1930s. He swept into the governorship in 1932 and remained at the center of politics throughout the decade. Langer, who was born on a farm near Casselton in 1886, was graduated from the University of North Dakota Law School and Columbia. As a young man in his twenties, he was elected state's attorney of Morton County, where he earned a reputation for being aggressive and tireless. By 1916, at age thirty, he had attracted enough attention to be endorsed for attorney general on the Nonpartisan League ticket and to win. In 1920 Langer opposed League candidate Lynn Frazier for governor. He gave Frazier a close race but lost. During the 1920s he left politics to practice law in Bismarck.

Langer, however, did not remain out of politics for long. By the late 1920s the Nonpartisan League had lost most of its political power and in the election of 1930 was soundly trounced by the IVA. Langer seized upon this opportunity. He knew that the League needed new and dynamic leadership if it were to survive as a political force. During the years 1929 to 1932, he made his move to capture the League. Using his own money and boundless energy, he reorganized the Nonpartisan League into his own political party. In the 1932 election, he easily won the governorship and carried the entire League ticket to victory, including both houses of the legislature. The state belonged to William Langer.

Governor William Langer signing a bill. (SHSND)

Above, the streets of Williston during the depression. Below, a Bowman area rancher sits in the shade of his sod house as the temperature soared to over 100 degrees. (FSA/UND-LC)

Langer came to power as the depression was casting its longest shadow across the state. He had run for office as a candidate who would give the people action, and he gave them action. Langer used the executive proclamation as his chief weapon to fight the depression. On April 17, 1933, he declared a moritorium on farm-mortgage foreclosures; this prohibited the forced sale of property to pay debts without the owner's written consent. A year later, he expanded the moratorium to protect renters and small businesses. When some sheriffs held foreclosure sales in spite of the moratorium, Langer called out the National Guard to put an end to the violations. In late 1933, he placed an embargo on wheat and on beef in an attempt to raise prices. He prohibited wheat and beef from leaving the state. Although he withdrew the embargoes in December, prices on the Minneapolis market did rise a few cents.

Although the embargoes did little to raise prices, the foreclosure moratorium, which was continued by his successors and later enacted by the legislature, kept many farmers on the land. Both were bold actions. Langer critics cried "dictatorship," but most people in the state saw his actions as expressions of genuine concern and personal involvement in the problems of the people.

Soon, however, Langer found himself in a series of legal and political battles which marked the most chaotic years of North Dakota politics. During his second year in office, the Roosevelt administration removed control of federal relief funds from Langer's office. On May 12, 1934, two months after he had received renomination for governor, a federal grand jury indicted Langer and eight associates on charges of conspiracy to solicit and collect money for political purposes from federal employees. After trial of nearly a month, presided over by Langer's arch foe, Judge Andrew Miller, Langer was sentenced to eighteen months in a federal penitentiary and fined $10,000. That same day, the North Dakota Supreme Court removed Langer from the governor's office and elevated Lieutenant Governor Ole Olson to that office.

Langer's enemies were overjoyed; his supporters staged protest marches and rallies. Most people thought that William Langer, convicted of a felony, was washed-up in politics. Langer, however, appealed the decision, and, on May 7, 1935, a federal circuit court of appeals reversed his conviction. Seven months later, Langer found himself in court again — charged once more with conspiracy. He was acquitted. Less than three weeks later, he was tried for perjury. He was acquitted. Four days after his acquittal for perjury, he was once again in court on conspiracy charges. He was acquitted.

While Langer was fighting for his political life in the courts, North Dakota politics became chaotic. After his first conviction, when Langer was stripped of his civil rights, his wife, Lydia, ran in his place as the Nonpartisan League candidate for governor in 1934. The court battle against Langer gave Thomas Moodie, a Democrat, the victory over Mrs. Langer. Langer supporters, however, found that Moodie had not met the state's residence requirement (five years) for governor because he had voted in Minneapolis in 1930. The North Dakota Supreme Court made Moodie's the shortest governorship in the state's history

Lydia Cady Langer. (SHSND)

when it removed him from office on February 4 — a month after he took office. This made Walter Welford, a Nonpartisan Leaguer, governor. North Dakota had had four governors within a little over six months.

In 1936 Langer ran for governor as an independent against League candidate Governor Welford and Democrat John Moses. To the dismay of many, he won, getting 36 percent of the vote in the three-way race. William Langer had risen from the political grave. His attempt to unseat two-term Senator Gerald P. Nye in 1938 failed, but in 1940 he beat three-term Senator Lynn Frazier and Thomas Whelan in another three-way race to become a Senator in Washington.

IV. The Moses Years

Langer's last term as governor, 1937-1938, marked the end of Nonpartisan League power. Langer had won in 1936 with only 36 percent of the vote, lost in 1938, and won in 1940 largely because the election was a three-way race. The Langer grip on state politics was over. The Nonpartisan League, which Langer used in his rise to power, would not win the governorship again until 1960, after it had merged with the Democrats.

The man responsible for taking the state away from Langer and his supporters was Democrat John Moses. Born in Norway, Moses was an energetic man who appeared to be sincere, honest, above politics and free of corruption. In 1936 he had done well as a Democratic candidate in his campaign against Langer and Welford. A lawyer from Hazen, Moses also farmed and dabbled in politics, serving as Mercer County state's attorney. When he received the Democratic nomination for governor in 1938, he received support from conservative IVA Republicans who detested Langer and from old-time Leaguers such as Lemke and Nye, who would not support a Langer candidate. The election of 1938 was a test for William Langer. Moses campaigned on a platform of honest and efficient government, implying that Langer had not represented these virtues. Moses easily defeated Langer's candidate, John N. Hagen, and Langer himself failed to win the Senate seat that he wanted so much.

During his first term in office, Moses was haunted by William Langer. Langer had initiated a measure to raise old-age pensions which had carried every county in the election of 1938. The 1939 legislature, under pressure from

Democratic Governor John Moses faces a Republican elephant in his office. (SHSND)

Governor Moses, refused to fund larger pensions. In a counterattack, Langer initiated three measures to finance the higher pensions: a gross transactions tax, municipal liquor stores, and diversion of highway funds. The campaign prior to the special election was a bitter battle between Langer and Governor Moses. Both worked tirelessly, and Moses won. The Langer proposal went down to a resounding 4 to 1 defeat.

Moses conducted large-scale investigations of state agencies, such as the State Hospital for the Insane, and reported many "irregularities" in their operations. He ordered sharp budget cuts of 18 percent in the operation of state agencies in an attempt to cut away at a $2,500,000 state deficit.

By 1940 the mood of the people was changing. In 1932 they had wanted a man who promised action — anything to fight the depression. William Langer had given them action. They stood by him through five trials and re-elected him in 1936. In 1940, partly out of gratitude for that action, they sent him to Washington. At home, though, with better times, North Dakotans were becoming more conservative, and John Moses became the man of the hour.

In Washington, four aggressive and capable men — all Nonpartisan Leaguers — worked on behalf of North Dakotans in the fight against depression: William Lemke and Usher L. Burdick in the House of Representatives, and Gerald P. Nye and Lynn J. Frazier in the Senate. Burdick, Lemke, and Frazier energetically created and supported farm legislation. In 1934 the Congress passed the Frazier-Lemke Farm Bankruptcy Act, which allowed farmers to recover lost property on easy terms. Lemke, a vocal and colorful spokesman for farmers, received the presidential nomination of the Union party in 1936. He carried no states, but became the only North Dakotan ever to run for the presidency.

V. Another World War, 1941-1945

Gerald P. Nye gained a national reputation as a crusading Senator. Editor of *The Sentinel-Courier News* in Cooperstown, Nye became Senator in 1925, when Governor Sorlie appointed him after the death of Senator Ladd. By the late 1930s, "Nye" was a household world in America. He headed the famous munitions investigation of 1934-1937 to discover what role financiers and munitions makers played in armament races and international conflict. The handsome and forceful North Dakotan probed the question with fierce intensity. In 1936 he came face to face with the renowned financier J.P. Morgan in an historic confrontation. Nye was convinced that munitions and financial leaders had led the United States into World War One.

During the Thirties, the world seemed to be moving toward another war. In 1931, Japan invaded China; in 1935, Italy, led by dictator Benito Mussolini, took Ethiopia in Africa; Germany under the control of Adolph Hitler began to rearm. Nye warned the nation against becoming involved in another world war. Because of Nye and other congressmen who agreed with him, Congress passed a series of neutrality acts which were intended to keep the country out of war. The acts prohibited the United States from selling arms or making loans to nations at war. Americans could not travel on the ships of warring countries. Most North Dakotans agreed with Nye and this policy. They wanted to do everything possible to avoid another war.

In 1939, war broke out in Europe; Hitler's German tanks rolled across Europe, and in a short time he had taken Norway, Denmark, Poland, Belgium, France, and the Netherlands. By 1940, Germany was preparing for its assault on England. The spread of the war alarmed Americans. North Dakota's congressmen warned against panic; they did not believe that the United States would be attacked. Nye spoke out strongly against drafting young men for the army, and against giving destroyers to England.

On December 7, 1941, Japan attacked the United States. As bombs were falling on Pearl Harbor, Nye was speaking at a rally demanding American noninvolvement in the war. But the Japanese had struck, and soon the United States would also be at war with Germany and Italy. The nation had no choice, and Senator Nye and all North Dakotans rallied to the cause of winning the war — a war they did not want.

North Dakota seemed very remote from the battles in Africa, Europe, and the Pacific during those years, 1941-1945. But distance from the raging war did not dampen the state's war effort. As they had done in 1917, North Dakotans rallied to the cause, giving the winning of the war against Hitler, Mussolini, and the Japanese top priority in their lives. To help finance the war, the people bought $397,000,000 in war bonds — an amazing sum for a state emerging from the destruction of the depression. In one of the bond drives, North Dakota led the nation in per capita bond buying. The state's colleges and universities became training centers for the armed forces. The people pitched in to collect paper, scrap

A 1938 campaign folder carried this picture with the caption: "Senator Nye challenges J.P. Morgan."

metal, and fat. Farmers worked longer hours to produce more food. Many goods were scarce; housewives waited months for a can of pineapple. Rationing of food and gasoline meant less on the table and no pleasure travel. Air-raid sirens wailed in the night as North Dakotans held practice alerts. And the soldiers, sailors, and marines who left the golden prairie to fight the enemy offered their lives in defense of freedom. Over 58,000 North Dakotans bravely served on the hot sands of North Africa, in the thick jungles of the South Pacific, and through the snows of Northern Europe. Many did not come home to the prairie; 1,939 died in the war.

The war caused hardship and heartbreak, but it ended the worst depression in the nation's history. Soon the WPA, the CCC, and the other New Deal programs were gone. They had kept North Dakota and the rest of the country alive during the Thirties. But now, with industry and agriculture booming because of the war effort, they were no longer needed.

North Dakota had record crops; the rains came and the dust settled. Wheat prices rose to over $1.50 per bushel, and cattle sold at $10.00 per hundred weight. A 1932 North Dakota law, which forced corporations to sell their land by 1942, placed more land on the market. Many began farming, and others expanded their farms. Because new land was for sale, land prices did not skyrocket in North Dakota as they did in other states.

Not everyone enjoyed the new prosperity. Many lost their farms in 1942, when the foreclosure moratorium came to an end. They did not have enough time to reap the bountiful wartime harvests in order to pay off delinquent loans. Defense plants in the cities needed workers at high wages, and thousands left North Dakota for steady jobs elsewhere.

*   *   *   *   *   *

The state suffered immensely during the years of depression. Many farmers lost their land, and those who survived paid a high price: falling land values, meager crops, and unsatisfactory prices. Per capita income was less than half the national average. Tied to the one-crop economy, North Dakota fell victim to drought. Both depression and drought ravaged the state. Federal programs which brought over $266,000,000 into the state meant survival, but almost 90,000 North Dakotans, their confidence shaken, gave up and sought greener pastures in California or Washington. Yet, those who stayed won the battle. During the dark days of 1934, John M. Gillette, the renowned rural sociologist at the University of North Dakota, had written: "You would be surprised to know how optimistic our citizens in this state are able to remain. They look forward to the future with hopefulness." Federal money helped keep North Dakota going during the Thirties; but the people, full of hope and determination, made the difference between victory and defeat. Against heavy odds, they held on and fought back. Through the swirling dust, they knew that the fields would blossom again. They did. World War Two ended the ugly depression. Farm prices rose; crops were good; prosperity was returning.

18 The Boom Years: Since 1945

The years since World War Two have been years of prosperity for North Dakota. The postwar generation experienced what its fathers and grandfathers had never experienced: thirty years of uninterrupted prosperity and economic growth. Not all years were equally prosperous, but nothing like the depression of the 1890s, the 1920s, or the 1930s happened. By the 1970s the state's economy had become more diversified because of the oil boom, coal development, and light industry. Yet, the key to North Dakota's well-being was still agriculture. And the key to a strong farm economy was wheat. In the 1970s it was still true that a healthy King Wheat meant a healthy North Dakota.

I. The Prosperous Generation

The economy of North Dakota has always been tied to agriculture. Because of the distance from major markets, large industries have not come to the state. The welfare of the farmers has determined the welfare of most North Dakotans. The agricultural economy, however, has always been subject to many forces that remain outside the control of those who grow the crops.

The economy of the state has been subject to good and bad times, due mainly to changes in wheat prices and crop yields. The years after the war, 1946 to 1949, were good years for agriculture. Wheat production averaged 140,000,000 bushels per year, and gross farm income was over $700,000,000 in 1947 and in 1948. This prosperity was reflected in the change of farm indebtedness. Now that prices were good and farmers received money, they began to pay off their debts.

Farm-mortgage debt was down to $67,000,000 by 1949. In the 1950s a change in the economic cycle occurred. Crop yields were not as good as they had been; with less income, farmers again had to borrow money. The farm-mortgage debt rose to $82,000,000 by 1959. The decline in farm prices during the 1950s and early 1960s was due in large measure to the lack of wheat consumption. Per capita yearly consumption dropped 39 pounds between 1945 and 1959. Underconsumption meant overproduction. The federal government responded and began several programs to help the farmers. During the 1950s, Congress devised programs to support the prices of agricultural products in order to make farming a more profitable business. These programs featured a land retirement system called the soil bank. The object of the plan was to take land out of use in order to bring production more into line with consumption. The federal government paid the farmer not to grow crops. During the 1950s, North Dakota had more land in the soil bank than any other state. Almost 8,000 whole farms were under the program. The "soil bank" program continued until 1970. With the new world food shortage and increased demand for the products of the farm, production controls were no longer needed.

In an effort to stimulate the grain trade, the 1959 state legislature created the North Dakota Wheat Commission. The Commission, directed by the growers, is supported by a 2-mill levy on wheat grown and marketed in the state. The purpose of the Commission is to increase the sale and use of wheat at home and abroad, to search for new uses for wheat, to provide information on the value of wheat products to processors and consumers, and to improve export quality. The Commission also surveys each year's crops and works with other agencies to promote wheat.

Farm prices, however, changed with world conditions in the 1970s. As the population of the world increased tremendously, more hungry mouths needed food. The export market for grain became an important factor for North Dakota farmers. In 1972 the Soviet Union, experiencing a poor harvest, came to the world market looking for grain. The sale of grain to Russia boomed the grain market, and the prices shot up, with wheat reaching $6.00 a bushel, bringing money into the pockets of the state's farmers. The need for grain in the world during the late 1960s and early 1970s terminated the huge grain storage program of the federal government, and grain reserves were sold on the world market. Agriculture experienced good years in the 1970s. Between 1947 and 1974, gross farm income in North Dakota increased from $700,000,000 to $2,417,000,000; the large share of that increase was due to the high wheat prices in the 1970s. The maxim "When King Wheat is healthy, North Dakota is healthy" remained true. Agriculture since World War Two has accounted for 25 percent of North Dakota's state income, or in the economist's term, gross state product (the market value of all goods and services produced in the state during a year). When wheat prices rose to all-time highs in 1973, the agricultural contribution to state income jumped to 41 percent. Between 1945 and the mid-1970s, the gross state product increased from $600,000,000 to

Harvesting time in the Red River Valley, 1950s. (GFH)

$4,000,000,000. The largest increase came between 1970 and 1973 — $2,000,000,000. Other factors also contributed to the increase: trade, 15 percent; government, 13.5 percent; finance, insurance, and real estate, 7.5 percent.

Since World War Two, however, North Dakota's per capita income has not been as high as the national average. Only in 1947 did it equal the national average, but in most of the other years it was about 20 percent lower. With high wheat prices, the North Dakota average began to rise. In 1973 it was $3,738 — still below the national average. By 1975, however, the state's per capita income climbed above the national average to $5,695. North Dakota was beginning to receive a greater share of the nation's wealth.

The economic growth of the state has been reflected in a building boom, especially since the mid-1950s. New schools, hospitals, clinics, swimming pools, college buildings, and business structures went up across the state. Seven thousand miles of hard-surface highways were completed. By the mid-1970s, North Dakota had interstate highway systems from Fargo to the western border, and in the Valley from Canada to near the South Dakota border. Many towns improved their streets and water and sewer lines. During the 1960s, Fargo, Bismarck, and Jamestown constructed huge civic centers. As the 1970s began, large shopping centers were built in Bismarck and Fargo, and others were planned.

On the farm, the greatest changes in styles of living came about. Electricity came to the farm. In 1935 only 2.3 percent of North Dakota's farms had electricity. Rural electric co-operatives were organized, the first at Cando in 1937.

Diversification brought more potato-growing. (SHSND)

The co-operatives borrowed money from the Rural Electrification Administration and began erecting power lines to serve the farms. By 1976 it would be hard to find a farm without electricity. Electrical power on the farm brought great changes. In their homes, people could have modern appliances and other conveniences that once only townspeople enjoyed. Many farmers modernized their homes. Most farm homes in 1976 were little different from the ones in the city. Modern technology was ending the isolation of farm life.

II. The Farm: Larger and More Diversified

The nature of farming has changed during the last generation. Farms became much larger; farming became very expensive; farming became more diversified. In 1940, North Dakota had 74,000 farms with an average of 500 acres. By the mid-1970s, the number of farms had dropped to less than 42,000 with an average size of almost 1,000 acres. Modern machinery, better farming methods, crop diversification, use of more fertilizers, and conservation practices made small farms increasingly impractical.

The investment needed to enter or continue in farming rose steadily after World War Two. Many farms were too small to compete. In 1959, 5,600 farms averaged a net income of less than $500 on an $18,000 investment. Land values were up sharply by the late 1960s. By 1976 some land in the Red River Valley was selling for $1,200 an acre. Farming now required a huge initial investment in land and machinery, and a farm which was large enough to be profitable.

North Dakota continued to produce wheat as its most important crop. The number of acres devoted to all types of wheat by the 1970s was about 10,000,000 — the same as in 1946. The state leads the nation in producing hard spring wheat, and that wheat accounts for 30 percent of farm income. The state also grows almost 90 percent of the nation's durum. Flax has been another valuable crop, and North Dakota grows about 50 percent of the nation's crop. Acres devoted to flax, however, have gradually decreased during the last fifteen years. Spring barley, used primarily in the malting and brewing industrty, has remained quite constant in acreage since World War Two — about 2,000,000 acres. The same holds true of oats. Farmers were devoting fewer acres to corn and rye by the 1970s.

Diversification of farming came with the expansion of some crops and the introduction of new ones. Acres for potatoes have increased gradually throughout the last thirty years. Especially in the Red River Valley, sugar beets became increasingly important as a good income crop. During World War Two, North Dakota averaged only 16,000 to 17,000 acres in beets. By the 1960s, this was up to 47,000; by 1970, 94,000; by 1974, 138,000. The "oil crops," sunflowers and soybeans, became important during the late 1950s and early 1960s. In 1949, only 7,000 acres of soybeans were seeded; by 1967, the acreage had reached 300,000. Soybean acreage declined some as wheat prices jumped in the 1970s. North Dakota leads the nation in sunflower production. In 1962, 13,000 acres were planted in sunflowers; by 1971, the figure climbed to 456,000 but dropped over 20 percent in the early 1970s as farmers again put more emphasis on wheat. Hog raising remained steady, but cattle production increased. Cattle and calves went up from about 1,500,000 in the 1950s to 2,600,000 in the mid-1970s. North Dakota's agriculture was more diversified by the 1970s. Wheat was still king, however, and still determined the health of the economy.

III. Organizing the Farmer

In the years 1945 to the 1970s, farm organizations grew rapidly. Two major groups became the dominant farm organizations in the state — the Farmers' Union and the Farm Bureau. The Farmers' Union, with 26,000 members in 1945, grew to 44,000 in 1960. By the 1970s its membership was down to 32,000, due, in part, to farm consolidation.

Farmers' Union policies and programs favored more federal legislation to help farmers and to preserve the family-type farm. Friendly to organized labor, the Farmers' Union supported progressive legislation regarding taxes, health insurance, and a guaranteed income for the family farm. Stronger in the western part of the state than in the east, the Farmers' Union tended to support the Democratic party. Although its membership has declined from its all-time high, the Farmers' Union was named by the state's political leaders in a poll taken in 1973 as the single most powerful organization within the state. The Farmers' Union was also a major force in the development of co-operatives. Two large regional co-ops of the organization have had amazing growth. The Grain Terminal Association (G.T.A.) began to buy elevators and market grain in 1938. By 1957 the G.T.A. owned 62 elevators in the state, and another 168 locally-owned elevators shipped grain to the G.T.A. In 1974 the G.T.A. was the state's largest handler of grain. A subsidiary of G.T.A., the Great Plains Supply, owns many lumber yards. The Farmers' Union Central Exchange, organized in 1931 in St. Paul, began to market oil products. Soon, it owned oil wells, pipelines, refineries, fertilizer plants, and machinery warehouses. In the mid-1970s, the Central Exchange was marketing its products with the brand name of Cenex; it is North Dakota's second largest retailer of gasoline. The newspaper, the *North Dakota Union Farmer*, is the voice of the Union.

The Farm Bureau, smaller than the Farmers' Union, grew from 3,000 in 1945 to about 18,000 by the early 1970s. The Bureau is strongest in the eastern part of the state and generally represents a more conservative attitude toward politics and government farm programs. The Farm Bureau has called for an end to government controls because they interfere with the free market. Favoring the free enterprise system, the Bureau favored stronger control of labor organizations, taxing the profits of the co-ops, and placing more stress on the individual efforts of the farmer. The Bureau's insurance program, called Nodak Mutual, is widely used in the state; and its publication, the *North Dakota Farm Bureau News*, presents its views on agricultural policy.

In 1968, a third farm organization entered North Dakota, the National Farmers Organization. This group is dedicated to achieving a fair price for the farmers' products. Through collective bargaining, it hopes to obtain a reasonable return on investment and production costs. Its actions in recent years have included holding products off the market until their prices rise.

Since the North Dakota economy rests on agriculture, these farm organizations, although they differ in their views, play a key role in the state. They have political power and work hard to achieve their objectives. Their approaches to questions vary, but all three work for a prosperous farm economy.

IV. The Labor Movement

In North Dakota the labor movement began in the 1880s. During the nearly one hundred years since that time, workingmen have organized to improve their lives. They have sought fair salaries, reasonable working hours and conditions, the right to bargain with employers, and laws which would strengthen the movement. During the 1890s workers generally toiled for a 10- to 12-hour day, had no sick leave, retirement or vacation plans, and received low wages. In 1910 Fargo carpenters and painters were getting $3.00 per day — about 60 percent of the national average.

The first unions were small and grew slowly. The public was generally unsympathetic to labor's efforts to organize. In 1880 a typographical union (newspaper typesetters) organized in Fargo, and soon Bismarck and Grand Forks had similar groups. By 1900, tailors, horseshoers, letter carriers, and cigar makers had formed unions in many of the towns. The largest and most successful early unions were those of the railroad workers.

Although several local unions were organized, labor believed that more coordination of efforts was essential for success. In 1906 the Trades and Labor Assembly was organized in Fargo. It brought together 13 local unions and coordinated their activities. Other city assemblies were organized during the decade that followed. In 1911 the North Dakota Federation of Labor provided a state-wide organization. Representing mostly the building trades, it gave more strength to the young movement.

In spite of these efforts membership grew slowly, and the unions were unable to win many concessions from employers. In 1906 the bricklayers had to strike in order to gain employer recognition for their union. After a week, they won recognition. In 1909 the Switchmen's Union demanded higher wages and an eight-hour day. They went on strike, but received only a five cent per hour wage increase. In 1910 the Fargo Leather Workers Union with twelve members struck for an eight-hour day. It lost but later received a 50 cent per day wage increase. The public and employers remained hostile to unionization. Workingmen fought for closed shops in which employers could hire only union members. Employers resisted. In 1913, Fargo contractors "locked out" union tradesmen and dealt the labor movement a severe blow. Many members left town. That same year the Industrial Workers of the World (IWW) made headlines in Minot by giving radical street-corner speeches. Several were sent to jail. The IWW had organized only a few farm workers in the northwestern part of the state, and its influence

Coal mining: underground operation. (SHSND)

was small in North Dakota. Even though the other unions were not sympathetic to the IWW, the Minot affair made all labor organizations appear to be radical in the eyes of many citizens.

When the Nonpartisan League came to power during World War One, labor supported it. The League legislature enacted labor-reform measures: workmen's compensation and an eight-hour day and minimum wage for women and children.

During the 1920s the labor movement made little progress. About 2,200 workers and 71 local unions were affiliated with the North Dakota Federation of Labor. The depression of the 1930s brought labor unrest and increased organizational activity. Several towns witnessed strikes. In 1934 and 1935, Fargo truck drivers who were affiliated with the International Brotherhood of Teamsters went on strike, demanding improved working conditions and a closed shop. The workers and police became militant. Trucks were overturned, and tear gas filled the air. Employers refused to bargain, and the strike was lost. The formation of the Congress of Industrial Organizations gave more voice to the non-trade or non-craft workers. In North Dakota new locals brought new people into the labor movement: teachers, meat cutters, packinghouse workers, foundry workers, and state employees at the Jamestown hospital and state penitentiary. Because of the growing influence of labor, the state's Department of Agriculture became the Department of Agriculture and Labor.

During the years since World War Two, North Dakota's workingmen have enjoyed better working conditions and higher wages due both to the general prosperity and the growing numbers of union members. Yet, in an agricultural-

Coal mining: surface, strip operation. (UND-A)

rural state, labor has had to struggle for recognition. In 1948 the movement received a setback when the voters approved a measure which made it illegal for labor and management to negotiate a "union shop" agreement. This meant that employers did not have to hire just union members. Although the 1950s began with a coal miners strike which lasted for six months, the decade was generally free from serious labor disputes. The merger of the American Federation of Labor and the Congress of Industrial Organizations in the mid-1950s brought more coordination to labor's efforts. During the 1960s and 1970s the three large labor groups — the AFL-CIO, the Teamsters, and the railroad unions — grew in numbers and strength. The unions became more politically active. The AFL-CIO's Committee on Political Education worked both for candidates and for legislation favorable toward labor. In 1967 North Dakota established a separate Department of Labor. By the mid-1970s about 18,000 North Dakotans were members of unions — a significant increase from the struggling days of the 1920s.

V. Industrial Growth

North Dakota long had hoped that major industry would locate in the state. Industry would diversify and strengthen the economy. The problem of distance from raw materials and markets remained a serious obstacle in attracting industry. Yet, North Dakota's economy was more diversified in the 1970s than it had been at the end of World War Two.

Many had explored for oil in North Dakota since 1919. In the 1930s, several major oil companies began to negotiate rights for drilling. On April 4, 1951, the Amerada Petroleum Corporation discovered oil at the Clarence Iverson No. 1 well. The oil came from the Nesson Anticline, a geological formation that is part of the Williston Basin, the giant saucer-like depression that underlies two thirds of the state. The discovery in 1951 set off an oil boom. Oilmen, speculators, brokers, and laborers flooded into the area around Tioga, crowding into all available living quarters, overburdening schools and community facilities, and creating a host of new businesses. The frenzy caused many to think that perhaps oil was under their land, and soon drilling leases were in high demand. Some mineral rights sold for as high as $700 an acre.

Drilling for oil was expensive because of the depth of the pools beneath the earth's surface. Amerada Corporation did most of the exploration, but other companies drilled wildcat wells. North Dakota oil production peaked in 1966 with 27,000,000 barrels from 1,965 producing wells. About 20,000,000 barrels from 1,963 wells were produced in 1975. Standard Oil of Indiana built a refinery at Mandan and a pipeline from Tioga to Mandan and from Mandan to Moorhead, Minnesota. A refinery was constructed at Williston, and gas processing plants were built at McGregor, Lignite, and Tioga. The oil and gas industry in North Dakota helped diversify the economy. In an effort to attract other industry to North Dakota, the 1957 legislature created the North Dakota Economic Development Commission. The Commission encouraged businesses, large and

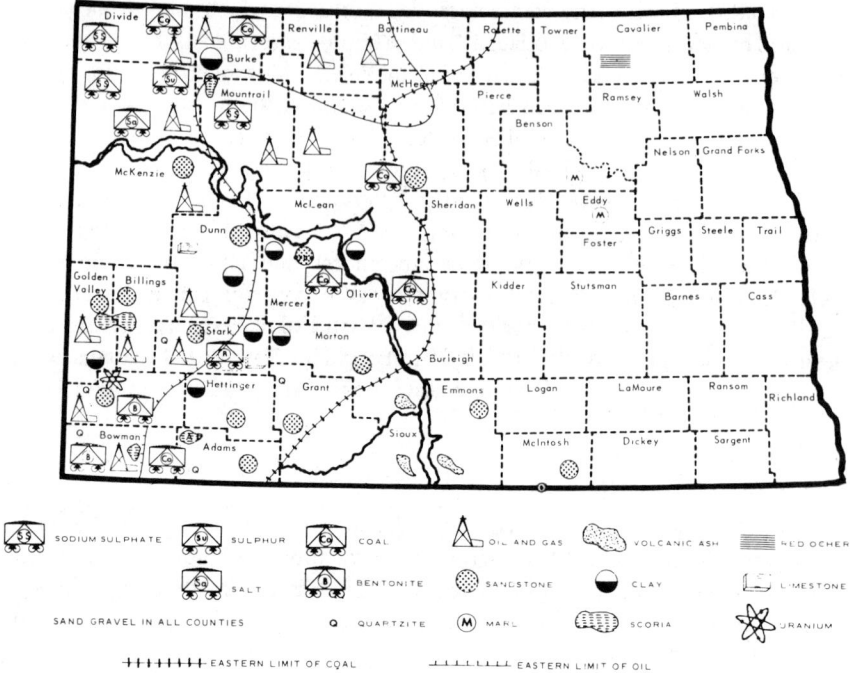

(ND-DPI)

small, to come to North Dakota. With its help and a law allowing towns to sell bonds to build and promote facilities for industries, some success was achieved.

Prior to the establishment of the Economic Development Commission, several industries had success in North Dakota. The Melroe Company began operations at Gwinner in 1947. Its Bobcat tractor was sold throughout the United States. In 1967, Melroe acquired the Reiten Manufacturing Company of Cooperstown. In the early 1970s Melroe was purchased by Clark Equipment, located in Michigan. The Gold Seal Glass Wax Company, headed by Harold Schafer, began in Bismarck. The company had great success and sponsored a national radio program starring Arthur Godfrey. Although its production plants are out of state, the home office is in Bismarck. In 1952 the Bulova Watch Company opened its Jewel Bearing Plant at Rolla. At Hebron, the state's only brick plant experienced growth after World War Two.

During the 1960s and into the 1970s, North Dakota developed in three industrial areas: agricultural-related, electric, and manufacturing industries. Food-related industries grew steadily. For example, 16 cheese plants were opened; beef packing began in West Fargo; sugar beet plants were built in Drayton and Hillsboro; pinto bean processing was started at Hatton; in 1968, a Roman Meal plant opened at Fargo; in 1970, a mustard processing plant began at Grand Forks; in 1971, a sunflower processing plant opened in Fargo.

The electrical industry expanded its plants significantly. Representative of this growth was Basin Elecric, which in 1962 received a $36,600,000 loan from R.E.A. to construct a large generating plant at Stanton. Minnkota Power Cooperative built a plant near Center.

Manufacturing and assembly-line industry showed progress, too. In 1962, Motor Coach Industries of Winnipeg opened an assembly plant in Pembina. It assembles all buses used by both Greyhound and Trailways. By the mid-1960s, a uranium ashing plant was going at Belfield, a salt plant in Williston, and a brewing company, Dakota Beer, in Bismarck; a briquet plant opened at Dickinson and a sulfur plant at Tioga. During the late 1960s and early 1970s, other plants opened in North Dakota: Steiger Tractor in Fargo, Western Gear (aircraft parts) in Jamestown, and Lockheed Aircraft in Minot.

Lignite coal is a rich North Dakota resource and important as an industry. North Dakota is estimated to have 27,000,000 acres of lignite lying under the ground in the western third of the state. This is a total of about 350,000,000,000 tons, about 22 percent of all United States coal. At the present time, 16,000,000,000 tons can be mined with present-day methods, strip mining. Coal mining operations began in 1884. In 1923 there were 259 operating mines, and by the early 1970s, 152,210,000 tons had been mined. Between 1965 and 1973, production doubled to 7,000,000 tons per year. Experts expect this to reach 12,000,000 in the near future. The Bureau of Mines built a lignite research laboratory in Grand Forks. As the demand for energy in the United States increased, North Dakota's lignite took on new importance. In 1973, about 18 percent of the nation's energy came from coal. By 1980, coal is expected to supply 53 percent more of the energy than at present. When burned, lignite releases less sulfur into the atmosphere than other kinds of coal. It also is much easier to mine, since strip mining requires only half the capital investment of underground mining. North Dakota's lignite is used in the state to fire giant generating plants for electricity at Stanton and Center. Utility companies are planning additional plants. North Dakota also exports its coal, mostly to be used as energy for industry. The Burlington Northern Railroad in 1974 averaged 31.5 trains of about 100 cars per week leaving the state with lignite. Lignite may also be exported as gas. Several companies hope to build plants that will convert the coal to gas. The gas would then be piped to the East.

By the mid-1970s, coal was more than a rich resource; it had become a political "hot potato." In an energy-starved world, North Dakota's coal had become "black gold." Voices began to cry out against large-scale, unrestricted mining. Questions were raised: What will the mining do to the land, and how will it affect the people and their lives? How should mining be controlled? How should it be taxed? Legislators hotly debated these issues. The 1975 legislature did enact a higher tax and set up a $2,000,000-agency, Regional Environmental Assessment Program, to study and assess the environmental, economic, and social impact of potential natural resource development.

Above, a power plant near Stanton. Below, a natural gas refinery near Tioga. (UND-LC)

It was logical that the rest of the country would eventually discover the scenic beauty and historical heritage of North Dakota. That discovery after World War Two boomed one of the state's potentially attractive industries — tourism. In 1961 a Travel Division was created in the Highway Department. The Division told the world about the Peace Garden State. Since 1961, travel into North Dakota has increased greatly. By the 1970s, tourism was the third largest industry in the state.

The coming of air bases and missile systems to North Dakota helped diversify the economy and brought the state into international politics. In 1954 the Department of Defense decided to build two air bases, one at Grand Forks and one at Minot. Operational by the early 1960s, the bases were home for the giant B52 bombers, K135 tankers, and fighter planes. In 1964 the Grand Forks Air Base became the launch-control site for Intercontinental Ballistic Missiles (ICBMs). Soon the northeastern part of the state had many deep concrete silos built into the earth. Each silo held a Minuteman Missile tipped with a nuclear warhead.

International events soon affected the state. The United States and the Soviet Union agreed that each nation could build an anti-ballistic missile defense system (ABM). After much debate, the government decided that an ABM system would be constructed in North Dakota to protect the Minuteman Missile complex. Construction began in 1968 at Nekoma near Langdon. Completed in 1975 at a cost of almost $6,000,000,000, the site contained defensive missiles and a huge radar installation. Critics of the system began to argue that the ABM complex in North Dakota was no longer needed. Congress agreed, and in 1976 the government began to dismantle the system.

Both the air bases and ABM installation brought thousands of people and millions of dollars into the state. The air bases stimulated the economies of both Grand Forks and Minot as well as near-by small towns. Langdon and surrounding towns boomed.

The expansion of old industry and the growth of new helped diversify the North Dakota economy. Industry touched more people's lives by the 1970s than ever before. The main obstacle to industrial development was still there: distance to and from markets and raw materials. New industries did have an impact on state income and especially on the communities where they located. As North Dakota passed through the 1970s, however, wheat was still king and the base of the economy.

VI. Garrison Diversion — A Continuing Question

On November 4, 1954, the last load of dirt was put in place on one of the world's largest rolled-earth embankments, the Garrison Dam. Located on the Missouri River 75 miles north of Bismarck, the dam contains 70,000,000 cubic yards of earth; it is one half mile in width at its base and is 60 feet wide at the top. Both a highway and a railroad cross the top of the dam, which is 12,000 feet long. The structure is a marvel of engineering and construction.

Tourism in North Dakota has increased sharply during the last few years. The Badlands region has especially attracted tourists. Above, the Theodore Roosevelt Hotel, restored by the Gold Seal Company, at Medora. Below, cattle branding near Medora. (SHSND)

Garrison Dam was built by the Army Corps of Engineers as one of the units in the overall plan for control, and later development, of the Missouri River Basin. The plan for such control and development was named Pick-Sloan Plan, after its co-authors, General Lewis A. Pick and W. O. Sloan. The project, authorized by the Federal Flood Control Act of 1944, was to achieve six main objectives: flood control, water for irrigation, improvement of navigation, production of hydro-electric power, water for improvement of health and sanitation conditions, and facilities for recreation and fish and wildlife preservation.

Of the six objectives, the control of flooding was foremost; and flooding has been controlled in the Bismarck area. The reservoir that the dam has created is a huge lake with over 609 square miles of water surface. The shore line of the reservoir, named Lake Sakakawea, is approximately 1,500 miles long, making it the largest man-made body of water within the confines of a single state. Recreational activities have flourished. The lake and smaller reservoirs created by the dam have become game refuges for migrating water fowl on their trips to and from Canada. Recreational benefits have enriched the lives of many people who like the outdoors. The dam has also provided the generation of electrical power.

An irrigation project in western North Dakota. (SHSND)

The question of irrigation has produced a controversy that began to swirl throughout the state by 1970. Irrigation, which would bring water to areas with little rainfall, had been a dream of North Dakotans during the dry 1930s. The Missouri River with its great volume would be the ideal source of water for irrigation. If that water could be diverted to other parts of the state, it could be pumped over the fields, bringing moisture at just the right times during the growing season.

Authorized by the act of 1944, the original diversion plan, called the Missouri-Souris Unit, was to irrigate a million acres in the Crosby-Mohall region. When surveys revealed in 1947 that, because of the density of the soil, the region would not be suitable for irrigation, the plan was dropped. By 1957, however, the Bureau of Reclamation reported on a new plan to irrigate one million acres in the drainage basins of the James and Sheyenne rivers southwest of Devils Lake. This plan, the Garrison Diversion Unit, called for huge pumps to lift the water from Lake Sakakawea into the Snake Creeek Reservoir near Garrison Dam. From there, the water would flow down a 73-mile-long McClusky Canal to the Lonetree Reservoir at the headwaters of the Sheyenne River. The plan included canals that would carry the water from Lonetree to areas to be irrigated, and to Devils Lake, which had lost much of its water during the drought-ridden Thirties.

Although the plan was very costly, the Bureau of Reclamation pointed out that in the long run the project would pay for itself. The cost — estimated in 1956 to be $529,000,000 — and the long time for completion — up to 60 years — discouraged congressional authorization and financing. In 1959 the Bureau presented a revised plan that would irrigate only 250,000 acres at a cost of $183,000,000. Again, Congress would not support the program. In 1962 the Bureau of Reclamation unveiled a new plan at a cost of $212,000,000. In 1965, Congress authorized the Garrison Diversion Plan. Work on the pumping station started in 1968, and the McClusky Canal was begun in 1970.

On the state level, other governmental action was taken in connection with Garrison Diversion plans. In 1955 the legislature passed an act allowing the establishment of a Garrison Conservancy District. The District is a 25-county area that would be affected by the diversion. The purpose of the Conservancy District was to promote the development of Garrison Diversion, to contract with the United States government and the state of North Dakota for construction, operation, and maintenance of the Garrison Diversion Unit, to operate and maintain the water supply and irrigation works serving the lands within the district, and to levy a tax, not to exceed 1 mill annually, to finance the District contracts and operations. Since 1966, the Conservancy District has levied the 1-mill tax, which amounts to about $400,000 dollars per year.

As Garrison Diversion progressed, some began to raise questions about its long-run benefit to the state. Some argued that the installation of an irrigation system would be so costly to the farmer that he might be better off investing his money in better equipment and other means of improving his operation. The farmer would pay $1.20 per acre for 40 years to help finance the cost of

Missile site construction. (GFH)

construction. In addition, he would pay $5.00 to $8.00 per acre a year for operation, maintenance, and repair of the system which brought water to his land. He would also have to pay for his own irrigation system.

Ecological concerns entered the debate. The Bureau of Reclamation projected that North Dakota would receive an annual benefit of millions of dollars from increased waterfowl, food production, and hunting and fishing. Opponents claimed that loss of wetlands would occur, resulting in the annual loss of 40,000 to 120,000 ducks. Fearing the concentration of undesirable substances in reservoir waters, and the introduction of rough fish into streams, the critics held that fishing would not improve because of the project.

Quality of water and pollution of rivers raised another issue. Those critical of the Diversion project claimed that irrigation runoff would pollute the streams into which it flows. They held that runoff into the Sheyenne River and other streams that flow into the Red River would pollute the Red to the point that it would be unacceptable to the Canadians. Because of this concern, government officials in the province of Manitoba voiced their objection to the Diversion project. In 1975 the International Joint Commission began to study the international river question.

In 1972, opponents of further development of the project formed the Committee to Save North Dakota. The Committee went to court to stop the work on the McClusky Canal until after the full impact of Diversion could be studied. By the mid-1970s, Garrison Diversion had joined the coal development issue as a major and controversial concern of the people of North Dakota.

*   *   *   *   *   *

The years since World War Two were marked by economic expansion and a general prosperity. Income generated in the state increased almost seven times. Although the health of King Wheat had a relapse during the late 1950s and early 1960s, it had never been better than in the late 1960s and 1970s. Agriculture and the state's economy moved toward diversification. Economic problems troubled the 1976 North Dakotan, especially Garrison Diversion and coal development, but at the same time, the state was economically sounder and better off than at any time in its history.

19 Political Change: Since 1945

The years that followed World War Two witnessed far-reaching political change in North Dakota. The Republican Organizing Committee (ROC) emerged out of the war years as the political force in the state. Although it could never defeat its arch-foe, William Langer, it took control of the Republican party away from him and the Nonpartisan League. For 16 years the ROC held the governorship and, most of the time, the legislature. Its success forced a merger of the old Nonpartisan League with the Democrats in 1956. North Dakota became a two-party state: Republican and Democratic-Nonpartisan League. The merger gave the Democratic-NPL new strength, and after 1960 it controlled the governorship for 16 years — although it controlled the legislature only once.

Many complex political issues faced the state as it moved toward and into the 1970s. Among the many political questions that faced North Dakotans, constitutional reform, the Equal Rights Amendment, and reapportionment illustrate the complexity of the the state's political concerns.

I. A New Political Force: The ROC

In 1943 a group of state senators — Joseph B. Bridston, an insurance man and founder of First Federal Savings & Loan of Grand Forks; Rilie Morgan, an editor from Grafton; Fred G. Aandahl, a farmer from near Litchville; and Milton R. Young, a farmer from near Berlin — succeeded in forming the Republican Organizing Committee (ROC). The movement for such an organization had begun in 1942, when a coalition of anti-Langer people, calling themselves

"Progressive Republicans," united against Langerism to return Democrat John Moses for a third term as governor.

By 1944 the ROC was a well-organized political faction. It had a permanent state committee with headquarters in Bismarck, and a state-wide organization. Rilie Morgan served as ROC chairman, and the campaign manager was Milton Young. Its first convention was held at Bismarck in 1944. In a statement of its principles, the ROC accepted the state industries and called on all groups — labor, farmers, and business — to unite to work for the prosperity of North Dakota. The ROC gained support from anti-Langer Republicans, from some farmers (especially the Farm Bureau), and some businessmen (especially the Greater North Dakota Association). The ROC leaders stressed honesty and efficiency in government; they firmly believed that Langer and his Nonpartisan League had stood for neither of these qualities.

In 1944 Gerald P. Nye was up for re-election to the United States Senate. At its nominating convention, the ROC backed Nye for senator; William Lemke, an anti-Langer Nonpartisan Leaguer, for the House of Representatives; and Fred Aandahl for governor. The Democrats endorsed John Moses for the Senate. Moses agreed to run for the Senate only if the Democratic party guaranteed him a federal appointment if he lost. Lynn Stambaugh ran for the Senate as an independent third candidate.

During the campaign, both Aandahl and Lemke supported Nye. Moses became ill and in September underwent surgery; Moses, assuring his supporters that he was completely recovered, won the election. Stambaugh had taken enough votes away from Nye to give Moses the victory. The ROC won the governor's chair with the victory of Aandahl, and other ROC candidates took state offices. John Moses died shortly after taking office as United States Senator; Governor Aandahl appointed Milton R. Young to fill the vacant office. Hard work and energetic leadership had paid dividends; the ROC had won its first battle.

After the 1944 election, the ROC became the dominent political faction within the state. Fred Aandahl won re-election for governor in 1946, and the ROC controlled both houses of the legislature. In a special election for John Moses' former Senate seat, Young won the post to which he had been appointed earlier. Joseph B. Bridston waged a strong campaign to unseat Langer in the primary, but he lost. Langer went on to win in the fall.

The 1947 legislature witnessed a battle between the ROC and the Farmers' Union. The struggle centered around bills which were aimed at the Farmers' Union insurance program and the taxing of surplus earnings of its co-operatives. The battle with the Farmers' Union insurance program had started in 1946, when the state Insurance Commissioner, Otto Krueger, an ROC member, had denied the Farmers' Union Insurance Department, known as the National Union Security Association, a renewal of its license. The company, however, was still able to offer its policies in the state as a fraternal order; competing insurance firms claimed that the Farmers' Union was selling insurance without a license.

Send These Republicans to Washington
UNITED STATES SENATORS

JOSEPH B. BRIDSTON

MILTON R. YOUNG

REPRESENTATIVES IN CONGRESS

JOHN HJELLUM

WILLIAM LEMKE

The 1946 ROC primary election campaign poster. Milton R. Young and William Lemke won. NPL Senator William Langer defeated Joseph B. Bridston, and NPL Representative Usher L. Burdick beat John Hjellum. (UND-LC)

Senator Langer chats with his political foe, Governor Fred Aandahl, 1952. (GFH)

Grand Forks attorney Carroll Day, who represented several insurance companies as legal counsel, spearheaded the campaign against the Farmers' Union. When the bills opposed by the Farmers' Union passed the Senate, Senator Day initiated a full Senate investigation of the Farmers' Union insurance business. The ROC-controlled Senate began its probe. The Farmers' Union countered with an all-out newspaper campaign. It prepared a fact sheet entitled the "Legislative Strangle," the first page of which pictured a black hand covering the state. Farmers' Union President Glenn Talbott gave a radio talk about what was happening in the legislature, stating that "war had been declared on the Farmers' Union." In the end, the bills against the farm organization were defeated, and the Farmers' Union hailed this as a victory and declared that it would fight to protect itself.

The battle in the 1947 legislature brought the Farmers' Union squarely into politics. In June 1947, President Talbott convened a meeting at Jamestown of county officers, directors of co-operative affiliates, and the State Farmers' Union Board of Directors. He called on the Farmers' Union to rally its voting strength behind progressive candidates. The meeting adjourned as an official Farmers' Union meeting and reconvened as a political action group, known as the "Farmers' Union Progressive Alliance." This group, together with organized labor and the Nonpartisan League, formed the Committee for Progressive Unity

Senator Young campaigning with President Dwight D. Eisenhower in 1952. (GFH)

in 1948. At its state convention, the League endorsed a ticket that represented the three groups which had formed the Committee for Progressive Unity. It was successful at election time. The League elected Usher L. Burdick to the United States House of Representatives; it captured a majority of the House in the state legislature, and a few state offices. But it lost in its bid to capture the governorship; the ROC's Fred Aandahl could not be beaten.

By 1950 the Farmers' Union was leaning toward the Democratic party. It wanted a party that would unite the liberals. The Farmers' Union adopted a resolution urging the Nonpartisan League to file its candidates in the Democratic column for the upcoming primary election; the League rejected the proposal. In the 1950 election, the ROC was again victorious. Milton Young was re-elected as senator; Fred Aandahl won election to the House of Representatives, and Norman Brunsdale became governor. The ROC held control of both houses of the state legislature. Two years later, in 1952, the ROC went all out to beat its old enemy, William Langer. The popular three-time governor, Fred Aandahl, gave Langer a hard fight for the Senate seat, but lost. The ROC did send Otto Krueger to the House of Representatives. Usher Burdick, long-time Leaguer, retained his seat. Ten years after its birth, the ROC still controlled the governorship, and in Washington one House and one Senate seat.

II. The Birth of a Two-Party State

At the beginning of the 1950s the Nonpartisan League was split into two factions — the liberals, called the insurgents, and the conservatives, called the old guard. The old guard supported the Republican party and wanted to keep the Nonpartisan League in the Republican column. They were generally anti-Farmers' Union and anti-labor. The insurgents, in contrast, who supported the Farmers' Union and labor, believed that they were more in tune with the politics of the Democrats. Both the ROC and NPL insurgents wanted party realignment: the old guard Leaguers should join with the ROC, and the insurgents in the League should merge with the Democratic party.

In 1956, the shift came about. The Nonpartisan League convention, controlled by the insurgents, voted to place its candidates in the Democratic column. Later, the Democratic convention endorsed the League candidates and accepted its platform. The ROC held a unity convention and welcomed the old guard Leaguers. North Dakota had become a two-party state. The Democratic-Nonpartisan League party would now oppose the Republican party. The confusion over the various political factions would end. Candidates identified themselves as Republicans, Democratic-Nonpartisan League, or independents. The 1956 election saw victory for the united ROC and old guard Leaguers when John Davis became governor and Milton Young was returned to the Senate. Some old-time Leaguers such as Usher L. Burdick and William Langer remained in the Republican party because they had run as League Republicans for so many years.

Even after the merger, the Democratic-NPL party was a minority party. As time went on, however, it gained strength in the state legislature. In 1958, Fargo attorney Quentin N. Burdick, the son of Usher L. Burdick and a strong Farmers' Union supporter, won a seat in the United States House of Representatives — the first Democrat to do so in the history of the state. John Davis was returned to the governor's chair, giving the ROC continued control in the state.

Senator Langer and Senator Young in the mid-1950s. (GFH)

William Guy takes the oath of office to begin his twelve-year career as governor. (GFH)

III. The Democratic-Nonpartisan League in Power

In 1960 the tide turned. Langer, who had been re-elected in 1958 without campaigning at all, died in late 1959. In a special election to fill Langer's seat, Quentin Burdick defeated Governor John Davis. That fall, Democratic-Nonpartisan Leaguer William L. Guy, a farmer from Amenia, defeated Republican C.P. Dahl, Davis' lieutenant governor, to become the governor — a post he would hold for an unprecedented 12 years. In 1962, Guy defeated Mapleton farmer Mark Andrews by 2,007 votes; and in 1964, when the term of governor was changed from two to four years, Guy won over Don Halcrow of Drayton by a comfortable margin. Again, in 1968, Guy won, defeating Robert McCarney, a Bismarck auto dealer, who had challenged the endorsed candidate in the Republican primary and won. Guy was followed in office by fellow Democratic-NPLer Arthur Link — a farmer from Alexander, a long-time member of the North Dakota legislature, and a one-term congressman. In 1972, Link defeated Richard Larson from Grand Forks.

In the United States Senate, Republican Milton Young and Democratic-NPL Quentin Burdick continued to hold their seats. Burdick's strongest challenge came in 1964, when he defeated Thomas Kleppe by 35,000 votes. In 1974, Young was almost unseated by Governor Guy. The campaign debate centered around Young's many years in the Senate and his age. The Republicans claimed that because of Young's long years, he had seniority — a valuable asset to North Dakotans. The Democrats downgraded the seniority claim and argued that after

Governor William Guy with former governor, John Davis. (GFH)

29 years it was time for a change. The election, one of the closest in North Dakota history, was so close that a recount of all ballots took place. Six weeks after the election, Milton Young was declared the winner by only 177 votes.

In the elections for the United States House of Representatives, the Republicans fared better than the Democrats. Democrats won only three House elections: Burdick in 1958, Rolland Redland in 1964, and Arthur Link in 1970. In a special election in 1963 to fill the seat made vacant by the death of Hjalmar C. Nygaard, Republican Mark Andrews won over John Hove by 4,692 votes. Andrews retained his seat in the House, and in 1972 became North Dakota's sole representative after the 1970 census showed that the state was entitled to only one seat in the House.

Presidential elections have favored the Republicans with one exception. In 1964, Democrat Lyndon Johnson carried the state over Barry Goldwater. North Dakota's voters chose Richard Nixon in 1960, 1968, and 1972.

During the 12 years of Governor Guy's administration, 1961 to 1973, North Dakota, like the nation, experienced many changes. Government became more complex as it attempted to meet the problems of the modern world. State government moved toward new approaches to problem solving. There are many examples of this. The voters approved a three-day organizational session in December for the legislature. These three days are not counted in the 60 days that the legislature can meet under the state's Constitution., The Legislative Council, a body that meets between the biennial sessions to plan and review new legislation, has increased from eight subcommittees in 1961 to 17 in 1971-73; it does much to help the legislative process. A State Planning Commission was created in 1963; in 1969 it was transferred to the Department of Accounts and Purchases, an agency set up in 1959 to handle the state's fiscal affairs. The office of Tax Commissioner was given additional responsibilities, and district offices were established to give taxpayers information on a year-around basis. In 1967 the legislature established the North Dakota Combined Law Enforcement Council to set standards and provide training for police officers, sheriffs, and court personnel, and to standardize and inspect jails. The State Highway Patrol established training programs, and in 1970 a Law Enforcement Training Center was begun.

The Public Service Commission was given jurisdiction over matters regarding natural gas and strip mining. The State Water Commission expanded its activity regarding the state's water resources. In 1967 the State Water Pollution Control Board was established. The legislature set up the North Dakota State Park Service in 1965 to oversee the state parks. By the 1970s, North Dakota had 10,452 miles of hard-surfaced city and rural roads, and in 1972 the administration of the highways became the responsibility of the Traffic Safety Programs Division, an independent agency. The Department of Social Services replaced the Department of Public Welfare in 1971. These changes were all part of modernizing and bringing state government up to date to meet new problems and challenges.

IV. An Attempt at Constitution Making

One of the significant political developments of the postwar generation was an attempt to revise and update the state Constitution. The need to revise the Constitution had been discussed for years. The original Constitution, written in 1889, has been amended 95 times.

Most experts on state constitutions agreed that the North Dakota document has several basic weaknesses. The governor is made responsible for the administration of state government, yet he does not have enough power to carry out that responsibility; he is surrounded by officials who are elected and are not directly responsible to him. The state Constitution also includes laws that should have been left to the legislature to decide. Laws that ordinarily could be changed by the legislature can be changed only by constitutional amendments. For example, Article Eleven contains 2,250 words to detail how the administration of public and school bonds should be handled. Written after a time of abuses by territorial officials, the Constitution left many decisions to the people themselves. Apparently because public officials can not be trusted to make appointments, the

On the campaign trail. Above, Senator Quentin Burdick. Below, Representative Mark Andrews. (GFH)

Governor Arthur Link. (GFH)

voters must elect many officials and understand the qualifications for such offices. In addition, the voters must know what proposed amendments to the Constitution are about and to make decisions as to their impact. As time went on and North Dakota moved toward a modern society, constitutional deficiencies became evident to many.

In 1963 the legislature set up a special commission of prominent citizens and legislators to make recommendations for change. The 1965 legislature revised and rewrote some of the commission's proposals and submitted them to a vote of the people; they were defeated. The 1967 legislature again submitted constitutional proposals to the people. The people once more rejected the proposals. In 1969 the legislature decided to ask the people to call a Constitutional Convention. In the 1970 primary election, the people agreed by a vote of 56,734 to 40,094.

That fall, people elected 98 delegates from the state's legislative districts. The delegates held a three-day organizational meeting at Bismarck in April 1971. At this meeting a slate of officers was selected and six committees were formed to study specific parts of the present Constitution. These committees held a series of meetings throughout the state in order to let the citizens express their views.

The Convention opened January 3, 1972, with Frank Wenstrom of Williston as president. The sessions were open to the public, and at committee meetings citizens expressed their views to the delegates. Each proposal made by a committee was brought to the Convention floor for debate and vote. The Convention accepted the proposed constitution by a vote of 91 to 4 (three delegates were absent and finished its work on February 17. The proposed constitution would go to the people for a vote.

The proposed constitution was modern. Among other things, it gave the governor more responsibility by allowing him to appoint some state officials who had formerly been elected. It also made some changes on limits of state bonding debt, property taxation, the power of government to take land under eminent domain, and bail for criminal offenses. It allowed the legislature to establish less than 12-man juries. The Convention placed four specific proposals on the ballot for the voter to decide upon: a one or two-house legislature; a change in the number of signatures required for initiatives, referenda, and initiated constitutional amendments; adult status for 18 year-olds; and a prohibition against the legislature's authorizing lotteries and gift enterprises. The proposed constitution also contained a controversial "right to work" provision. This allowed a person the right to join or not to join a labor union. Labor attacked the new document because of the "right to work" provision. Other groups joined in the battle to convince the voters not to accept the proposed constitution. The delegates, who had already spent months in study and debate, defended the new document and explained misunderstandings. On election day in April 1972, the proposed constitution was defeated by a convincing vote of 107,643 to 64,073. North Dakotans seemed to prefer a piece-meal approach to changing the Constitution. The 1975 legislature passed a resolution that directed the Legislative Council to study constitutional revision and report its findings to the 1977 legislative assembly.

V. The ERA Battle

To amend the United States Constitution, three fourths of the states in the Union must agree to the proposed amendment. Congress decides how the states shall express agreement, and in the case of the proposed 27th amendment, it was to be done by the state legislatures. The 27th amendment is the Equal Rights Amendment, or ERA. To become the supreme law of the land, 38 states must approve it. The amendment reads: "Equality of rights under the law shall not be denied or abridged by the United States or by any state on account of sex. The Congress shall have the power to enforce, by appropriate legislation, the provisions of this article."

This proposed amendment caused a storm of controversy in the United States, perhaps more than the 19th Amendment, which gave women the right to vote. The Supreme Court has ruled that although one legislative session rejects a

Keli Rylance (daughter of Representative Daniel Rylance) votes for ERA during the 1975 legislative session.

proposed amendment, the following one can approve it. Supporters of the 27th amendment realized that if passage were to be had in the 1975 legislative session, a well-organized campaign would be necessary. To conduct such a campaign, a new organization, the Coordinating Council for the Equal Rights Amendment, was formed. The Council had the support of the League of Women Voters, the North Dakota Business and Professional Women's Clubs, the American Association of University Women, Common Cause, the North Dakota Education Association, and others. The Council began its efforts by sending letters to the wives of incumbent legislators and candidates during the fall elections. Headquartered in Bismarck, the ERA forces were well organized and lobbied tirelessly for their cause.

The amendment passed the Senate, 28 to 22. To secure passage in the House required greater efforts. After intensive lobbying by ERA supporters, the House passed the measure by only a one-vote majority. North Dakota was the only state to ratify the 27th amendment in 1975.

VI. The Reapportionment Question

The question of reapportionment has been a lively and complex political issue. Representation in the legislature was provided for in the Constitution written in 1889. The legislature is to have a Senate of not more than 50 members

President Harry Truman campaigns through North Dakota in 1952. (GFH)

nor less than 30; the House of Representatives, no more than 140 nor less than 60. Senators are to be elected from districts with no more than one senator per district, and the House members are elected at large from these districts. The legislature is supposed to make adjustment in representation to take into account population shifts as reflected in state and federal censuses. Such an adjustment is called reapportionment. Reapportionment is to insure that each member of the legislature represents as closely as possible the same number of people. The state legislature failed to reapportion itself after 1931; by the 1960s there was over-representation from the rural areas that had lost population and under-representation from the cities which had gained population. Such a situation is called malapportionment. During the 1960s, the United States Supreme Court ruled that both houses of a state legislature must be apportioned on the basis of population: "one man, one vote." The federal government would force reapportionment where needed.

In 1965, a three-judge federal district court decided that North Dakota was malapportioned and ordered a new plan. The new plan provided that 49 senators and 98 representatives were to be elected from 39 legislative districts. This plan was in effect until 1972. Because the 1971 legislature failed to reapportion itself, in 1972 the federal court ordered a new plan that was to be in effect for the 1973 legislative session only. The 1973 legislature did pass a new apportionment plan, but Governor Link vetoed it. One of the reasons the governor vetoed the plan was that it contained districts from which more than one senator would be elected. There were five such multi-senatorial districts. The legislature, controlled by the Republicans, overrode the veto, and the plan was to go into effect. However, by means of referendum procedure, the plan was referred to a vote of the people. Also to be voted on was an initiated constitutional amendment which would have created a commission to reapportion the state with single-member senatorial districts. In the special election held in December 1973, the people of the state voted "no" on both questions, leaving the state without a reapportionment plan.

In 1974 the federal district court again ordered the 1972 plan to be in effect until the 1980 federal census. The plan was appealed to the United States Supreme Court. In its decision, the Court ruled that the district court decision was unacceptable because the 1972 plan contained multi-senatorial districts and because there was a variance of 3,488 people between the largest and smallest districts.

Because of the Supreme Court action, the 1975 legislature formed a joint committee to draw up a new plan. The plan provided for 51 senators and 102 representatives to be elected from 38 districts. There were 39 numbered districts because the legislature decided to leave out unlucky number 13. The plan also provided for single-member districts in the state's five largest cities: Grand Forks, Minot, Fargo, Jamestown, and Bismarck. A two-senator district in the northern part of Minot was an exception. The governor allowed the plan to become law without signing it.

The plan was again challenged in the courts; a federal district court presented a new reapportionment plan in December 1975. The new plan called for 50 senators and 100 representatives. It also provided for single-member senatorial districts. The legislature now would more truly reflect the population shifts that had taken place in North Dakota since World War Two.

*   *   *   *   *   *

Compared with the politics of the generation prior to World War Two, the politics of the last thirty years have been more stable and more conservative. The eruption of the Nonpartisan League with its "state socialism," removal from office of the governor and two other high officials, and the political chaos of the 1930s were reflections of a state attempting to deal with economic problems over which it had little control. When times were good and King Wheat was healthy, the people of North Dakota have been less inclined to "rock the boat." Prosperity breeds more conservative approaches to economic questions. Neither the ROC nor even the Democratic-NPL proposed anything approaching the radicalism of the old NPL. Yet, North Dakota's problems grew more complex as new issues arose: an unwieldly Constitution, reapportionment, coal development, Garrison Diversion, equal rights for women, and a web of other environmental and governmental concerns. The approach to answering these questions has been more deliberate, more cautious, and more orderly.

20 Progress of a People

World War Two ushered in a generation of progress. In many respects, North Dakota in the 1970s was a better place to live than it had been in the 1940s. During this generation, North Dakota, with more money in its treasury and more federal funds, moved, sometimes slowly and painfully, toward solving its "people problems." North Dakota seemed to come out of the depression with a renewed determination to give its children a better education and its people a better life. After 1945 the state moved forward; it did not solve all its problems, but it did bring about changes that improved the quality of life.

I. Profile of the People

Since 1920, two population patterns describe North Dakota: out-migration from the state, and a rural-to-urban shift within the state. In 1930 the North Dakota population reached its highest point with 681,000 people. The second boom of settlers after 1900 had doubled the population from 319,000 in 1900 to 647,000 in 1920. When drought and depression hit in the 1930s, some concluded that the land could not support so many people; many lost their farms; others gave up. People began leaving the state; this pattern of out-migration has continued to be characteristic of North Dakota's population. By 1940 the population had declined to 642,000, and by 1950 to 620,000. During the 1950s the population increased slightly, reaching 632,000 in 1960; but by 1970 it was down to 618,000. People have left North Dakota for many reasons. The main one, however, has been lack of economic opportunity. Mechanization and large farms discouraged many in farming; lack of significant industrial growth provided few new jobs.

Within the state, the movement of people has been away from the farms and small villages toward the larger cities. This trend became evident during the 1930s. By 1940, 131,923 North Dakotans lived in towns with a population over 2,500; by 1970, the number had reached 273,442. Since 1950 the farm-to-city shift has been pronounced. Between 1950 and 1970, Fargo's population grew 32 percent, to 53,500; Grand Forks, 44 percent to 40,000; Bismarck, 69 percent to 35,500; Minot, 48 percent to 34,200; Dickinson, 57 percent to 13,000.

During these same twenty years, rural counties lost many people: McLean lost 40 percent of its population; Sheridan, 38 percent; Logan, 33 percent; Billings, 32 percent; Kidder, 29 percent; Renville, 29 percent. All counties without urban centers lost population. Some small towns grew between 1950 and 1970, especially during the 1950s; Bowman, 27 percent; Cooperstown, 25 percent; Bottineau, 19 percent; Langdon, 18 percent. Most, however, remained about the same or lost people: Mott declined 13 percent; Hettinger, six percent; Oakes, two percent; Lakota, six percent. The Velva area illustrates the rural-to-town movement of people: between 1950 and 1970 the village of Velva gained six percent, while the rural Velva area lost 36 percent of its people. In 1940, 89,000 people worked on farms; in 1970 only 35,000 listed themselves in the census report as "farmers and farm managers"; another 8,300 called themselves "farm laborers." North Dakota's economy was still agricultural, but fewer people worked the land.

North Dakota's population changed in other ways, too, during the last generation. The immigrants who had come in droves had become Americanized. In 1900, one person in three in North Dakota was an immigrant. By 1940, one in 12 was foreign-born; and by the mid-1970s, the day of the immigrant was nearly over. Foreign-language newspapers were gone; only on special occasions did churches hold foreign-language services. One can still hear Icelandic on a street in Mountain, or German at Strasburg, or Norwegian in Northwood, but this is the exception. The postwar era, and especially the coming of air bases, brought blacks to North Dakota. To see a black on the streets of Grand Forks in 1940 was rare; by the 1970s, it was common. Over 2,500 blacks claim North Dakota as home.

The North Dakota Indian population has increased steadily, from 6,969 in 1900 to 10,114 in 1940. By 1970, 14,369 Indians lived in the state, a little over two percent of the total population. About half lived on or near the Turtle Mountain Indian Reservation in Rolette County; about 2,000 at Fort Berthold; 1,700 at Fort Totten; and the rest on the North Dakota part of Standing Rock.

By 1900, the spirit of the Indian people had been broken. The government's Bureau of Indian Affairs attempted to force the Indian into white society by making the Indian a land owner and educating him in white values. Torn between white society and traditional Indian ways, many Indians became apathetic and disillusioned. By the 1920s, some reformers began to call for changes in

INDIAN RESERVATIONS IN NORTH DAKOTA

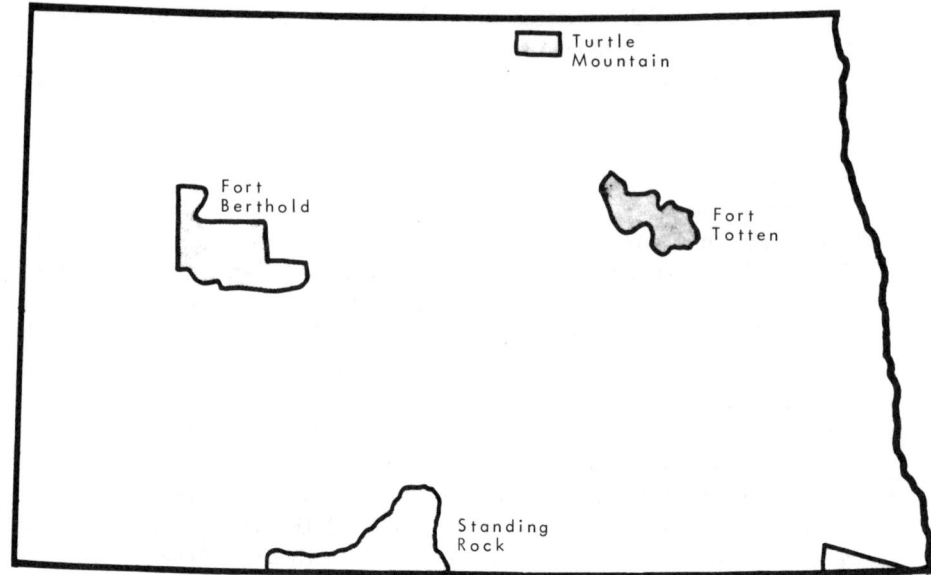

(ND-DPI)

government policy toward the Indian. In 1924 all Indians received United States citizenship. In 1928 the Brookings Institute in Washington conducted a survey of conditions among the Indians. Its report showed that poverty was wide-spread and that most Indians were extremely discouraged about the future. In response to this report, Congress passed the Indian Reorganization Act of 1934. This act gave Indian tribes the right to approve their own constitutions, elect councils, and appoint business committees. Funds became available for loans to finance agricultural and business enterprises and for higher education. The Reorganization Act represented an attempt to deal with the Indians in a new way.

The new tribal government produced new Indian leaders and provided more Indian voice in reservation matters. For example, the Three Tribes at Fort Berthold set up a Tribal Council of ten, elected from five districts for two-year terms. This Council elects the chairman. On some reservations the Chairmen are elected at-large by the people. Councils have promoted the welfare of their people, especially with the expansion of federal programs in the 1960s. For example, in the mid-1960s the Council at Standing Rock established a Housing Authority to build low-rent housing, a short-term loan program, and a Community Action Program under the Economic Opportunity Act for the improvement of education, youth programs, and housing.

In the years since World War Two, the life of the North Dakota Indian has improved. The Bureau of Indian Affairs (BIA) lessened its drive to make the Indian into a white; federal programs brought better housing and education. Yet, in spite of this, the standard of living is low; many are eligible for welfare. Some farm, and some ranch. Employment opportunities near the reservations are very few. For example, of the Turtle Mountain Chippewa, about 500 work for the government or government programs; 100 work at the Jewel Bearing Plant at Rolla; 100 work for the state at San Haven Hospital. Some Indian groups have begun their own businesses, such as the Four Bears Motel complex near New Town.

The more relaxed control by the BIA, and the development of tribal self-government have developed a growing belief in progress among many Indians. By the late 1960s, a revival of Indian culture and history was beginning. Special educational materials on Indian history and life were becoming available. Colleges and universities began Indian Studies Programs. The American Indian Movement was calling attention to Indian affairs. During the early 1970s, four new Indian colleges, one on each reservation, were established and funded by the federal government. Indian students now have a chance to study their heritage as well as receive a general education near their homes. Over 300 full- and part-time students were enrolled in these colleges in 1975.

II. The Revolution in the Public Schools

Between 1900 and 1920, the number of students in North Dakota's schools more than doubled, from 78,000 to 168,000. More than half of them attended the state's 5,000 one-room schools. The small rural schools continued to offer less extensive educational opportunities than the town schools. School years were shorter; attendance was poorer; teachers had much less training and worked for very low wages. Of the 9,500 high-school students in 1920, most were from the towns. But many high schools were small; of the 144 in the state in 1920, half had less than 50 pupils.

Some educators believed that North Dakota had built too many schools for its population and that the state needed to reform its system. Men such as Webster Merrifield, the President of the University, and Neil C. Macdonald, a well-educated, former rural school teacher, called on the legislature to make improvements. In 1911 a reform-minded legislature passed a school reform measure. This law gave state aid to rural schools that would raise standards, and it established the position of school inspector. Macdonald, as inspector and later as State Superintendent, worked hard to improve the schools.

By 1920 the rural schools were improving. Attendance increased, and more students finished the eighth grade. Many more farm children completed high school. Yet, most rural schools were still of poor quality. Only one in 45 teachers had attended college, and only a little over half had completed high school. Most rural schools had a new teacher every year because of the low pay.

In spite of a shaky farm economy during the 1920s, North Dakota continued to spend a high percentage of its revenues on education — it ranked eighth in the nation. More and more children were going to school; high-school enrollments

Many school buildings which had served the people since the turn of the century were replaced by new, modern structures. Above, the old school. Below, the remains of the old in the shadow of the new. (GFH)

NORTH DAKOTA: THE HERITAGE OF A PEOPLE

doubled during the decade. Rural teachers were better prepared; by 1930 only one in 100 had not completed high school, and one in three had attended a teacher-training school. Yet, the rural schools struggled. Salaries for teachers were among the lowest in the nation; the small schools could not afford the newest books and equipment. North Dakota was not getting a fair return on its investment in education. Too many schools with too few students made education very expensive.

The depression of the 1930s brought a crisis to the classroom. Farmers lost their crops; many city folks were unemployed; thousands could not pay their taxes. Funds available to run the schools declined; many school boards faced empty treasuries. Teachers had their salaries cut drastically; many lost their jobs. To help keep the classrooms open, the legislature passed a two-percent sales tax. It was not enough. Federal government programs employed many teachers and kept the schools open. Over 600 rural schools were forced to close; even so, by 1940 there were still over 3,500 one-room schools in the state.

The years after World War Two brought far-reaching changes to North Dakota's school system: an increase in state financial support, the consolidation of small schools, more qualified teachers, and higher standards. Many North Dakotans came to realize that these changes would have to come if the state's children were going to be prepared to live in a much more complex world — a world of atomic energy, computers, and space flights.

A typical North Dakota classroom of the 1940s. (FSA/UND-LC)

In 1947 the legislature passed legislation which began a revolution in North Dakota education — a better and fairer method of financial support, and a reorganization plan. County "equalization funds" — a tax on all property in a county — brought more money. Later, a special county fund was set up to support high schools. This "equalized" taxation for education. Before, many people had not paid taxes to support a high school, since 80 percent of the school districts did not have high schools. Those in districts without high schools sent their children to other districts, but paid no taxes to support that school. In 1959 the legislature established a foundation program to finance public education; county taxes and state funds were to pay 60 percent of the cost of educating a student. Payments were made to school districts on a teacher-pupil basis for elementary schools, and on an average daily attendance basis for high schools. Since 1959 state support has continued to increase.

The reorganization plan permitted counties to consolidate districts with the approval of the state and of the voters in the districts. Reorganization came slowly. Many rural people had strong attachments to the schools which they and their parents had attended, and they did not want to see them abolished. Small towns hated to see their basketball or football teams hang up their uniforms for the last time. It was hard to set the past aside for educational change. Yet, reorganization came. Improved roads and state funds for transporting students made consolidation more acceptable. In 1947 the state had 2,271 school districts; by 1973 it had only 372. The real movement toward consolidation came during the 1960s. In 1959 over 20,000 children still attended one-room schools; by the early 1970s only 335 children went to the small, rural schools, while almost 98,000 were in graded elementary schools.

Mayville State College in the 1920s.

Reorganization and improved funding worked a revolution in North Dakota's school system. More students were now receiving a better education from more qualified teachers. In 1930, less than 40 percent of the students finished the eighth grade; 51 percent of those who began high school finished their work. By 1950, about 65 percent were finishing both. Twenty years later in the 1970s, over 80 percent completed the eighth grade, while of those who went on to high school, nearly 90 percent got their diplomas. North Dakota had much better qualified teachers by the 1970s. Eighty percent of the elementary teachers had completed college. In the high schools, 99 percent had college degrees; 39 percent had done graduate work.

The day of the little country school house was over. North Dakotans had come to realize that they had built too many schools for too few people. The adjustment was slow and painful. Sixty years after Neil Macdonald began the fight to improve the state's schools, the battle was won.

III. Higher Education in a Changing World

In 1920, less than 2,000 students were enrolled in the state's schools of higher education. The normal schools such as Valley City and Mayville trained elementary teachers in two-year or summer programs. The normal schools also offered high-school work. During the years before World War One, both the University and the Agricultural College expanded their programs and facilities. Both trained high-school teachers. The University added programs in law, engineering, and medicine; and the Agricultural College developed programs in pharmacy, engineering, architecture, and veterinary medicine.

The schools played vital roles in the development of a young state. At Fargo, researchers such as Henry L. Bolley and Lawrence Waldron developed new kinds of wheat and helped farmers with their problems. At Grand Forks, geologist Arthur G. Leonard studied North Dakota's mineral resources; Earle J. Babcock pioneered lignite research; John M. Gillette investigated rural social problems; Orin G. Libby reorganized the State Historical Society. The normal schools helped improve teaching.

During the 1920s, college enrollments more than doubled to 6,000 students; half attended the University and Agricultural College. The state had nine public institutions of higher learning; Jamestown College was the only private liberal arts college in North Dakota. The normal schools — Valley City, Mayville, Minot, Ellendale, and Dickinson — became four-year teachers colleges and grew rapidly. The University began the state's first graduate program. The depression of the 1930s dealt the colleges a severe blow. Enrollment during this period increased about 15 percent, but financial support was cut in half. A state without money could not support its schools. Faculty salaries were cut in half, and many professors left. Programs suffered; schools and programs lost accreditation. The depression had robbed the state of many of its dedicated teachers and quality programs. World War Two took away the students; enrollments fell from 7,000 to 1,900.

Technological revolution: students in the laboratory. Above, 1910s. Below, 1970s. (UND-UR)

Progress in education. Above, the University of North Dakota, 1910s. Below, a part of the University of North Dakota campus, 1970s. (UND-UR)

PROGRESS OF A PEOPLE

By the late 1940s, more employers were demanding college graduates. A desire for expansion marked the postwar attitude toward higher education — more money, more students, more schools, more buildings, more programs, more faculty. And the universities and colleges boomed. By 1950, enrollments were again over 7,000; and in 1960 over 14,000 students entered the state's college classrooms. By 1974, enrollments had mushroomed to over 27,000. Appropriations jumped from less than $4,000,000 in 1945 to $88,000,000 in 1975.

The teachers colleges began to offer liberal arts programs, and Minot embarked upon a graduate program in education. The universities (in 1960 the Agricultural College was renamed North Dakota State University of Agriculture and Applied Science) entered new fields and expanded existing programs. In 1974 the University began a four-year medical school. Graduate programs, especially, prospered as the world demanded more specialized training. For example, in 1945 the University granted only 16 graduate degrees. In 1975 it gave 344.

New schools were founded; old ones took on new life; one died. Bismarck Junior College opened in 1939; Devils Lake Junior College (Lake Region), in 1941; and Williston, in the 1950s. In 1956, Mary College became the second four-year private college in the state. The State School of Science at Wahpeton grew as the demand for people with trades increased. In 1967, Williston became a branch of the University; and shortly thereafter, the School of Forestry at Bottineau became affiliated with NDSU. In 1961, Ellendale became a state teachers college, and in 1965 became a branch of the University. A fire at Ellendale in 1970 led to its closing. Two years later the voters removed Ellendale from the Constitution's list of state institutions.

By the 1970s the quality of both teaching and scholarship in the colleges and universities was high. More faculty members than ever before had their doctorates. Federal funding stimulated research and writing — especially in the sciences. The Universities' researchers produced a flood of new scholarship to help North Dakotans better understand their land, their heritage, and themselves. Elwyn B. Robinson, Professor of History at the University of North Dakota, in his *History of North Dakota* (1966) represents the dedication to excellence in scholarship of the postwar faculties. His twenty years of painstaking research and writing produced one of the nation's best state histories. And North Dakotans better understand themselves because of it.

IV. Progress: Libraries and Health

Between 1900 and 1920 most of North Dakota's larger towns developed public libraries. The first came at Grafton in 1897. Andrew Carnegie, the steel millionaire, built hundreds of libraries across the nation in towns which pledged to support a library. He had built eleven library buildings in North Dakota by 1916. Many wealthy local people donated funds to begin libraries. For example, the Grandin brothers gave Mayville $8,000 for a library.

Governor Arthur Link signs the bill which made the initial appropriation for construction of a Heritage Center, March 30, 1973. (SHSND)

Although people in the larger towns had access to books, most rural and small-town folks did not. To help remedy the problem, in 1907 the legislature established the Public Library Commission. Headquartered in Bismarck, the Commission set up traveling libraries to reach booklovers in smaller places. By 1920, over 300 such libraries circulated around the state. Through the 1920s and 1930s, library service grew slowly. Private library associations attempted to collect books and set up small local libraries, but by 1940 there were less than 40 such collections. The State Library Commission (formerly the Public Library Commission) tried to get books into rural North Dakota through its traveling libraries, but in 1946 had no more traveling libraries than it did in the 1920s. It was an impossible task.

The boom in library service expansion came after 1957. In 1956, Congress passed the Library Service Act, which provided federal funds to be matched by the

An early-century photograph of the Grafton State School.

state to develop library services for rural regions. The 1957 legislature provided matching funds and permitted counties to levy a two-mill tax to support the county libraries. Two counties, Divide and Stutsman, had already set up county libraries, but after 1957 the library boom was on. Soon, bookmobiles joined the grain elevator as symbols of rural North Dakota.

The State Library Commission actively promoted a plan for regional libraries and came to serve more as a resource center for regional and community libraries. It contracted with other libraries to help serve the state. Federal money was the key to up-grading North Dakota's libraries. In 1957 the State Library Commission received $40,000 in federal support; in 1968 such support peaked at almost a half million dollars. By the early 1970s, federal financial help had greatly improved the state's library services.

By the 1970s, North Dakota had developed a network of hospitals and agencies to provide good care for its sick and its disadvantaged. The framers of the Constitution realized the need to care for what it then called the "insane." During the early years, the State Hospital at Jamestown had only a few patients, but they usually stayed a long time and often died there. With the development of new approaches for helping the mentally ill, more people sought help at the hospital, and fewer people stayed year after year. In 1970-1971, the Hospital admitted over 3,000 patients for treatment; the length of hospitalization has decreased sharply. During the 1960s and 1970s more emphasis has been placed

New hospitals served the people. To the left, the University of North Dakota Medical Center Rehabilitation Hospital and, to the right, Grand Fork's United Hospital, 1976. (UND-UR)

on drug and alcohol rehabilitation. A network of mental health centers supported the Hospital's work and improved care.

Since 1904 the Grafton State School has been concerned with the mentally retarded; it cares for those who cannot function in society and educates and trains those who can. By the early 1970s, about 1,000 North Dakotans were receiving help at the school. The State School for the Blind, which was founded in 1908 at Bathgate and in 1961 moved to Grand Forks, provides education for the visually handicapped. Since 1890, the State School for the Deaf at Devils Lake has given educational opportunities to the deaf.

County welfare boards handle funds for the needy and the handicapped. By the 1950s, federal programs greatly expanded the area of social services. To coordinate social services and assist the county welfare boards, eight area social service centers have been created in the state. By the 1970s, social service programs had grown rapidly: food stamps, medical assistance, adoption assistance, foster care. Like regional libraries, and regional health centers, area social service centers made life on the plains better.

In the mid-1970s, North Dakota's people lived the longest and had a lower infant death rate than any other state in the nation. Yet, medical service has always been a major concern of people living in sparsely settled areas. In 1918, North Dakota had 604 physicians. In 1950, it had 450; and in 1975 about 500 — half the national per capita average. Although many small towns had lost their

Philanthropist Chester Fritz, who provided funds to build both the Chester Fritz Library and Chester Fritz Auditorium at the University of North Dakota, shakes hands with Governor Guy, 1961. (GFH)

doctors, the caliber of medical treatment and facilities was good. Most physicians worked in the larger towns which had long-established clinics and hospitals. Ninty-five percent of North Dakota's people, however, live within 30 minutes of medical help. Good roads and an excellent ambulance service — rated the best in the nation — have brought the people closer to the doctors. Regional clinics and the development of "trap line" medical service has made medical care more available to sparsely populated areas. For example, the clinic at Hettinger has a dozen physicians who serve a large North Dakota, South Dakota, and Montana area. "Trap lines" — the sending out of doctors from larger clinics to small towns for a day — have expanded medical care. In 1973 the legislature approved a four-year medical program for the University. With a program that stressed community-based primary-care, the Medical School graduated 40 M.D.s in 1976.

Although North Dakota had fewer physicians in 1976 than it did in 1920, medical care was vastly better. New medical knowledge, better equipment, and improved organization have upgraded the health of North Dakotans.

V. "God Giveth the Increase": The Churches

During the early years of settlement, the churches played a crucial role in the lives of their members. They ministered to the spiritual needs of new people in a strange land. The churches were not only religious bodies, but also social organizations. The schools brought the young together; the churches were the most important organizations to bring adult North Dakotans together. The people worshipped, but they also chatted, exchanged ideas about farming, met others

New churches of many architectural styles were built during the postwar generation.

who spoke the language of the old country, and socialized. On the isolated prairie, that was important.

During the years since World War One, the churches have continued to play a vital role in the lives of their people. At the same time, they have changed. They have grown in numbers; they have become Americanized; they have gone through some re-organization and consolidation; they have shared in the prosperity of the post-World War Two era.

North Dakota churches have grown more rapidly than those in most other states. Since 1920, North Dakota church membership has doubled, while the state population has declined. In 1920, one in three North Dakotans belonged to a church. By the 1970s, almost three of every four were members. The Lutheran Church grew the fastest. By 1970, almost half of the state's church membership was Lutheran. Roman Catholics accounted for about a third.

Like the people whom they served, the churches went through a process of Americanization. Before 1920, over 70 percent of North Dakotans were immigrants or sons and daughters of immigrants. The Lutheran and Roman Catholic became immigrant churches. They brought the Gospel to the Germans and Scandinavians in the language of the old country. Their switch to English church services symbolized the Americanization process. The town churches changed first, usually by the early 1920s. In many rural and small town churches, German and the Scandinavian languages continued to be used into the late 1930s. In some cases, German held out to the 1960s. The change to English services made the Lutheran church more appealing to non-Scandinavians and contributed to the phenomenal growth of Lutheranism.

The churches experienced some re-organization and consolidation. With confidence during the early years in future growth, the church bodies built more churches than would be needed in a North Dakota with good roads and sparse population. Congregations, especially in the rural areas, were small and struggled to get and maintain pastoral care. By 1920, the state had over 2,500 church buildings. During the depression of the 1930s, many of the country and small village churches were forced to close. Since 1920, the number of North Dakota church buildings has declined about 20 percent. Many churches, however, have merged or formed a single parish of several churches. During the early 1960s, the merger of several national Lutheran bodies into the American Lutheran Church and the Lutheran Church in America has brought more cooperation and some consolidation to North Dakota Lutheranism.

The churches have shared in the economic prosperity of the post-World War Two generation. Contributions have increased sharply; ministers' salaries, which had been depressed for so long, gained respectability. New church building sprang up across the state as symbols of the new prosperity. For example, in Grand Forks only one Lutheran church did not replace its old building with a larger, new one. And that one remodeled and built a large addition. Like the schools and the hospitals, the churches had found good days.

* * * * * *

The generation of North Dakotans after World War Two experienced what their forefathers had never experienced: thirty years of prosperity. This prosperity had its ups and downs, but North Dakota was much better off than ever before. Prosperity and expanded federal programs and funding brought the quality of life to the highest point in the state's history. By the mid-1970s, schools were vastly improved; libraries were more accessible; churches were stronger; health care, physical and mental, was better. Tied to the outside world by a network of television stations and three airlines, North Dakota was not as remote. When North Dakota became a site for the nation's missile complex, a national television newsman told his viewers that North Dakota had become the world's third-ranking nuclear power. The state was very much a part of the world. Population was still declining, but those who stayed in the good land had a better life.

Epilog

North Dakota became a state in 1889. The story of its people, however, goes back hundreds of years. Through those years the region developed through four stages. The first stage began as the Mandan made their way into the Missouri Valley and ended as the white man began to settle the prairies and plains. During that period of almost three hundred years, the Mandan, the Hidatsa, the Arikara, the Sioux, and the Chippewa came into the region. They left the wooded lands of the East to begin new lives in the West. They adjusted to the semi-arid plains and established themselves in a new country. They built homes, hunted the plains, and fished the rivers. Each tribe developed its own way of living, its own view of the world, and its own way of worshipping the Great Spirit. They fought among themselves, but they all agreed that this was their land. Soon, however, their land began to attract others. As the frontier of settlement moved westward, news spread that the land of the Upper Missouri and the Red River was rich in beaver. Fur companies invaded the Indian's domain. The army followed and by the 1860s was building a chain of forts throughout the land. Hungry for new farm lands, whites started to settle the fertile prairies of Dakota. Angry about the coming of whites, the Indians fought to hold their land. They lost. A reservation system kept the Indian in restricted areas and opened the land to large-scale white settlement.

The second stage of North Dakota history began with the influx of white pioneers and ended with World War One. During these 60 years, North Dakota was turned into a land of ranches, farms, and towns. The bonanza farms proved that North Dakota was a bountiful land that could provide a rich livelihood. North Dakota attracted people from many parts of the nation and the world. The new pioneers came from as far away as Russia and Sweden. The thousands of immigrants and American easterners who were lured to the state were people in search of a new life. Like the Indians who had come to the region, they had to adjust to a new environment. Life on the frontier was not easy. In spite of the hardships and difficulties, the settlers had an unbounded faith in the future. This was a time of optimism and expansion. With feverish intensity, they built schools, churches, railroads, and towns. Some talked in terms of the day when the land would support a population of a million, or perhaps two or three million. The first twenty years of the twentieth century were prosperous, and settlers continued to arrive. World War One further boosted the economy and the confidence of the people.

The third stage — the 1920s and 1930s — brought drastic change which threatened to kill both the faith and the spirit of the people. These twenty years brought economic trouble. The land turned against its people: drought and grasshoppers struck in the midst of a national depression. Crops were wiped out; banks failed; over half the people in the state had no means of support. Beaten by nature and the depression, thousands left the state. Despair gripped the people. Their unbounded confidence in the future was shaken. The depression years caused North Dakotans to reassess the meaning of living in a semi-arid country. The people began to ask the questions: Can this land support the people who are already here? Could people support so many institutions?

The fourth stage of development began with the return of prosperity during World War Two. The postwar generation came to grips with the questions raised during the depression. As population declined, North Dakotans concluded that a large state with a small population needed to consolidate its resources. The painful move toward consolidation of schools and churches symbolized this. The regional approach to libraries, health care, and social services is a response to the need for consolidation. This adjustment, along with prosperity, has brought the quality of life to the highest level in the state's history.

Just as optimism and confidence characterized the early people, they characterize the contemporary North Dakotan. Supported by a strong economy, the people today have the same faith in the future as their fathers and grandfathers had. They are more realistic in their approach to life and its problems, and the state is stronger because of that realism. The problems of the modern world are quite different from those which faced the people 300 or 50 years ago; yet, the same qualities of courage and determination are needed today if North Dakota is going to continue to prosper and progress. That slogan of so many years ago is fitting for today: "Nothing was ever lost by an abiding faith in North Dakota."

NORTH DAKOTA ATLAS

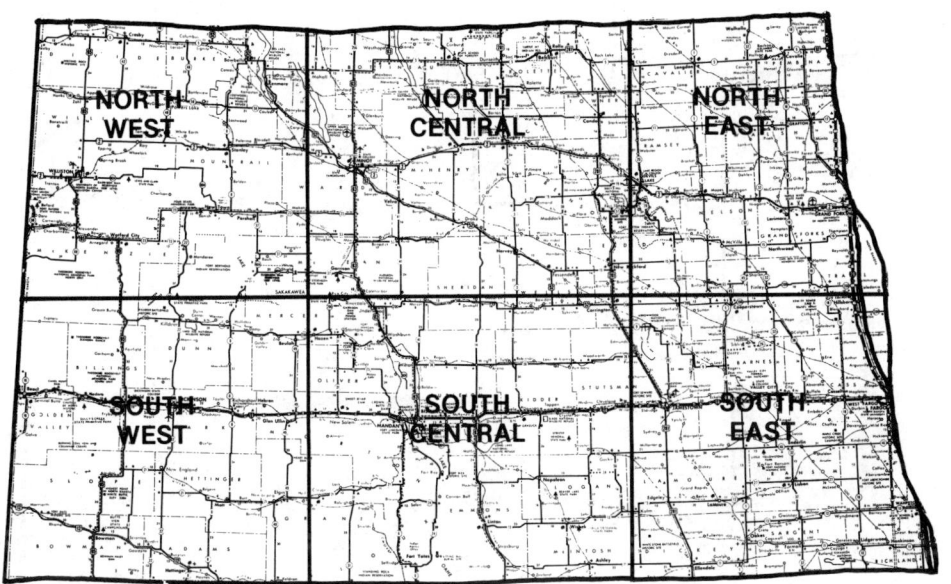

The map in this section is used through the courtesy of the North Dakota State Highway Department.

NORTH WEST NORTH DAKOTA

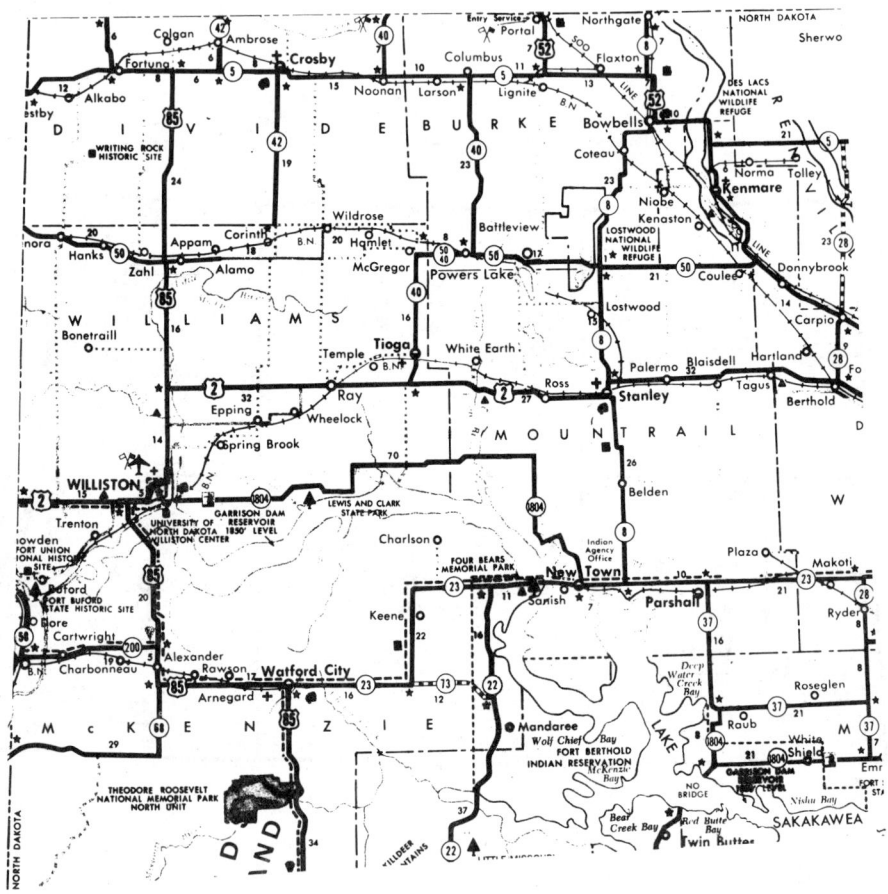

NORTH CENTRAL NORTH DAKOTA

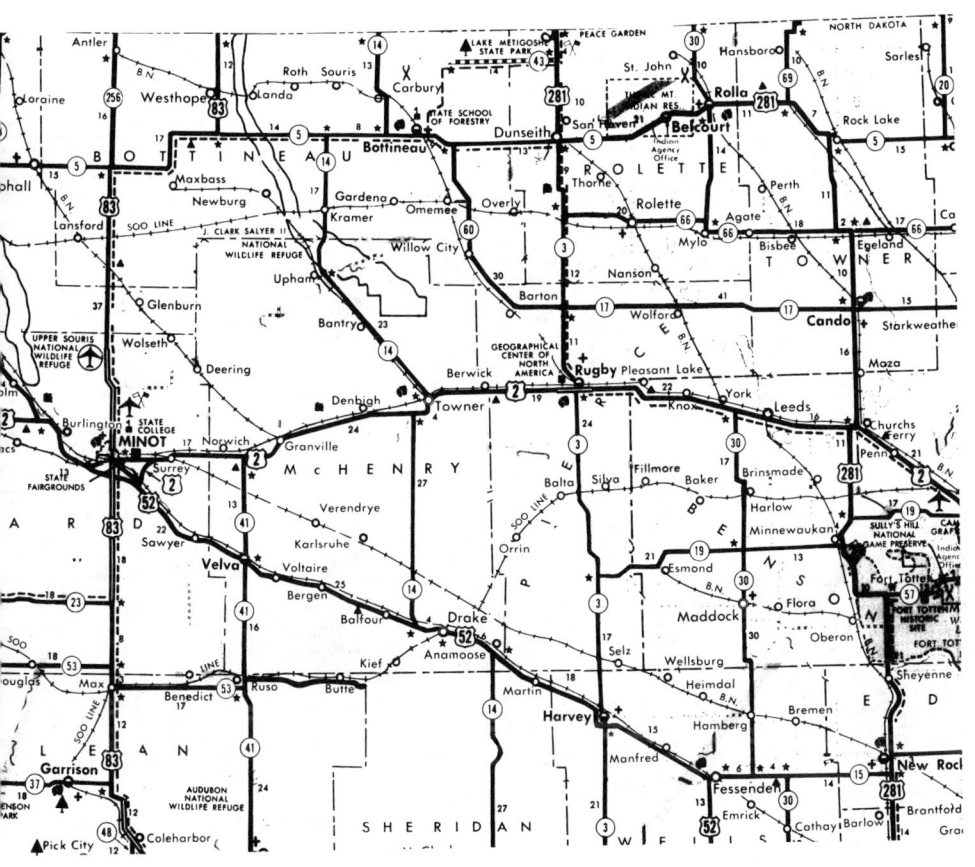

NORTH EAST NORTH DAKOTA

SOUTH WEST NORTH DAKOTA

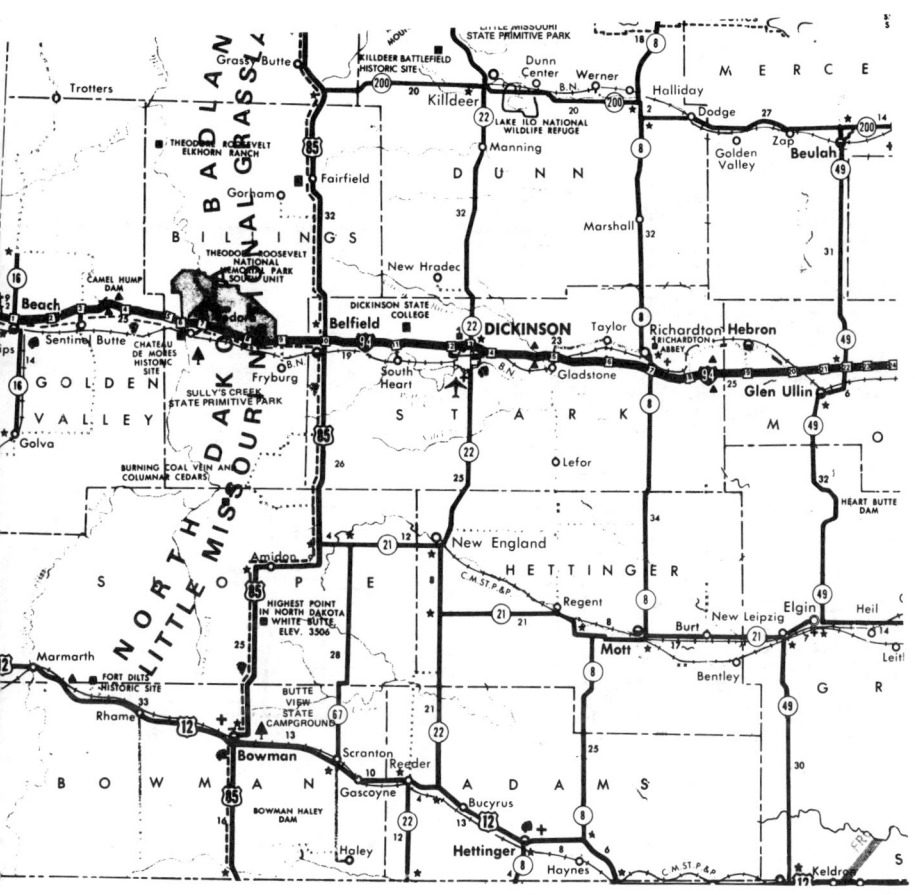

SOUTH CENTRAL NORTH DAKOTA

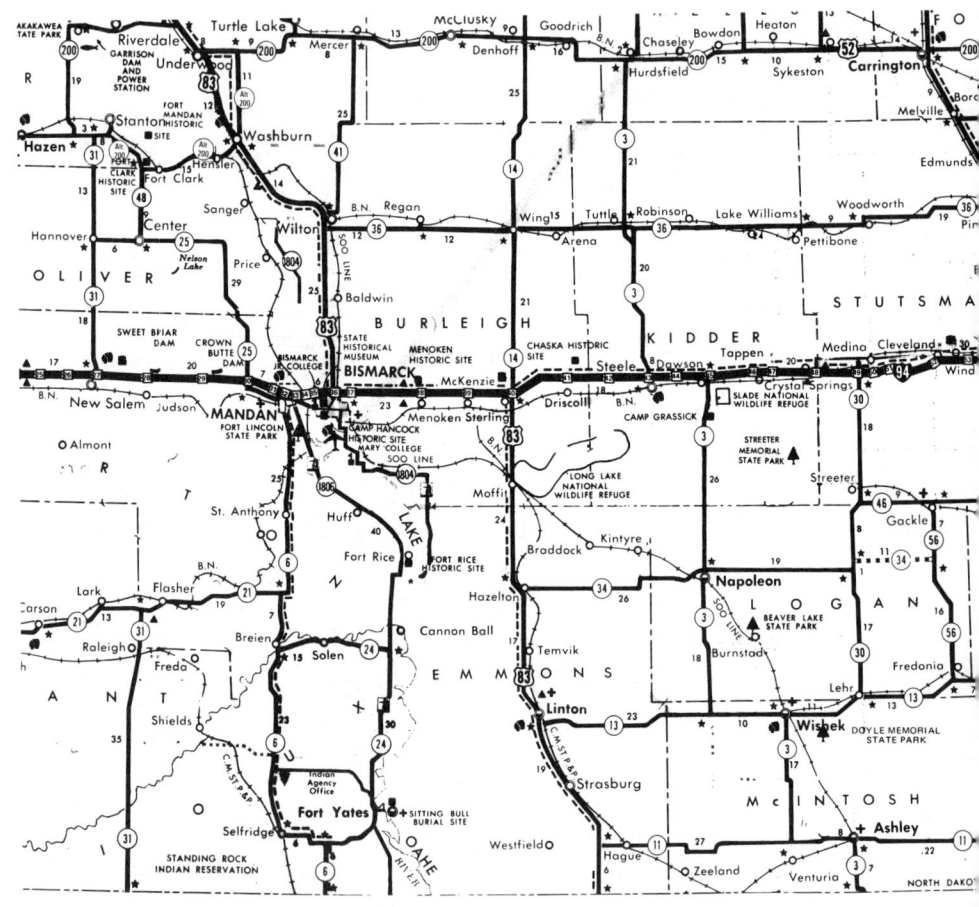

SOUTH EAST NORTH DAKOTA

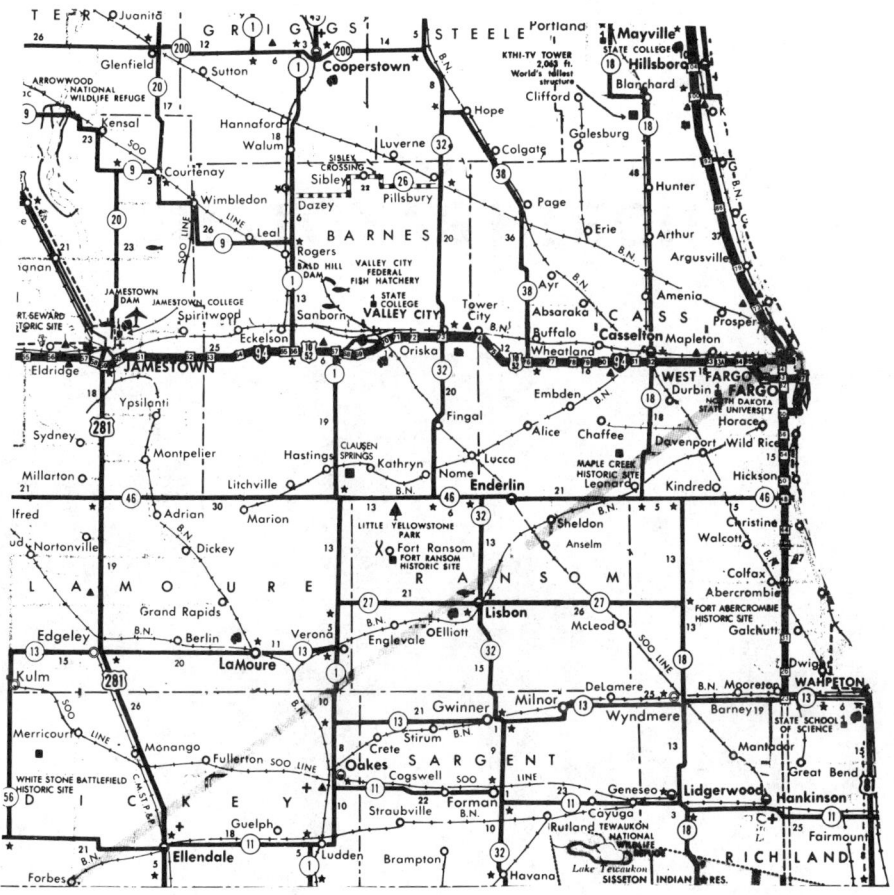

PICTURE ALBUM OF NORTH DAKOTANS

Children, 1930s.

Working a Western North Dakota Homestead, 1910s.

Working in the towns, 1910s. (SHSND)

Indians dancing, immigrants arriving. (SHSND)

Fun with basketball and automobiles, 1904. (SHSND)

Parades: Grand Forks and Dickinson. (SHSND)

232   NORTH DAKOTA: THE HERITAGE OF A PEOPLE

People: Boarding a steamer and enforcing prohibition. (SHSND)

North Dakotans dedicate the U.S.S. Grand Forks. (GFH)

INDEX

Aandahl, Fred G., 185-186, 189
Agricultural Adjustment Act (AAA), 157
Agriculture, Mandan, Hidatsa and Arikara, 41; Selkirk Colony, 53-54; Métis, 54; on reservations, 61-62, 124; bonanza farming, 83-86; pioneer farming, 95-96; in 1890s, 112; 1900-1915, 128-131; and Nonpartisan League, 135-144; 1920s, 147-149; 1930s, 155-157; World War Two, 165; 1945-1970s, 167-172; and Garrison Diversion, 181-184
Air Force, U.S., air bases and missiles, 179
Akicitas, 19, 28
Algonquian language, 29, 46
Allin, Roger, 112-113
Alpha (steamboat), 70
Amerada Petroleum Corporation, 175
American Association of University Women, 197
American Farm Bureau Federation, 152
American Fur Company, 51-52, 54, 71
American Indian Movement, 203
American Lutheran Church, 216
Amidon, Charles F., 134
Andrews, Mark, 191-192
Animal life, 12-13
Arikara, 17-18, 26, 31, 40-46, 49-51, 60, 61
Army, U.S., arrival in Dakota, 56-57; Sully-Sibley campaigns, 57-58; building of forts, 59-60; Indian policy of, 61-62; Battle of Little Big Horn, 64; Battle of Wounded Knee, 65
Ashley, William H., 51
Assiniboin, 18, 30-31, 40-46, 47-48, 55
Assiniboin (steamboat), 71
Astor, John Jacob, 51-52, 54-55
Atkinson, Henry, 51
Automobiles, 139, 152-154

Babcock, Earle J., 207
Badlands, the, 5-6, 13, 78, 87-89
Badlands Cattle Company, 88
Baer, John M., 139
Baker, I.P., 72-73
Bank of North Dakota, 142-144, 146, 149, 154
Banks, state control of, 111, 112; state-owned, 142, 143; failures, 149, see Bank of North Dakota
Baptists, 119
Basin Electric, 177
Basset, Arthur, 137
Bathgate, ND, 213

Beach, ND, 114, 137
Beach, Rex, 132
Belcourt, Father George A., 117
Belfield, ND, 74, 177
Berwick, ND, 156
Big Mounds Battle, 57
Billings County, 2, 201
Billings, Frederick, 78
Binford, ND, 57, 164
Birds, 15
Bismarck, ND, 71-74, 81, 92, 99, 107-108, 111-112, 126-127, 133, 154, 159, 169, 176-181, 186, 191, 197, 199, 201, 210, 211
Bismarck Tribune, 98
Black Hills, 24, 45, 61, 62, 73, 87, 89
Black Mouth Society, 43
Blackfoot (Sihasppa), 31, 51
Blakely, Russell, 68
Blizzards, 9
Bolley, Henry L., 207
Bonanza farming, 83-86
Bottineau County, 109, 115
Bottineau, ND, 80, 201, 210
Bowman, ND, 5, 146, 201
Bridston, Joseph B., 185-186
Briggs, Frank, 112
Brisben, James E., 86
Brown, W.H. and Company of Chicago, 128
Brules (Teton Sioux), 17
Brunsdale, Norman, 189
Buffalo, 12, 24, 26, 32, 33, 39, 41, 53, 55, 61, 66
Burbank, John A., 104
Burdick, Quentin N., 190-191
Burdick, Usher L., 163, 189-190
Bureau of Indian Affairs, 122, 201-202
Bureau of Mines, 177
Bureau of Reclamation, 182-184
Burke, Andrew, 112
Burke, John, 132, 140
Burleigh County, 112
Burleigh, Walter A., 104
Burlington Northern Railroad, 177
Burtness, Olger B., 151

Caddoan language, 41
Camp Atchison, 57
Canadian Pacific Railroad, 79
Canadians, 115

Cando, ND, 80, 156, 169
Casey, Lyman R., 111
Cass-Cheney bonanza farm, 85
Cass, George W., 83-84
Casselton, ND, 80, 84, 140, 159
Cattle, see ranching
Cavalier County, 115
Center, ND, 177
Central Lowlands, 4-6
Chaboillez, Charles Jean Baptiste, 53
Charbonneau, Toussaint, 49
Chauteau, Pierre Jr., 71
Cheney, Benjamin, 83-85
Cheyenne, 17, 29, 31, 40-46
Cheyenne (steamboat), 70
Chicago-Milwaukee and St. Paul Railroad, 81, 126
Chicago and Northwestern Railroad, 81
Chippewa (Ojibwa), 17-18, 29-39, 40-46, 48, 55, 60, 68, 203
Choteau, Pierre, 49
Christian, George C., 83
Church, Lewis K., 104
Churches, see religion
Civilian Conservation Corp (CCC), 158, 165
Clark, William, 12, 40, 47-55
Climate, general description, 7-11; influence of on man, 15, 155-157
Coal, formation of, 2; development of industry, 177
Columbia Fur Company, 51, 54
Committee for Progressive Unity, 189
Committee to Save North Dakota, 184
Constitution, state, making of, 107-109; content, 109-110; attempt to make new constitution (1972) 193-196
Continental Land and Cattle Company, 88
Cooke, Jay and Company, 76-77
Cooper, Thomas, 130
Cooperstown, ND, 151, 164, 176, 201
Coulson Line (Missouri Transportation Company), 71, 73
Coulson, Sanford B., 71
Crazy Horse, 62
Cree, 18, 29-31, 40, 46-48
Crook, General George, 62
Crosby, ND, 114, 182
Crow, 40, 45, 50
Custer, General George Armstrong, 60-62, 72
Custer Trail Cattle Company, 87

Dahl, C.P., 191
Dakota (dialect), 16-17
Dakota Farmers Alliance, 112
Dakota Territory, organized, 103; structure of government, 103-106; statehood movement, 106-107
Dalrymple, Oliver, 85
Davis, John, 190-191
Dawes Allotment Act, 124
Dawson, ND, 57
Day, Carroll, 188
Deadwood, SD, 73-74
Depression, Panic of 1873, 77; 1890s, 102, 112; 1920s, 148-149, 151-152; 1930s, 155-163, 165-166, 205
DeSmet, Father Pierre Jean, 117
Devils Lake, ND, 12, 40, 59-61, 73, 80, 93, 108, 110, 126-127, 132, 154, 182, 210, 213
Dickinson, ND, 9, 74, 121, 177, 201
Dickinson State College, 207
Dickson, Robert, 52, 53
Divide County, 147, 157, 212
Douglas, Thomas (5th Earl of Selkirk), 53
Drake, ND, 143
Drayton, ND, 176, 191
Drift Prairie, 4-6, 11, 15, 80, 92, 125, 127
Driscoll, ND, 57
Duis, George E., 152
Duluth, MN, 76-77, 135
Dumoulin, Father Sévére Joseph, 54, 117

Eaton, Howard and Eldon, 87-88
Economic Opportunity Act, 202
Edgeley, ND, 81, 126, 156
Edmunds, Newton, 104
Education, see schools and higher education
d'Eglise, Jacques, 48
Elections, 1889 Constitutional, 109; 1889 general, 110; 1892, 112; 1906, 132; 1908, 133; 1910, 133; 1916 primary, 140; 1918, 141-142; 1920, 144; 1921 recall, 144; 1922, 149; 1924, 149; 1926, 149; 1928, 150; 1930, 150; 1932, 159; 1934, 161; 1936, 162; 1938, 162; 1940, 163; 1944, 186; 1946, 186; 1948, 189; 1950, 189; 1952, 189; 1956, 190; 1958, 190; 1960, 191; 1962, 191; 1964, 191; 1968, 191-192; 1970, 192; 1972, 191-192; 1974, 191; 1972 (constitution) 196
Elevators, proposed state owned, 113, 137; and grain trade, 135-136; co-ops, 136; state owned, 142, 143
Elk Valley bonanza farm, 84
Ellendale, ND, 121-122, 207, 210

El Paso (steamboat), 71
Emery bonanza farm, 84
Equal Rights Amendment, 185, 196-197
Equity Co-operative Exchange, 136, 140
Esmond, ND, 125

Family life, Sioux, 19-20, 22; Chippewa, 31, 38; Mandan and Hidatsa, 43; pioneer farm, 97-98
Far West (steamboat), 72
Fargo, ND, 6, 8, 11, 78, 79, 81, 92, 97-99, 108, 121, 125, 127, 130, 133-134, 140, 154, 169, 176-177, 190, 199, 201, 207
Farm Bureau, 171-172, 186
Farmers' Union, 152, 171-172, 186-190
Farming, see agriculture
Faulk, Andrew J., 104
Federal Emergency Relief Administration (FERA), 157-158
Federal Flood Control Act of 1944, 181
Ferris, Sylvane and Joseph, 88
Fish, 13, 15
Fisk, Charles J., 132
Floods, 11; control of, 158, 181-182
Fort Abercrombie, 56-57, 59, 68
Fort Abraham Lincoln, 60
Fort Atkinson, 51, 56
Fort Benton, 73
Fort Benton Transportation Company (Power Line) 72-73
Fort Berthold, 46, 59, 61, 64, 122, 124, 201-202
Fort Buford, 59
Fort Clark, 51
Fort Garry, Canada (Winnipeg), 56, 66-70
Fort Lisa, 50
Fort Mandan, 49
Fort McKeen, 60
Fort McKenzie, 51
Fort Pembina, 60
Fort Pierre, 51, 56
Fort Randal, 56
Fort Ransom, 59-60
Fort Rice, 58-59, 61
Fort Seward, 60
Fort Stevenson, 59
Fort Tecumseh, 71
Fort Totten, 59-62, 64, 73, 122, 124, 201
Fort Union, 46, 51-52, 71, 75
Fort Yates, 59, 73, 117
Foster County, 84
Fram (steamboat), 70

Francher, Fred, 112
Frazier-Lemke Farm Bankruptcy Act, 163
Frazier, Lynn, 140-141, 143-144, 146, 149-150, 159, 162-163
French and Indian War (1754-1763), 48
Fur trade, Chippewa, 29; on Missouri to 1812, 47-50; on Missouri, 1812-1860s, 50-52; on Red River, 52-55; role of Red River cart in, 66-67

Gall, 62, 64
Garrison Dam and Diversion, 178, 181-182, 199
Geology, 1-3
Germans and German-Russians, 115
Ghost Dance, 65
Gillette, John M., 134, 166, 207
Glaciers, 2-3, 5
Gold Seal Glass Wax Company, 176
Grafton, ND, 185, 210
Grafton State School, 213
Grain trade, and steamboats, 68, 73; and railroads, 81; state control of, 111, 112, 141; and elevators, 135-136; co-operative movement, 136-137
Grand Forks County, 84
Grand Forks Herald, 132
Grand Forks, ND, 11, 53, 70, 77-81, 92, 97-99, 108, 121, 127, 132-134, 143-144, 149-155, 176-177, 185, 188, 191, 199, 201, 207, 213, 216
Grand Forks (steamboat), 70
Grand River Agency, 61
Grandin brothers, 83-84, 210
Grandin (steamboat), 70
Grass, 11-12, 87
Great Dakota Boom, 83
Great Northern Railroad, 73, 78-80, 125-126, 130
Great Plains, 4-6, 48
Great Sioux Reservation, 122
Greater North Dakota Association, 186
Griggs, Alexander, 68, 70
Gronna, Asle J., 134, 145
Gros Ventre of the Missouri, see Hidatsa
Guy, William L., 191-193
Gwinner, ND, 176

Hagen, John N., 143, 162
Halcrow, Don, 191
Hall, Thomas, 143, 151
Hanna, Louis B., 145
Hanna, Mark, 132
Hanna, ND, 125

Hansboro, ND, 126
Hansbrough, Henry C., 110
Hatton, ND, 176
Hawley, W.L., 88
Hazen, ND, 162
Health and health care, 61, 212-214
Hebron, ND, 176
Henry, Alexander, 13, 31, 53
Hettinger, ND, 201, 214
Hidatsa (Gros Ventre of the Missouri), 31, 40-46, 49, 51, 60-61
Higher Education, 121-122, 203, 207-210
Highways and roads, 152-154
Hill, James J., 68-, 70, 78-80, 130
Hillsboro, ND, 176
Home Building Association, 142-144
Homestead Act, 94-95, 127
Horses, 24, 31, 33
Hove, John, 192
Howard, William A., 104
Hudson's Bay Company, 48, 52, 54, 55, 68-70
Huidekiper, A.C., 87-88
Hunkpapa (Teton Sioux), 17, 60, 62
Huron, SD, 112

Immigrants, 114-117; see also specific nationalities
Independent Voters Association (IVA), 142, 144, 149-152, 159, 162
Indian policy, U.S. government, 18, 61-62, 122-124, 201-203
Indian Reorganization Act of 1934, 202
Indians, see specific group
Industrial Commission, 142, 144
Industry, 175-179
International Joint Commission, 184
International (steamboat), 68
Itazipchos (Teton Sioux), 17
Iverson, Clarence, 175

James River Valley, 58
Jamestown College, 207
Jamestown, ND, 60, 80, 92, 99, 108, 118, 127, 169, 176-177, 199, 212
Jamestown State Hospital, 163, 212
Jayne, William, 104
Jewel Ball Bearing Plant, Rolla, ND, 176, 212
Johnson, Sveinbjorn, 144
Jusseaume, Rene, 48

Kenmare, ND, 125, 151
Kidder County, 201
Killdeer Mountains, 58
Killdeer, ND, 155

Kitchen, Joseph A., 144
Kitse-manito, 35-36
Kittson, Norman, 55, 66-70
Kleppe, Thomas, 191
Knauf, John, 132
Kositsky, Karl, 143
Kountz Line, 72
Krueger, Otto, 186, 189

Labor, and bonanza farming, 86; and Nonpartisan League, 143; movement, 1880s-1970s, 172-175
Ladd, Edwin F., 133, 150, 164, 176
Laidlaw, William, 51
Lakota (dialect), 16
Lakota, ND, 201
Lamont, Daniel, 51
LaMoure, ND, 78
Land, formation of, 2-3; features of, 4-5; soils, 6; influence of on man's activity, 6; ways of acquiring, 94-95; speculation, 102, 128-129; declining price of, 148
Land Laws, 94-95, 127
Langdon, ND, 80, 201
Langer, Lydia, 161
Langer, William, 140, 143, 146, 159-163, 185-186, 189-191
Laramie Treaty, 61
Larimore bonanza farm, 84
Larimore, ND, 80
Larson, Richard, 191
League of Women Voters, 197
Leavenworth, Colonel Henry, 51
Legislative assemblies, first, 110-111; 1893, 113; 1907, 133; 1911, 133; 1917, 141; 1919, 142-143; 1927, 150; 1939, 162; 1947, 186-188, 206; 1963, 195; 1969, 195; 1973, 198-199; 1975; 177, 196, 197, 199
Lemke, William, 139-140, 144, 149, 163, 186
Leonard, Arthur G., 207
LeSeuer, Arthur, 137
Lewis, Merriweather, 12, 40, 47-55
Libby, Orin G., 207
Libraries, 210-212
Library Service Act, 211
Lignite, see coal
Lignite, ND, 175
Linçoln, Abraham, 57, 75, 104, 122
Link, Arthur, 191-192, 199
Linton, ND, 125-126
Lisa, Manuel, 50, 55
Lisbon, ND, 59, 109

Litchville, ND, 185
Little Big Horn, 62
Little Crow, 57
Little Shell's Band, 122
Loftus, George S., 136
Logan County, 201
Lonetree Reservoir, 182
Louisiana Territory, 48-49
Lutherans, 116, 118, 215-216
Lutheran Church in America, 216

Macdonald, Neil C. 203, 207
Maddock, Walter, 150
Maltese Cross Ranch, 88
Mandan, 31, 40-46, 47-55, 60, 61
Mandan, ND, 60, 125, 154, 175
Manitoba Escarpment, 4
Manitoba Railroad (Great Northern Railroad), 73, 79-80, 93
Mapleton, ND, 191
Marquis, wheat variety, 129
Marty, Abbot Martin, 117
Mary College, 210
Mayville, ND, 80, 84, 108, 121-122
Mayville State College, 207, 210
McCanna bonanza farm, 84
McCarney, Robert, 191
McClusky Canal, 182-184
McCumber, Porter J., 134, 145
McHenry County, 109, 138
McIntosh County, 92
McKenzie, Alexander, 107, 112-113, 128, 131, 132-135, 138
McKenzie, Kenneth, 51, 71
McLaughlin, 126
McLean County, 201
Mdwakantowan (Santee Sioux), 17
Medora, ND, 74, 89-90
Mellette, Arthur C., 104
Melroe Company, 176
Menoken, 48
Mercer County, 162
Merrifield, A.W., 88
Merrifield, Webster, 203
Methodists, 119
Métis, 37, 54-55, 66
Michigan, ND, 176
Michilimackinac Company, 53
Midewiwin, 33-35
Midland Continental Railroad, 126
Miller, Judge Andrew, 161
Miller, John, 110, 112
Miniconjou (Teton Sioux), 17

Minneapolis, MN, 79, 81, 83-84, 125-126, 128-130, 135-136, 154, 161
Minnesota and Pacific Railroad, 78
Minnesota Stage Company, 68
Minnesota Territory, 55
Minnewauken, ND, 73
Minnie H (steamboat), 73
Minnkota Power Co-operative, 177
Minot, ND, 11, 80, 93, 121, 127, 137, 154-155, 157, 177
Minot State College, 217
Missionaries, 54, 117
Mississippi River Valley, 40, 54
Missouri Coteau, 5
Missouri Escarpment, 5
Missouri Fur Company (Commercial Company for the Discovery of the Nations of the Upper Missouri), 49-50
Missouri Plateau, 5-6, 11-12, 15, 92, 127
Missouri River Valley, 41, 45
Missouri Transportation Company (Coulson Line), 71
Missouri Valley, 117
Mohall, ND, 125
Montana-Idaho Transportation Company, 71
Moodie, Thomas, 161
Moorhead, MN, 67, 77, 175
de Morès, Marquis (Antone Amédée Marie Vincent Amat Mancade Vallombrosa), 89-90
Morgan, Rilie, 185-186
Morton County, 92, 140, 159
Moses, John, 162-163, 186
Motor Coach Industries of Winnipeg, 177
Mott, ND, 126, 155, 201
Mountain, ND, 201

Naca Ominicia, 19
Nakota (dialect), 16-17
National Farmers Organization, 172, 196
National Youth Administration (NYA), 158
Neche, ND, 80
Nelson County, 116
Nesson Anticline, 175
Nestos, Rangvold A., 144, 149-150
New Town, ND, 203
Newspapers, 98, 132, 139, 143, 172
Nonpartisan Leader, 139
Nonpartisan League, 135-146, 149-152, 159-163, 185-190, 199
North Dakota Better Farming Association, 130
North Dakota Business and Professional Women's Club, 197

North Dakota Economic Development Commission, 175-176
North Dakota Education Association, 197
North Dakota Farmer's Union, 152
North Dakota Mill and Elevator Association, 142-144, 146, 149-150, 154
North Dakota State School for the Blind, 213
North Dakota State School for the Deaf, 213
North Dakota State University, (Agricultural College), 130, 133, 150, 207-210
North Dakota Supreme Court, 131-132, 140, 142, 161
North Dakota Wheat Commission, 168
North Dakota Wheat Growers Association, 152
Northrup, Anson, 68
North Star (steamboat), 68
Northwest Company of Montreal, 48, 52-53
Northern Pacific Railroad, 71-74, 75-81, 82-84, 87, 91, 94, 107, 112, 117-118, 125-126, 129-130, 140
Northwestern Express and Transportation Company, 73
Northwood, ND, 201
Norwegians, 114-116
Nye, Gerald P., 150, 163-164, 186
Nygaard, Jhalmar C., 192

Oakes, ND, 81, 125, 201
O'Fallon, Benjamin, 51
Oglala (Teton Sioux), 77
O'Hare, Kate Richards, 146
Ohio Valley, 16
Oil, formation of, 2; discovery of, 175; development of industry, 175-176
Ojibwa, see Chippewa
Okipa, 44
Okitsita, 32
Olson, Ole, 161
Omaha, 17, 26, 41
"The One-Eyed" (Chief of Hidatsa), 49
Oohenonpas (Teton Sioux), 17
Ordway, Nehemiah G., 104, 106-107

Pagek (Bony Spectre), 36
Panic of 1873, 72, 77, 79
Park River, ND, 80
Parshall, ND, 8
Pawnee Nation, 41
Pembina County, 108, 115
Pembina, ND, 4, 12, 31, 53-56, 66-68, 114, 117
Pembina Escarpment, 4
Pembina Hills, 4
Pemmican, 55, 56

Pennington, John L., 104
Pierce County, 1
Pierce, Gilbert, 104, 111
Pierre, SD, 71, 73
Pilcher, Joshua, 51
Pioneer (steamboat), 68
Plants, 11-12
Population, Yankton Sioux, 17; Teton Sioux, 17; Arikara, 18, 41; Mandan, 40; Hidatsa, 40; Assiniboin, 46; Northern Dakota, 1878-1890, 92, 102; foreign-born in 1890, 93; 1880s, 107; 1890s, 113; 1900 census 114-115; Indian, 1900, 122; growth, 1900-1915, 127; loss, 1930s, 166; patterns 1920-1970s, 200-201
Power, James B., 83, 91
Power, Thomas, 73
Prairie Coteau, 4
Preemption Act, 94-95
Presbyterians, 119
Provencher, Father Joseph Norbert, 54, 117
Pryor, Ensign Nathanial, 49
Public Library Commission (State Library Commission), 211-212
Public Service Commission, 193
Radio, 154
Railroads, competition with steamboats, 70, 73, 74; Northern Pacific, 75-78; Great Northern (St. Paul, Minneapolis, and Manitoba), 78-81; Northern Pacific and bonanza farming, 83-84; promotion and sale of land, 91-92; and settlement, 92-93; state control of, 111, 112, 113, 133; expansion and branch lines, 125-126; promote diversified farming, 130; and politics, 131-132; and coal, 177
Rainfall, 7, 8, 155
Ranching, 86-89; Theodore Roosevelt, 88-89; Marquis de Morès, 89-90; 1930s, 156
Red Cloud (steamboat), 72
Red River Transportation Company, 79
Red River Valley, 4-6, 7-12, 30, 33, 52, 55, 66, 73, 79-84, 92, 107, 115, 117, 129, 157, 170-171
Red Thunder, 53
Redland, Rolland, 192
Regional Environment Assessment Program, 177
Reiten Manufacturing Company, 176
Religion, Sioux, 20-22; Chippewa, 35-38; Mandan, Hidatsa, and Arikara, 43-44; at Pembina and Selkirk colony, 54, 117; Sioux Ghost Dance, 65; on reservations,

62, early organization, 117-119; churches, 1920-1970s, 214-216
Renville County, 201
Republican Organizing Committee (ROC), 185-191, 199
Reservation, 61-62, 122-124; 201-203
Richardton, ND, 128
Richland County, 84, 110
Robinson, Elwyn B., 158, 210
Rolette, Joseph, 55
Rolla, ND, 176, 203
Rollette County, 109, 115, 201
Roman Catholics, 117-118, 215
Roosevelt, Franklin D., 157, 161
Roosevelt, Theodore, 88-89, 131
Rugby, ND, 1
Rural Electrification Administration (REA), 170, 177
Russell, Charles Edward, 139

St. Boniface, Manitoba, 117
St. Cloud, MN, 67-68, 79
St. Louis, MO, 48-50, 73
St. Paul, MN, 55, 57, 66-70, 75, 78-79, 81, 125-126, 136, 152, 156, 172
St. Paul and Pacific Railroad, 78-79
St. Thomas, ND, 79
Sakakawea, 49
San Haven Hospital, 203
Santee Sioux, 16-28, 29-30, 57
Sarles, Elmore Y., 132
Sault Ste Marie Railroad (the "Soo"), 81, 125-126
Schafer, Harold, 176
Schools, 64, 121, 157, 203-207
Scott, A.J., 152
Seasons, 8-11
Selkirk Colony (Red River Settlement), 53-55
Selkirk (steamboat), 70
Sevareid, Eric, 81
Shafer, George F., 150
Shanley, Bishop John, 118
Sharon and Amenia Land Company, 84
Shawnee, 29
Sheridan County, 201
Shortridge, Eli C.D., 112
Sibley, Henry Hastings, 55, 57-58
Sihasppa (Teton Sioux), 17
Sinclair, James H., 151
Sioux, 16-28, 29-39, 40, 43-44, 55, 57-61, 64, 68, 107, 146, See also Teton Sioux, Yankton Sioux, Santee Sioux
Sisseton (Santee Sioux), 17, 28, 61

Sitting Bull, 60, 62, 64-65, 107
Slaughter, Linda Warfel, 59
Smallpox, 43, 55, 157
Sod houses, 96
Soils, 6
"Soo Line", 81, 125-126, See Sault Ste Marie Railroad
Sorlie, Arthur G., 149-150, 164
Souris, ND, 125
Sports, 26, 34, 99
Stages and freighting, 68, 73-74
Stambaugh, Lynn, 186
Standing Rock Agency, 61
Standing Rock Indian Reservation, 59, 64-65, 122, 124, 201-202
Stanton, ND, 177
Starkweather, ND, 126
State Historical Society of North Dakota, 207
Statehood movement, 106-107
Steamboats, and fur trade, 52; on Red River, 68-70; on Missouri, 71-73; on Devils Lake, 73; decline of, 74
Steele, ND, 8, 155
Steiger Tractor, 177
Stevens, Isaac, 75
Strasburg, ND, 201
Stutsman County, 84, 132, 212
Sully, General Alfred, 57-59
Sun Dance, 18, 21-22, 32, 36, 39, 43-44, 122
Surrey, ND, 125

Talbott, Charles C., 152
Talbott, Glenn, 188
Tappen, ND, 57
Television, 216
Teton Sioux, 16-28, 40-46, 51, 56-65, 122
Thatcher, M.W. "Bill", 152
Thierry, Chateau, 146
Thoresen, T.H.H., 150
Three Tribes (Arikara, Hidatsa, and Mandan), 40-46, 61, 64, 122, 202
Timber Culture Act, 12, 94-95
Tin Lizzy, 154
Tioga, ND, 175, 177
Tiospaye, 19
Tornado, 8
Towner County, 115, 139
Townley, Arthur C., 137-146, 149
Towns, influence of steamboats on, 70, 71, 73; influence of railroads on, 77, 78, 79, 80; founding of Medora, 89-90; early growth of, 92-93; early life in, 98-99; growth of

1900-1915, 127; population patterns, 1940-1970s, 201
Trade Dance, 36, 39
Traill County, 157
Traverse de Sioux, 67
Trees, 12
de Trobriand, General Régis, 59
Turtle Mountains and Reservation, 4, 12-13, 122-124, 201-202

Union Pacific Railroad, 75
Union Party, 163
United States House of Representatives, 110, 186, 189, 192
United States Senate, 103, 151, 186
United State Supreme Court, 105, 131, 157, 196-199
University of North Dakota, 134, 140, 159, 166, 203, 207-210, 213-214

Valley City, ND, 108, 121-122, 151
Valley City State College, 207
de Varennes, Pierre Gaultier, 47
Velva, ND, 81, 201
de la Vérendrye, Sieur, 47-48
von Hoffman, Medora, 89

Wadsworth, H.B., 88
Wahpekute (Santee Sioux), 17
Wahpeton (Santee Sioux), 17, 28, 61
Wahpeton, ND, 56, 80, 114, 121, 210
Wakan Tanka, 20
Wakincuzas (Santee Sioux), 19
Waldron, Lawrence, 207
Walhalla, ND, 117, 125
Walsh County, 115
War of 1812, 50-51
Ward County, 109
Washburn, ND, 126
Washburn, William D., 126
WDAY, 154
Welford, Walter, 162
Wells County, 84

West Fargo, ND, 176
Wenstrom, Frank, 196
Whelan, Thomas, 162
Wheat, milling process, 83, bonanza farming, 83-86; new varieties, 129; prices, 1920s, 148; prices and crops, 1930s, 155-156; Langer embargo on, 161; prices and crops during World War Two, 165; Federal programs, 1930s, 157; crops and prices, 1945-1970s, 167-168; wheat Commission 168
White, Frank, 132
Whitestone Hill Battle, 58
Whope, the Beautiful One, 20-21
Wicasa Yatapickas, 18-19, 28
Wihtigohanek (Ice Giants), 36
Williams, Erastus A., 107
Williston Basin, 175
Williston, ND, 5, 127, 175, 177, 196, 210
Wilson, Woodrow, 131, 145
Wimbledon, ND, 126
Winnipeg, Canada (Fort Garry), 53, 68-70, 79-80, 126, 177
Winship, George, 132
Wisconsian glacier, 2
Wood, Fred B., 138
Wood, Howard, 138
Works Progress Administration (WPA), 157, 16
World War One, 125-126, 129, 134, 147-148 154, 164, 207, 215
World War Two, 166-184, 185, 199-200, 202 205, 207, 215-216
Wounded Knee Creek, 65

Yankton Sioux, 16-28, 122
Yankton, SD, 71, 73, 106-107, 112
Yanktonnais (Yankton Sioux), 17, 28, 45, 61
Yellowstone (steamboat), 52, 71
Yellowstone River Valley, 46
Young, George M., 151
Young, James C., 128
Young, Milton R., 185-186, 189-191